Neoclassical Realist Theory
of International Politics

Neoclassical Realist Theory of International Politics

Norrin M. Ripsman, Jeffrey W. Taliaferro,

and

Steven E. Lobell

OXFORD
UNIVERSITY PRESS

OXFORD
UNIVERSITY PRESS

Oxford University Press is a department of the University of Oxford. It furthers
the University's objective of excellence in research, scholarship, and education
by publishing worldwide. Oxford is a registered trade mark of Oxford University
Press in the UK and certain other countries.

Published in the United States of America by Oxford University Press
198 Madison Avenue, New York, NY 10016, United States of America.

Library of Congress Cataloging-in-Publication Data
Names: Ripsman, Norrin M., author. | Taliaferro, Jeffrey W., author. |
Lobell, Steven E., 1964– author.
Title: Neoclassical realist theory of international politics / by
Norrin M. Ripsman, Jeffrey W. Taliaferro, and Steven E. Lobell.
Description: New York, NY : Oxford University Press, 2016.
Identifiers: LCCN 2015040763 (print) | LCCN 2016000647 (ebook) |
ISBN 978–0–19–989923–4 (hardback) | ISBN 978–0–19–989925–8 (paperback) |
ISBN 978–0–19–989924–1 (E-book) | ISBN 978–0–19–060304–5 (E-book) |
ISBN 978–0–19–060305–2 (Online Component)
Subjects: LCSH: International relations. | International relations—Philosophy. |
Realism—Political aspects. | BISAC: POLITICAL SCIENCE / International Relations /
General. | POLITICAL SCIENCE / International Relations / Diplomacy. |
POLITICAL SCIENCE / Political Freedom & Security / General.
Classification: LCC JZ1307 .R56 2016 (print) | LCC JZ1307 (ebook) | DDC 327.101—dc23
LC record available at http://lccn.loc.gov/2015040763

To our families

CONTENTS

ACKNOWLEDGMENTS

This book is the result of a twelve-year collaboration that began at the International Studies Association conference in Portland, Oregon, in February 2003. All three of us individually were struggling with the same theoretical problems with the international relations literature. We had each studied aspects of international security, but were frustrated with the paradigmatic rigidity of debates in the field. Our own work had crossed both paradigmatic lines and levels of analysis in the interest of explanatory power. Yet we strongly believed in the importance of both structural constraints on state behavior and the utility of a systematic theory of foreign policy and international politics. Ben Frankel, the founding editor of *Security Studies*—who mentored young scholars and built them into a network—introduced us and encouraged us to explore our common interests in enriching realism.

Gideon Rose coined the term "neoclassical realism" in a review article of four books published in the spring 1998 issue of *World Politics*. In that article, Rose claimed those four books (by Thomas J. Christensen, Fareed Zakaria, Randall Schweller, and William C. Wohlforth, respectively) constituted a new school of mid-range foreign policy theories. Neoclassical realism, as he envisioned it, sought to blend the central insight of the structural realism (or neorealism) of Kenneth N. Waltz about the constraints an anarchic international system imposes upon states with the practical insights about statecraft and the complexities of state-society relationships found in the twentieth-century classical realism of Hans Morgenthau, Arnold Wolfers, E. H. Carr, and others.

In truth, none of the three of us used the term "neoclassical realism" in our respective first single-authored books, but we identified with it. We concluded that neoclassical realism was more than just a one-off moniker for the four books that Rose reviewed. We also believed that neoclassical realism could be a coherent research program. Neoclassical realist theories could explain far more than just the occasional anomaly for structural realism, provided that we could define a coherent scope and content for neoclassical realism to prevent it from being merely a descriptive theory or simply being an underspecified eclectic approach.

The co-edited volume *Neoclassical Realism, the State, and Foreign Policy* (Cambridge: Cambridge University Press, 2009) was the first step of our efforts to establish the parameters and scope of neoclassical realism. Growing out of a conference at Concordia University in Montreal, we delineated the neoclassical realist understanding of the state as prerequisite for understanding foreign policy decision making. Our second co-edited volume, *The Challenge of Grand Strategy: The Great Powers and the Broken Balance between the World Wars* (Cambridge: Cambridge University Press, 2012), further developed our thinking about neoclassical realism, specifically the importance of different great powers' strategic environments. The present book introduces what we term "Type III" neoclassical realism, a body of theories that purports to explain phenomena ranging from short-term crisis decision-making by individual states up to and including broader patterns of international outcomes and structural change.

Our collaboration would have been considerably more difficult before the advent of the Worldwide Web, virtual networks, and Voice over Internet software. We posted draft chapters on a WebDAV hosted at the College of Social and Behavioral Sciences at the University of Utah. Skype greatly facilitated the completion of this book. For the past two years, we held weekly (or at least, bi-weekly) Skype meetings that frequently last two hours. We also held face-to-face writers' workshops in Chicago (February 2013), Boston (January 2014), and Salt Lake City (January 2015).

We are indebted to several institutions for research support: Norrin Ripsman received research support from the Fonds de recherche du Québec – Société et culture, and the Social Science and Humanities Research Council of Canada. Jeff Taliaferro received research support from the Office of the Dean of the School of Arts and Sciences and the Faculty Research Awards Committee (FRAC) for the Schools of Arts and Sciences and Engineering at Tufts University. Steven Lobell received a University Research Committee (URC) Faculty Research Award at the University of Utah.

Over the years, we (both individually and collectively) have received comments from Sammy Barkin, Beth Bloodgood, Mark Brawley, Dale Copeland, Timothy Crawford, Michael Desch, David Edelstein, Mark Haas, Paul Kowert, Rob Krebs, Peter Jackson, Jonathan Kirshner, David Lake, Patrick James, Christopher Layne, Jack Levy, Dan Lindley, Michael Lipson, Sébastien Mainville, Benjamin Miller, Hans Mouritzen, Tudor Onea, John Owen, T. V. Paul, Joseph Parent, Galia Press-Barnathan, Jeremy Pressman, Alex Reichwein, Evan Resnick, Sebastian Rosato, Larry

Rubin, Randall Schweller, Scott Silverstone, Jennifer Sterling-Folker, Asle Toje, Stephen Walt, and Anders Wivel. We are indebted to each of them.

We individually tested our arguments and presented parts of this book at Cornell University, the University of Connecticut, Florida International University, University of Haifa, McGill University, the University of Notre Dame, and the Norwegian Nobel Institute.

We received excellent research assistance for this manuscript from Brittany Griffin, Shoghig Mikaelian, and Aleksandra Vuldzheva. Brittany also helped format the manuscript.

We are particularly grateful to Oxford University Press. We especially want to thank our editor, Dave McBride, who first encouraged us to write this book and who has offered us much encouragement along the way. We are also indebted to Katie Weaver of Oxford University Press for helping us navigate the production process.

The three of us also thank our families from the bottom of our hearts for their love and support throughout this long endeavor. Without them this book would simply not have been possible.

Norrin M. Ripsman   Jeffrey W. Taliaferro   Steven E. Lobell
Toronto, Canada   Boston, MA   Salt Lake City, UT
                                              September 2015

Introduction

Neoclassical Realist Theory of
International Politics

BEYOND AN APPROACH TO THE STUDY
OF FOREIGN POLICY, TOWARD A THEORY
OF INTERNATIONAL POLITICS

In this book, we forge a neoclassical realist research program for the study of international politics. We argue that neoclassical realist theory can explain political phenomena ranging from short-term crisis decision-making, foreign policy behavior, and patterns of grand strategic adjustment of individual states, to systemic outcomes, and ultimately to the evolution of the structure of the international system itself. We, thus, go well beyond the theories of foreign policy behavior associated with the extant neoclassical realist literature, which address anomalous cases for structural realism or seek to explain foreign policy behavior.[1] Our objective here is to develop a comprehensive neoclassical realist research program of international politics, which provides greater explanatory leverage than the conventional alternatives, including structural realism, liberalism, or constructivism.

As we will explain in detail in Chapter 4, the sharp distinction that Kenneth Waltz draws between theories of foreign policy and theories of

---

1. Structural realism is often referred to as neorealism. See Richard K. Ashley, "The Poverty of Neorealism," *International Organization*, vol. 38, no. 2 (1984), pp. 225–286. In this book, we use the term structural realism, which is more expressive of the causal mechanism.

international politics is overdrawn and counterproductive.[2] Clearly, the international system influences foreign policy, as states must tailor their policies to respond to the threats and opportunities it provides. Yet, over time, the strategic choices of states—particularly the great powers—have an important effect on both international outcomes and the structure of the international system itself. For example, if particular great powers fail to balance adequately against rising threats or pursue expansionist policies that provoke others, these choices might have ramifications for the outbreak of war, its diffusion, and eventually its outcome. The outcome, such as the defeat or weakening of a great power in war, in turn may affect the structure of the international system, which might change from multipolar to bipolar or from bipolar to unipolar under these circumstances. Therefore, in advancing the neoclassical realist program, we maintain that it would be problematic to divorce the international realm completely from the realm of crisis decision-making, foreign policy, and grand strategy. The domestic-level variables that are relevant to explain the latter therefore have at least some causal relevance for the former. One purpose of this book is to specify the conditions under which they are relevant for explaining crisis decision-making, foreign policy, grand strategy, international outcomes, and structural change in the international system, the degree to which they matter, when they have greater influence, and how they interact with systemic causes.

THE VALUE-ADDED OF NEOCLASSICAL REALIST THEORY

We argue that theories from other major international relations research programs—structural realism, liberalism, and constructivism—actually elucidate comparatively little about foreign policy or international politics. Consider structural realism; only in rare circumstances does the international system provide clear information to states about the external constraints and opportunities they face. Thus, for example, confronted in June 1967 with the Egyptian mobilization, a blockade of the Straits of Tiran, and the withdrawal of the United Nations peacekeeping force in the Sinai, Israel had crystal-clear information about the threat with which it was presented and a greatly restricted range of policy options with which to address it.[3] Similarly, the Soviet Union's introduction of

2. Kenneth N. Waltz, *Theory of International Politics* (Reading, MA: Addison-Wesley, 1979).
3. Michael Oren, *Six Days of War: June 1967 and the Making of the Modern Middle East* (Oxford: Oxford University Press, 2002).

offensive nuclear missiles into Cuba in the autumn of 1962 presented a clear and present danger to the physical survival of the United States, greatly restricting its range of options. Under these circumstances, even though there was room for debate over the optimal policy response—as witnessed by the Executive Committee of the National Security Council's deliberations—international imperatives, rather than domestic political considerations, severely limited the range of potential options.[4] The international system rarely provides that level of clarity and certainty. In most circumstances, there is greater room to debate the nature of international threats and opportunities. Thus, the British Cabinet in the early to mid-1930s could debate whether Germany or Japan constituted the greater threat to British interests, and US policymakers and academics in the 1990s and 2000s could debate whether a rising China presented a threat to be contained or a rival to be engaged.[5]

Similarly, by downplaying international pressures, *Innenpolitik* approaches can tell us very little about the foreign policy choices and grand strategies of states, especially during periods of high-stakes external challenges. Only in extreme cases, when leaders are threatened with imminent deselection in an election, revolution, or coup, do states make policy choices almost exclusively, or even mainly, for domestic political reasons. Thus, when Egyptian president Anwar Sadat—who was relatively new in office and far less popular than his predecessor, Gamal Abdel Nasser—faced intense domestic pressure to regain the Sinai in the early 1970s, he calculated that he was unlikely to remain in power without waging a war with a far more powerful Israel.[6] Similarly, in 1982, Argentine president Leopoldo Galtieri risked war with a more powerful Great Britain, which was the United States' closest ally, with no hope of the other superpower

---

4. This is borne out by the secret recordings of the Executive Committee of the National Security Council meetings. See Sheldon M. Stern, *Averting "The Final Failure": John F. Kennedy and the Secret Cuban Missile Crisis Meetings* (Stanford, CA: Stanford University Press, 2003).

5. Aaron L. Friedberg, *A Contest for Supremacy: China, America, and the Struggle for Mastery in Asia*, 1st ed. (New York: W. W. Norton, 2011); Michael Beckley, "China's Century? Why America's Edge Will Endure," *International Security*, vol. 36, no. 3 (2011), pp. 41–78; Zachary Selden, "Balancing against or Balancing with? The Spectrum of Alignment and the Endurance of American Hegemony," *Security Studies*, vol. 22, no. 2 (2013), pp. 330–364; and Evan Braden Montgomery, "Contested Primacy in the Western Pacific," *International Security*, vol. 38, no. 4 (2014), pp. 115–149.

6. Alvin Z. Rubinstein, *Red Star on the Nile: The Soviet-Egyptian Influence Relationship since the June War* (Princeton, NJ: Princeton University Press, 1977). See also Janice Gross Stein, "Calculation, Miscalculation, and Conventional Deterrence I: The View from Cairo," in *Psychology and Deterrence*, ed. Robert Jervis, Richard Ned Lebow, and Janice Gross Stein (Baltimore and London: Johns Hopkins University Press, 1991), pp. 34–59; Raymond A. Hinnebusch, "Egypt under Sadat: Elites, Power Structure, and Political Change in a Post-Populist State," *Social Problems*, vol. 28, no. 4 (1981), p. 454.

(the Soviet Union) intervening when he concluded that his *junta*'s control over the Argentine state was threatened by a severe domestic economic and political crisis and that asserting national control over the Falkland Islands/Las Malvinas might save his government.[7] As we indicate in Figure I.1, however, foreign policy and international politics are typically conducted between these polar opposites, without either domestic or international pressures dictating the course of events on their own; agents and structure combine to produce outcomes. Even in the rare and extreme situations discussed above, neither domestic nor systemic theories were completely determinative (which is why the curve never intersects the asymptotes). Thus, for example, even during the Cuban Missile Crisis, President John F. Kennedy was aware that an insufficiently forceful response would have incurred the wrath of Congress and the American public a month before the midterm election.[8] Similarly, during the 1973 war, Sadat launched only a limited incursion into the Sinai for fear that a full-scale assault on the Sinai or the Negev would provoke a nuclear-armed Israel to escalate the conflict dangerously. Therefore, while in extreme circumstances the system or domestic environment may dominate, they do not determine. Consequently, *Innenpolitik* theories are never sufficient; they are most useful in explaining only a narrow range of cases near the left asymptote. Similarly, systemic theories alone are insufficient and provide the greatest explanatory leverage only over the small range of cases at the right asymptote.

Liberal international relations theories are an influential subset of the *Innenpolitik* approach. As Andrew Moravcsik maintains, liberalism, which subsumes various democratic (or liberal) peace theories, commercial liberalism, and liberal inter-governmentalism, "rests upon a 'bottom up' view of politics in which the demands of individuals and societal groups are treated as analytically prior to politics."[9] For liberals, the state is not an

---

7. T. V. Paul, *Asymmetric Conflicts: War Initiation by Weaker Powers* (Cambridge: Cambridge University Press, 1994), pp. 155–164; and Amy Oakes, "Diversionary War and Argentina's Invasion of the Falkland Islands," *Security Studies*, vol. 15, no. 3 (2006), pp. 449–451.

8. Stern, *Averting "The Final Failure,"* pp. 159–175, 178–179, and 204.

9. Andrew Moravcsik, "Taking Preferences Seriously: A Liberal Theory of International Politics," *International Organization*, vol. 51, no. 4 (1997), p. 518. Classic liberal works include Bruce M. Russett, *Controlling the Sword: The Democratic Governance of National Security* (Cambridge, MA: Harvard University Press, 1990); Bruce Russett and John R. Oneal, *Triangulating Peace: Democracy, Interdependence, and International Organizations* (New York: Norton, 2001); James Lee Ray, *Democracy and International Conflict: An Evaluation of the Democratic Peace Proposition* (Columbia: University of South Carolina Press, 1995); John M. Owen, IV, *Liberal Peace, Liberal War: American Politics and International Security* (Ithaca, NY: Cornell University Press, 1997); and Spencer R. Weart, *Never at War: Why Democracies Will Never Fight One Another* (New Haven, CT: Yale University Press, 1998). Major works on economic interdependence include Robert

Figure I.1
Relative Causal Importance of Systemic and Domestic Variables

autonomous or independent actor, but rather chooses policies that reflect the aggregate preferences of the dominant societal coalition. Therefore, these societal actors, rather than international pressures, are the driving forces of foreign policy and international politics.

Even the (neoliberal) institutionalist theories of Robert O. Keohane and his students and the systemic liberal theories proposed by G. John Ikenberry and Daniel Deudney are essentially *Innenpolitik* because they hold that the state and, by extension, the international institutions they construct ultimately rest upon the consent of the governed.[10] International

O. Keohane and Joseph S. Nye, *Power and Interdependence*, 3rd ed. (New York: Longman, 2001); Patrick J. McDonald, *The Invisible Hand of Peace: Capitalism, the War Machine, and International Relations Theory* (New York: Cambridge University Press, 2009); and Quan Li and Rafael Reuveny, *Democracy and Economic Openness in an Interconnected System: Complex Transformations* (Cambridge and New York: Cambridge University Press, 2009). For a critical analysis of commercial liberalism, see Norrin M. Ripsman and Jean-Marc F. Blanchard, "Commercial Liberalism under Fire: Evidence from 1914 and 1936," *Security Studies*, vol. 6, no. 2 (1996–1997), pp. 4–50.

10. Robert O. Keohane, *After Hegemony: Cooperation and Discord in the World Political Economy* (Princeton, NJ: Princeton University Press, 1984); Robert O. Keohane and Helen V. Milner, eds., *Internationalization and Domestic Politics*, Cambridge Studies in Comparative Politics (Cambridge: Cambridge University Press, 1996); Helga Haftendorn, Robert O. Keohane, and Celeste A. Wallander, eds., *Imperfect Unions: Security Institutions over Time and Space* (Oxford and New York: Oxford University Press, 1999); Robert O. Keohane, *Power and Governance in a Partially Globalized World* (London: Routledge, 2002); G. John Ikenberry, *After Victory: Institutions, Strategic Restraint, and the Rebuilding of Order after Major Wars* (Princeton, NJ: Princeton University Press, 2001); Daniel Deudney, *Bounding Power: Republican Security Theory from the Polis to the Global Village* (Princeton, NJ: Princeton University Press, 2007); and G. John Ikenberry, *Liberal Leviathan: The*

institutions can facilitate mutually beneficial and sustainable cooperation between rational egoists in mixed motive situations, even under conditions of anarchy. States build and participate in international institutions because doing so allows them to achieve efficiency gains through lower transaction costs, greater transparency, issue linkages, monitoring compliance, adjudicating disputes, and the like. This, in turn, enables the participating states to provide absolute gains for their respective societies. The causal mechanism of liberal institutionalism, therefore, is the efficiency gain provided to society as a whole, whether it pertains to economic wealth or military security. This means that institutionalism, like other variants of liberalism, follows an *Innenpolitik* causal logic.

Our critique of liberalism is not that liberal democracy, international institutions, trade flows, or levels of economic interdependence between states are epiphenomenal. Rather, we contend that by downplaying the relative distribution of power and by focusing on institutions, liberal democracy, and trade, to the exclusion of power politics, liberal theories are limited in explaining many aspects of international politics.[11] Moreover, in aggregating societal preferences to explain state behavior, liberalism ignores the central role of the foreign policy executive, the ministers and officials who are tasked with making foreign and security policy and who stand at the intersection of domestic politics and the international arena.

A third leading approach to the study of international politics—constructivism—also provides us with little leverage over foreign policy making or the dynamics of international politics. Constructivists assume that neither the international system nor the domestic political environment can have an independent or uniform effect on state behavior. Instead, actors who are steeped in culture (both domestic and international) must interpret and intersubjectively ascribe meaning to their external environment, international interactions, and the behavior of other actors. Simply put, what actors do in the international arena, the interests those actors hold, and the structures within which those actors operate arise from social norms and ideas, rather from an objective material reality.[12] However, since states and leaders are influenced by competing

Origins, Crisis, and Transformation of the American World Order (Princeton, NJ: Princeton University Press, 2011).

11. We recognize that some liberal theories do posit interactions between systemic (international) and unit-level (domestic) variables. Nonetheless, we maintain that in general liberal theories downplay the causal importance of the relative power distributions.

12. J. Samuel Barkin, "Realist Constructivism," *International Studies Review*, vol. 5, no. 3 (2003), p. 326. Leading social constructivist theories of international relations include: Nicholas G. Onuf, *World of Our Making: Rules and Rule in Social Theory and International Relations* (Columbia: University of South Carolina Press, 1989); Peter J. Katzenstein, ed., *The Culture of National Security: Norms and Identity in World Politics*

international and domestic norms and cultures and juggle multiple, and often conflicting, identities, this means that it would be extremely difficult to make a priori predictions about their foreign policy choices, nor could we explain past behavior except through ex post facto stipulations. This is unsatisfying both from a scientific point of view and from the perspective of scholars who wish to generate policy-relevant advice. Of course, some constructivists and critical theorists would reject these pragmatic, positivist objectives.[13] Again, this is unsatisfying. To be clear, our criticism of constructivist theories is not that ideas, norms, and identities are epiphenomenal. Rather, we contend that by downplaying or even rejecting the importance of the relative distribution of material power, constructivist theories, like liberal theories, are limited in explaining many aspects of international politics.[14]

Neoclassical realist theory addresses these shortcomings. It identifies consequential variables at several levels of analysis and demonstrates how they can produce a range of outcomes at the levels of foreign policy, grand strategic adjustment, international outcomes, and structural change, which makes it a far more powerful explanatory tool than its competitors.

Some might object to our casting our discussion in paradigmatic terms. David Lake, for example, has charged that the paradigmatic debate that dominated the subfield of international relations in the past is unhelpful and should be rejected in favor of problem-driven research agendas.[15] John Mearsheimer and Stephen Walt have observed, much to their dismay, that international relations scholars have, in recent years, eschewed the pursuit of grand theory in favor of hypothesis testing.[16] At a time when much of mainstream international relations—at least in the United States—has moved away from grand theory and paradigmatic debates, why have we

(New York: Columbia University Press, 1996); Alexander Wendt, *Social Theory of International Politics* (Cambridge: Cambridge University Press, 1999); and Nicholas G. Onuf, *Making Sense, Making Worlds: Constructivism in Social Theory and International Relations* (London: Routledge, 2012).

13. Richard Price and Christian Reus-Smit, "Dangerous Liaisons? Critical International Theory and Constructivism," *European Journal of International Relations*, vol. 4, no. 3 (1998), p. 272; and Stefano Guzzini and Anna Leander, "Wendt's Constructivism: A Relentless Quest for Synthesis," in *Constructivism and International Relations: Alexander Wendt and His Critics*, ed. Stefano Guzzini and Anna Leander (London: Routledge, 2006), pp. 78–79.

14. Stefano Guzzini, *Power, Realism and Constructivism* (New York: Routledge, 2013), pp. 15–46.

15. David A. Lake, "Why 'Isms' Are Evil: Theory, Epistemology, and Academic Sects as Impediments to Understanding and Progress," *International Studies Quarterly*, vol. 55, no. 2 (2011), pp. 465–480.

16. John J. Mearsheimer and Steven M. Walt, "Leaving Theory Behind: Why Simplistic Hypothesis Testing Is Bad for International Relations," *European Journal of International Relations*, vol. 19, no. 3 (2013), pp. 427–457.

elected to write a book about neoclassical realism? We would argue that, while we too agree that paradigmatic rigidity and stale internecine disputes across paradigms are unhelpful, we should not throw the baby out with the bath water. Paradigmatic approaches can help us understand the dynamics of international politics and its regularities in a holistic manner, rather than simply focusing on largely disconnected empirical results. Furthermore, as Mearsheimer and Walt emphasize, grand theory can help us guide our empirical research by generating important theoretical questions in the first place and helping us develop hypotheses that are worth testing.[17] As long as it is not impervious to the insights generated by other paradigms—and, by its very nature, neoclassical realism, is not—a powerful paradigmatic approach can inform a useful policy-relevant empirical research agenda.

Our main contributions in this book are as follows. First, we organize, clarify, and advance the neoclassical realist research agenda. We set out the core assumptions of the approach and explain how neoclassical realist theory builds upon some of the key insights of structural realism about the importance of international structure. However, as will quickly become apparent, we do not merely see neoclassical realism as an attempt to explain empirical anomalies for particular structural realist theories, especially balance-of-power theory, or to incorporate insights from twentieth-century classical realists like Hans Morgenthau, E. H. Carr, Arnold Wolfers, and Henry Kissinger into the language of modern social science. Nor do we see neoclassical realism as merely the logical extension of structural realism. Rather, we advance neoclassical realism as its own research program in the study of international relations.[18] This neoclassical realist research program is part of the broader philosophical tradition of *Realpolitik*, as is structural realism, yet it is also informed by key insights of *Innenpolitik* and constructivist critics of structural realism.

Second, we provide a systematic treatment of neoclassical realist variables. We identify the range of independent variables, including both the structure of the international system and also structural modifiers that together form the structural realist baselines from which neoclassical realist theories depart. We then organize the domestic-level intervening

17. Ibid.

18. We use the terms "paradigms," "research program," or "school" to denote empirical theories that proceed from the same core assumptions and that identify related independent variables. In this book, we do not engage the debates about meta-theory (or philosophy of science) and the criteria that political scientists ought to employ to measure scientific progress. For debates over the latter, see Jennifer Sterling-Folker, "Realist Environment, Liberal Process, and Domestic-Level Variables," *International Studies Quarterly*, vol. 41, no. 1 (1997), p. 6.

variables—which hitherto have been treated in a rather ad hoc manner by neoclassical realists—into four coherent clusters (leader images, strategic culture, state-society relations, and domestic institutions) and specify the domestic-level processes that they can influence. In addition, we discuss the extended range of dependent variables over which neoclassical realism can provide leverage, expanding over time from crisis decision-making and foreign policy responses to structural change in the international system. This alone is a very important contribution, which both overcomes the impression that neoclassical realists select variables in an ad hoc manner and specifies the scope and domain of neoclassical realism beyond structural realism's focus on international outcomes.

Third, we distinguish neoclassical realism from other approaches that are frequently mistaken for it because they, too, combine either levels of analysis or the insights of multiple approaches or paradigms. Thus, we explain why analytical eclecticism and foreign policy analysis, among other approaches, cannot correctly be classified as neoclassical realism. In this regard, we clear up the conceptual confusion surrounding neoclassical realist theory.

Fourth, we provide a unique discussion of methodology and research design for those employing and/or testing neoclassical realist theories. Notably, we address all aspects of the theory-building and theory-testing processes, including foundational issues of identifying appropriate research questions and puzzles and the underlying epistemology of neoclassical realism.

Fifth, we demonstrate the value-added of neoclassical realism by illustrating how it can resolve longstanding theoretical disputes within the field. In particular, we address four central debates in the international relations literature: how states respond to threats, the systemic effects of unipolarity, when states are likely to select freer trade over protectionism, and the relative influence of material interests versus ideology in influencing state behavior and international outcomes. In each case, we develop a neoclassical realist theory to demonstrate neoclassical realism's greater explanatory power over these important topics than structural realist, liberal, and constructivist alternatives. In so doing, we illustrate how a focus on international constraints and opportunities moderated by domestic-level processes can provide a more nuanced and theoretically contingent understanding of these phenomena than existing approaches. Moreover, neoclassical realist theory can elucidate the conditions under which each of the leading approaches are likely to be useful, as well as the limitations of these approaches.

Two important caveats are in order. Our purpose here is to advance the neoclassical realist research agenda. In so doing, we are building a broad but coherent approach. Like other broad approaches or paradigms, this approach can encompass many, often competing, theories that nonetheless share the same set of core assumptions about the way states navigate their international and domestic environments. In this regard, neoclassical realism is analogous to the liberal paradigm, which unites democratic peace theory, commercial liberalism, and liberal institutionalism— theories that make very different predictions and employ different causal mechanisms to explain the occurrence of peace or international coop- eration, but nonetheless begin with a common set of liberal assumptions about the role of self-interested individuals, preferences, and political institutions in world politics.[19] Thus, for example, while democratic peace theorists would expect less conflict from a pair of democracies that do not trade with each other than from a mixed pair of democratic and authori- tarian states with a high volume of bilateral trade, commercial liberals would expect the reverse. Neoclassical realism is also comparable to its intellectual ancestor, structural realism, which encompasses both Waltz's balance-of-power theory and Gilpin's hegemonic theory of war and change, which are purely systemic, but competing theories of the causes of war under anarchy.[20] Therefore, there can be many neoclassical realist theories of international politics. For example, Randall Schweller's theory of underbalancing, Jeffrey Taliaferro's theory of resource mobilization, and Nicholas Kitchen's theory of grand strategy formation may use differ- ent variables to explain different phenomena and may even conflict par- tially, but they are all united by the assumptions about foreign policy and international politics that we identify in this book.[21] Consequently, it is possible to have both inter-approach debates (between neoclassical real- ism and structural realist or liberal theories) and intra-approach debates (between different neoclassical realist theories).

To illustrate this dynamic, in Chapter 6 we develop four of our own neoclassical realist theories of international politics to address four per- sistent debates amongst international relations theorists. Our theories fit

19. Michael W. Doyle, *Ways of War and Peace: Realism, Liberalism, and Socialism* (New York: W. W. Norton, 1997), pp. 205–212; 301–314; Colin Elman and Miriam Fendius Elman, eds., *Progress in International Relations Theory: Appraising the Field* (Cambridge, MA: MIT Press, 2003).

20. Robert G. Gilpin, "The Richness of the Tradition of Political Realism," *International Organization*, vol. 38, no. 2 (1984), pp. 287–304. For an argument that hegemonic theory and balance-of-power theory are not necessarily theoretical competitors see Randall L. Schweller and William C. Wohlforth, "Power Test: Evaluating Realism in Response to the End of the Cold War," *Security Studies*, vol. 9, no. 3 (2000), pp. 73–75.

21. Randall L. Schweller, *Unanswered Threats: Political Constraints on the Balance of Power* (Princeton, NJ: Princeton University Press, 2006); Nicholas Kitchen, "Systemic Pressures and Domestic Ideas: A Neoclassical Realist Model of Grand Strategy Formation," *Review of International Studies*, vol. 36, no. 1 (2010), pp. 117–143; and Jeffrey W. Taliaferro, "State Building for Future Wars: Neoclassical Realism and the Resource Extractive State," *Security Studies*, vol. 15, no. 3 (2006), pp. 464–495.

within the parameters of the approach we advance in this book, but not all scholars using a neoclassical realist approach will subscribe to them or agree with them. Ultimately, judging their utility will require careful empirical testing of the type we describe in Chapter 5 to see if they provide greater explanatory leverage over other neoclassical realist theories, as well as those drawn from other conventional approaches.

Second, neoclassical realist theory, like all other approaches to the study of international relations, builds upon insights from its antecedents to create a unique approach to the discipline. Thus, while some—though not all—of the critiques of structural realism detailed in Chapter 1 that neoclassical realists take as their point of departure stem from the insights of liberals, constructivists, and cognitive psychologists, they do not render the research endeavor merely a composite of other theories. Indeed, while Waltz utilized John Herz's concept of the security dilemma to build his structural theory of international politics, it would be unfair to dismiss his novel and influential structural realist theory as merely a restatement of Herz and Waltz's other antecedents.[22] Similarly, while Robert Gilpin's hegemonic theory of war and change was heavily influenced by Simon Kuznets' writings, it would be a mistake to label his important contribution merely derivative of Kuznets.[23] By the same token, the coherent approach we present in this book represents a systematic approach to international politics, privileging international systemic variables filtered through domestic-level intervening variables in a clearly specified manner, which distinguishes it from the structural realist, classical realist, liberal, constructivist, and other influences on our work.

ORGANIZATION OF THE BOOK

We organize the book in the following manner. In Chapter 1, we begin with a discussion of neoclassical realist theory and its improvement on structural realism as a means of explaining the foreign policy and grand strategic responses of states to external challenges and opportunities. We start with an overview of structural realism and its implications for

22. See Waltz, *Theory of International Politics*, pp. 184–186. For concise discussions of how the treatments of the security dilemma by Waltz, Robert Jervis, John Mearsheimer, and other structural realists draw upon the earlier writings of classical realists John Herz and Herbert Butterfield, see Shiping Tang, "The Security Dilemma: A Conceptual Analysis," *Security Studies*, vol. 18, no. 3 (2009), pp. 587–623; and Ken Booth and Nicholas J. Wheeler, *The Security Dilemma: Fear, Cooperation, and Trust in World Politics* (New York: Palgrave Macmillan, 2008), pp. 21–41.

23. Robert Gilpin, *War and Change in World Politics* (Cambridge: Cambridge University Press, 1981), pp. 159–160.

the foreign policy choices of states in an anarchic international system, taking care to explain why Waltz's claim that structural realism is not a theory of foreign policy is unsatisfying and technically incorrect, since the structural effects Waltz and other structural realists posit obtain only through the agency of states responding, on average, rationally to systemic incentives. We then identify four key shortcomings of the structural realist approach: (1) leaders do not always perceive systemic imperatives correctly, even when they are clear; (2) the international system itself does not always present clear signals about threats and opportunities; (3) decision makers do not always respond rationally to systemic imperatives, even when they perceive these imperatives correctly; and (4) states are not always able to mobilize their available resources efficiently and effectively. Consequently, it is essential to modify structural realist theory by incorporating the intervening-level processes and variables that can affect the manner in which states respond to systemic stimuli.

We thus consider the extant neoclassical realist literature, of which we identify two distinct types, which sought to rectify these shortcomings of structural realism. Type I neoclassical realism, including those authors identified by Gideon Rose in his essay which coined the term "neoclassical realism," sought merely to fix structural realism by using domestic-level intervening variables to explain away empirical anomalies for structural realist theories.[24] Type II neoclassical realism, including the contributors to our 2009 edited volume, uses systemic stimuli, moderated by domestic-level intervening variables, to inform an approach to foreign policy more generally, since—except in rare circumstances—structural realism does not provide enough information to predict national strategic choices.[25]

In the next four chapters, we carve out a neoclassical realist research program of Type III—one that explains international politics—and provide a practical guide for neoclassical realist researchers. In Chapters 2–4, we identify the variables employed by neoclassical realism: the systemic independent variable, the domestic-level intervening variables, and the range of dependent variables. Chapter 2 outlines our conception of the international system, including Waltzian structural variables and structural modifiers. We also elucidate the important neoclassical realist variables of the permissiveness and clarity of the international system.

24. Gideon Rose, "Neoclassical Realism and Theories of Foreign Policy," *World Politics*, vol. 51, no. 1 (1998), pp. 144–172.

25. Steven E. Lobell, Norrin M. Ripsman, and Jeffrey W. Taliaferro, eds., *Neoclassical Realism, the State, and Foreign Policy* (Cambridge: Cambridge University Press, 2009).

Chapter 3 details and delimits the range of unit-level intervening variables employed by neoclassical realists. In particular, it identifies four broad classes of intervening variables, including: (1) leader images, (2) strategic culture, (3) domestic institutions, and (4) state-society relations. It then explains how each of these intervening variable clusters affects the three intervening-level processes identified in Chapter 1: (1) perception of the international system, (2) decision making, and (3) resource mobilization or policy implementation. Chapter 4 presents the range of the dependent variables that neoclassical realism can explain, growing over time from crisis decision-making, foreign policy responses, and grand strategic adjustment in the short- to medium-term to international outcomes in the medium- to longer-term and structural change in the long-term. It then delimits the scope of neoclassical realist theory by discussing what cannot be explained by the approach. Finally, it presents our first cut at linking the different intervening variables to specific dependent variables to assist in neoclassical realist theory building.

We provide a methodology for neoclassical realist research in Chapter 5. The chapter begins with guidelines on theory building, specifying how to identify appropriate research questions or puzzles, the epistemology of soft positivism that undergirds our approach, and the process of theory construction. This includes the specification of appropriate dependent and intervening variables together with the appropriate independent variables and structural realist baseline, and the establishment of scope conditions for the theory. The chapter then shifts its focus to the process of theory testing, with discussions on how to identify key actors for testing purposes; selecting alternative explanations;·and a primer on historiography, process tracing, and standards of evidence. In this regard, we provide a comprehensive discussion of research design and methodology for international relations theorists.

Chapter 6 demonstrates the utility of neoclassical realism by using the concepts developed in Chapters 2–5 to forge our own theories to resolve longstanding debates in the international relations literature. First, we address the debate amongst realists and between realists and *Innenpolitik* theorists over how states respond to threats. While balance-of-power realists expect states to balance against rising powers except under specific international structural circumstances, and while most *Innenpolitik* approaches expect their responses to vary depending on their domestic circumstances, we offer a more nuanced argument. We argue that when states face a restrictive international environment, they tend to balance, as balance-of-power realists would expect, although their domestic political environments may influence the types and the intensity of balancing strategies pursued. In more permissive international environments, whether and how states balance will depend on domestic political circumstances in the responding state.

Second, we address the debate between balance-of-power realists and power preponderance theorists on the consequences of unipolarity for the international system. Power preponderance theorists claim that unipolarity is stabilizing and promotes systemic cooperation, whereas balance-of-power realists assume that the unipole will be predatory, making unipolarity dangerous and encouraging the other states to resist it at all costs. We mediate between these two positions with a neoclassical realist argument that hinges upon the domestic political environment of the unipole. We argue that a domestically unconstrained unipole would be as threatening as balance-of-power theorists maintain and, consequently, would inspire fear and balancing. In contrast, a domestically constrained hegemon would pose a far lesser threat and, consequently, might inspire cooperation of the type predicted by power preponderance and hegemonic stability theorists.

Third, we consider the debate between realist and liberal theorists about the circumstances under which states prefer free trade to protectionism. Realists assume that great powers always prefer protectionism to free trade because of the relative gains problem, the fear of cheating, and the security externalities of trade. Liberals assume that it depends on the domestic coalition that controls the state; a nationalist coalition will select protectionism, whereas an internationalist coalition will opt for free trade. We propose a neoclassical realist position predicated first and foremost on the stability of the international environment and subsequently on the domestic coalition of the state. When facing a restrictive international environment, all great powers will prefer protectionism to free trade. When facing a more permissive international environment, however, domestic politics can have greater sway over foreign trade policy. States with inward-looking, nationalist coalitions will prefer protectionism, whereas states dominated by outward-looking coalitions will prefer freer trade.

Fourth, we address the debate between materialists and ideational theorists over whether ideology or material interests determine policy. We argue that in restrictive environments material factors determine the policy choices of all regimes. In permissive environments, however, ideology and ideas have the ability to influence policy.

Finally, in Chapter 7, we evaluate the trajectory of neoclassical realist research. We begin by engaging other approaches to international relations and foreign policy that utilize domestic political variables or seek to reach across paradigmatic lines or levels of analysis and explain how our research program differs from them. We then address a number of lines of criticism that have been leveled against our approach over the past few years and explain either why they miss the mark or how we have responded to them. We conclude with a discussion of our vision for the future of Type III neoclassical realist research and particularly promising avenues of inquiry.

CHAPTER 1

Neoclassical Realist Theory and the Limits of Structural Realism

Neoclassical realism is not sui generis, but instead is a logical extension of the realist tradition. More particularly, although it represents an alternative to constructivism and liberal approaches, as well, it was developed in response to shortcomings of structural realism identified by both realists and critics of realism. In this chapter, we will trace the origins of neoclassical realism and its specific correctives to the external determinist logic of structural realism.

STRUCTURAL REALIST ASSUMPTIONS ABOUT FOREIGN POLICY

The originator of structural realism, Kenneth Waltz, argued that to understand international politics, we must understand the nature of the international system—the political environment within which states interact. Explanations of patterns of international interaction, such as the recurrence of war, that were based on conceptions of human nature or the nature of states (Waltz's first and second images of international politics) were, at best, incomplete, as human nature theories could not explain why war does not always occur, while theories of national difference could not explain why states with different political systems behave similarly in similar circumstances. Furthermore, first- and second-image theories were insufficient because the prescriptions that followed from them required changes in the relations between states, which implies that the problem of war itself stemmed from the nature of the international system, his third image. In contrast, third-image theories, focusing on the anarchical structure of the international system and its consequences for states, were the most efficient explanations of war and other recurring macro-political outcomes between states, and they were sufficient as they required no reference to the types of states involved, human nature, or the particular leaders of specific states.[1] As a result, Waltz constructed a third image theory of international politics, which assumes that under anarchy states respond to the most important variable in the international system, the distribution of material capabilities.[2]

For Waltz and other structural realists, differential growth rates, which over time change the relative distribution of capabilities between states, are the driving forces of international politics.[3] Rising states pose a challenge to others and inspire them, almost automatically, to balance against the challenger either internally, by arming or emulating one another's military practices and technologies, or externally, by allying with other states. In addition, to ensure their long-term survival, states are compelled to anticipate future power shifts and forestall them through policies such as preventive war.[4] Furthermore, they should seek relative rather than absolute gains vis-à-vis other states and avoid the pursuit of cooperative agreements that provide their rivals with gains which can be converted to military advantage.[5] In an anarchic, self-help system, where security and survival are always at stake, states are thus compelled to obey systemic imperatives and do so regularly. While Waltz acknowledges that states do not always behave as the international system requires them to, he maintains that, because those who defy systemic imperatives are frequently defeated and eliminated, the international system socializes states over time to balance against rising great powers and to emulate the successful security behavior of their peers.[6] Consequently, regardless of their leadership and domestic political differences, structural realists generally

1. Kenneth N. Waltz, *Man, the State and War* (New York: Columbia University Press, 1959).

2. Kenneth N. Waltz, *Theory of International Politics* (New York: McGraw Hill, 1979).

3. Ibid.; A. F. K. Organski and Jacek Kugler, *The War Ledger* (Chicago: University of Chicago Press, 1980); and Robert Gilpin, *War and Change in World Politics* (Cambridge: Cambridge University Press, 1981).

4. See, for example, Jack S. Levy, "Declining Power and the Preventive Motivation for War," *World Politics*, vol. 40, no. 1 (1987), pp. 82–107; and Dale Copeland, *The Origins of Major War* (Ithaca, NY: Cornell University Press, 2000).

5. Joseph M. Grieco, "Anarchy and the Limits of Cooperation: A Realist Critique of the Newest Liberal Institutionalism," *International Organization*, vol. 42, no. 3 (1988), pp. 485–507.

6. Waltz, *Theory of International Politics*, pp. 118–128. See also João Resende-Santos, *Neorealism, States, and the Modern Mass Army* (New York: Cambridge University Press, 2007).

expect states to balance against rising challengers in a predictable and unproblematic manner.[7]

Structural realism can answer two general questions. The first question concerns which distribution of power is more stable, that is, less prone to war among the major powers. For most structural realists, following Waltz, the answer is that bipolar distributions are most stable, followed by balanced multipolar distributions. They conclude that the least stable systems are unbalanced multipolar distributions.[8] These scholars also view unipolarity as inherently unstable, as all other states fear that the unipole would act in a predatory manner and would naturally align against it to resist its designs and restore a balance of power.[9] Other structural realists, however, would follow Robert Gilpin in expecting unipolar systems to be the most stable, as none could anticipate a successful war against the unipole, which thus has unfettered power to create a stable order.[10] The second question concerns the strategies states use to secure themselves. More specifically, what are states likely to choose from a range of survival strategies, including balancing (internal and external), buck passing, bandwagoning, and other options?[11]

In this regard, although structural realism is designed to explain international outcomes rather than foreign policy, one can derive an externally driven model of state behavior from its premises.[12] For structural

7. See, for example, Kenneth N. Waltz, *Foreign Policy and Democratic Politics: The American and British Experience* (Boston: Little, Brown, 1967), esp. pp. 306–311, where he argues that the domestic differences between Great Britain and the United States had little impact on their foreign policy behavior.

8. Waltz, *Theory of International Politics*, pp. 161–193; John J. Mearsheimer, *The Tragedy of Great Power Politics* (New York: W. W. Norton, 2001), p. 335. For the converse argument that multipolarity is more stable than bipolarity, see Karl Deutsch and J. David Singer, "Multipolar Systems and International Stability," *World Politics*, vol. 16, no. 3 (1964), pp. 390–406.

9. See, for example, Kenneth N. Waltz, "Structural Realism after the Cold War," in *America Unrivaled: The Future of the Balance of Power*, ed. G. John Ikenberry (Ithaca, NY: Cornell University Press, 2002), pp. 29–67.

10. Robert Gilpin, *War and Change in World Politics* (Cambridge: Cambridge University Press, 1981); and Geoffrey Blainey, *The Causes of War* (New York: Free Press, 1973).

11. Other options available to states include appeasement, hiding from threats, and preventive war. See Randall L. Schweller, *Deadly Imbalances: Tripolarity and Hitler's Strategy of World Conquest* (New York: Columbia University Press, 1997), pp. 74–75; Paul W. Schroeder, "Historical Reality vs. Neo-realist Theory," *International Security* vol. 19, no. 1 (1994), pp. 108–148; Stephen M. Walt, *The Origins of Alliances* (Ithaca, NY: Cornell University Press, 1987), pp. 17–49; Mearsheimer, *Tragedy of Great Power Politics*, pp. 164–165; Jack S. Levy, "Preventive War and Democratic Politics," *International Studies Quarterly*, vol. 52, no. 1 (2008), pp. 1–24; and Norrin M. Ripsman and Jack S. Levy, "Wishful Thinking or Buying Time? The Logic of British Appeasement in the 1930s," *International Security*, vol. 33, no. 2 (2008), pp. 152–158.

12. See, for example, Colin Elman, "Horses for Courses: Why *Not* Neorealist Theories of Foreign Policy?" *Security Studies*, vol. 6, no. 1 (1996), pp. 7–53.

Figure 1.1
A Structural Realist Model of Foreign Policy

realists, states are compelled to select foreign policies that are the most appropriate responses to systemic circumstances. Domestic politics and leader characteristics play no significant role in determining policy, given the great dangers of acting inconsistently with systemic imperatives in an anarchic realm. Consequently, if faced with similar external threats and opportunities, states with different regime types, ideologies, and political institutions can be expected to behave in a similar manner. Indeed, if states did not routinely behave in accordance with systemic imperatives, the macro-level patterns that structural realists identify simply could not obtain. Therefore, structural realist theories of international politics actually depend upon the implicit theories of foreign policy upon which they are built being correct.[13] We will revisit this issue in greater depth in Chapter 2. For now, it is sufficient to point out that structural realism assumes that foreign policy is externally driven, as outlined in Figure 1.1.

THE PROBLEM OF EXTERNAL DETERMINISM

Neoclassical realists agree with structural realists that states construct their foreign security policies primarily with an eye to the threats and opportunities that arise in the international system, which shape each state's range of policy options. Since their very survival is at stake if they fail to secure themselves properly from without in an anarchic international system, where the slightest misstep could lead to defeat in war, the incentives are extremely high for states to focus on external stimuli and craft foreign policies to respond to them appropriately. As Jennifer Sterling-Folker describes, therefore, neoclassical realists share an environment-based ontology, granting primacy to the political environment within which states interact.[14] Nonetheless, they reject the implication that states necessarily respond as fluidly and mechanically to changing international circumstances as structural realist balance-of-power theories imply. In

13. Cf. ibid.; and James Fearon, "Domestic Politics, Foreign Policy, and Theories of International Relations," *Annual Review of Political Science*, vol. 1 (1998), pp. 289–313.
14. Jennifer Sterling-Folker, "Realist Environment, Liberal Process, and Domestic-Level Variables," *International Studies Quarterly*, vol. 41, no. 1 (1997), pp. 1–25.

particular, they note four important limitations to the structural realist model: the ability of leaders to perceive systemic stimuli correctly, the lack of clarity in the international system, the problem of rationality, and the difficulty of mobilizing domestic resources.

i. Perception and Misperception

The first problem is that state leaders do not always perceive systemic stimuli correctly. The international system may at times present states with relatively clear requirements, based on the relative distribution of capabilities and differential growth rates. Yet, as William Wohlforth points out, "If power influences the course of international politics, it must do so largely through the perceptions of the people who makes decisions on behalf of the states."[15] As Robert Jervis and others have noted, leaders, who are only human after all, frequently err in how they process information, their calculations of relative power, their identification of the options at their disposal, and their assessments of the likely consequences of their actions.[16] Such misperceptions can occur to any leader, particularly when faced with incomplete or contradictory information about other state's intentions, relative capabilities, and the likely consequences of one's behavior, or when experiencing an information overload.[17] But it can also result from a systematic bias in a particular leader's package of images and cognitions that comprise his/her cognitive filter, which is used to evaluate and process incoming information.[18] Therefore, a state's national security behavior may have more to do with its leaders' personality, beliefs, and images than objective systemic constraints and opportunities.[19]

In this vein, James McAllister argues that American leaders in the immediate post–World War II period did not behave as Waltz would have expected in a bipolar era—i.e., they pursued external balancing by

15. William C. Wohlforth, *The Elusive Balance: Power and Perceptions during the Cold War* (Ithaca, NY: Cornell University Press, 1993), p. 2.

16. Robert Jervis, *Perception and Misperception in International Politics* (Princeton, NJ: Princeton University Press, 1976); Geoffrey Blainey, *The Causes of War* (London: Free Press, 1973), pp. 35–56; Richard Ned Lebow, *Between Peace and War: The Nature of International Crisis* (Baltimore: Johns Hopkins University Press, 1981), pp. 101–119; and John G. Stoessinger, *Why Nations Go to War*, 9th ed. (Belmont, CA: Thomson Wadsworth, 2005).

17. Robert Jervis, "War and Misperception," in *The Origin and Prevention of Major Wars*, ed. Robert I. Rotberg and Theodore K. Raab (New York: Cambridge University Press, 1988), pp. 101–126.

18. Jervis, *Perception and Misperception in International Politics*, pp. 28–31.

19. Ibid., pp. 18–19.

rearming the Western Europeans rather than internal balancing and they sought to unite Western Europe, rather than to foster its dependence on American power—because they perceived not bipolarity but "a latent tripolar system" once German recovery occurred.[20] Wohlforth maintains that United States and Soviet leader's perceptions of the relative balance of power shaped the nature of superpower relations during the Cold War. While he maintains that, over time, these perceptions tended to follow the actual distribution of power, they led to crises when short-term perceptions masked longer-term trends.[21] And Victor Cha suggests that perceptions of the United States' level of commitment, rather than merely objective calculations of the balance of power, were the primary determinants of the ups and downs in relations between Japan and the Republic of Korea (ROK). Specifically, in periods when Japanese and South Korean leaders perceived a decline in the US defense commitment to East Asia, Japan-ROK relations exhibit significantly less contention over bilateral issues.[22] If leader perceptions of systemic constraints diverge from reality and differ from leader to leader, systemic theories of foreign policy and international politics would be, at best, incomplete, as the sources of a state's behavior may lie less in the external environment than in its leaders' psychological make-up.

ii. The Clarity of Systemic Signals

The second limitation of the structural realist model is that the international system does not always present clear signals about threats and opportunities.[23] In extreme circumstances, when states are faced with a clear and present danger—such as a rapid and imminent power transition—they can easily discern the threat and determine how to counter it given its time frame and the resources at their disposal. Thus, in 1967, when Egypt blockaded the Straits of Tiran, mobilized its armed forces on the Israeli border, and asked the United Nations peacekeeping

20. James McAllister, *No Exit: American and the German Problem, 1943–1954* (Ithaca, NY: Cornell University Press, 2000).

21. Wohlforth, *Elusive Balance.*

22. Victor Cha, "Abandonment, Entrapment, and Neoclassical Realism in Asia: The United States, Japan, and Korea," *International Studies Quarterly*, vol. 44, no. 2 (2002), pp. 261–291. See also idem., *Alignment Despite Antagonism: The United States-Korea-Japan Security Triangle* (Stanford, CA: Stanford University Press, 1999).

23. Steven E. Lobell, Jeffrey W. Taliaferro, and Norrin M. Ripsman, "Introduction: Grand Strategy between the World Wars," in *The Challenge of Grand Strategy: The Great Powers and the Broken Balance between the World Wars*, ed. Jeffrey W. Taliaferro, Norrin M. Ripsman, and Steven E. Lobell (Cambridge: Cambridge University Press, 2012), pp. 1–36.

forces to evacuate the Sinai, it was clear to Israeli leaders that they were in imminent danger and that a pre-emptive strike would be appropriate.[24] Most situations are not as clear-cut, however, leaving great ambiguity over the nature of both the challenges the international system presents and the appropriate responses to them. Thus, for example, it was unclear to British leaders whether the rise of American power and its emerging dominance over the Caribbean Sea in the late nineteenth century constituted a threat to British naval supremacy that should be resisted or an opportunity for the British to retrench and concentrate its naval power in regions of greater strategic importance, especially as American economic policies in the western hemisphere would further British economic goals.[25] It is also unclear whether the rise of China in the post–Cold War era requires the United States to respond in a competitive manner, requiring containment, or whether it necessitates an engagement strategy to moderate Chinese risk-taking behavior.[26] If the international system only rarely provides clear enough information to states to guide their policy responses, then a broad range of foreign policy choices and international political outcomes must lie outside the purview of a structural theory of international politics.

iii. Problems of Rationality

A third limitation is structural realism's implicit assumption of rationality.[27] Neoclassical realists note that leaders do not always respond rationally to systemic stimuli. Even if they correctly perceive the threats and incentives of the international system, they may follow suboptimal or irrational decision-making processes that could lead to policy responses at odds with systemic

24. Michael B. Oren, *Six Days of War: June 1967 and the Making of the Modern Middle East* (Oxford: Oxford University Press, 2002).

25. See Steven E. Lobell, *The Challenge of Hegemony: Grand Strategy, Trade, and Domestic Politics* (Ann Arbor: University of Michigan Press, 2003), pp. 53–63; and Gilpin, *War and Change in World Politics*, pp. 195–196.

26. See Aaron L. Friedberg, "The Future of US-China Relations: Is Conflict Inevitable?" *International Security*, vol. 30, no. 2 (2005), pp. 7–45; and Robert S. Ross and Zhu Feng, eds., *Rising China: Theoretical and Policy Perspectives* (Ithaca, NY: Cornell University Press, 2008).

27. While Waltz argues that balance-of-power theory does not require an assumption of rationality, most structural realists do make rationality a core assumption of structural realism, since if states were not rational, there is no way that systemic threats and opportunities could reliably do any heavy lifting in a theory of international politics. See, for example, Miles Kahler, "Rationality in International Relations," *International Organization*, vol. 52, no. 4 (1998), pp. 919–941; and John J. Mearsheimer, "Reckless States and Realism," *International Relations*, vol. 23, no. 2 (2009), pp. 241–256.

imperatives. As with perception, these problems could relate to cognitive limits on the ability of human beings to process information, particularly in a crisis, when time is short and the stakes are high.[28] As a result, leaders may fail to identify the entire range of policy alternatives available to them or may choose between them in a suboptimal manner, rather than selecting the option likely to maximize the expected payoff at the lowest possible cost. They might even become paralyzed by indecision and fail to react in a decisive manner, as Barbara Tuchman claims Russian Tsar Nicholas II was on the eve of World War I, when he vacillated between competing mobilization plans in response to Austrian action against Serbia.[29]

Nonetheless, particular decision makers might be especially susceptible to failures of rationality, due to their unique temperaments, cognitive flaws, eccentricities, or historical experiences.[30] Thus, both German chancellor Adolf Hitler and Soviet general secretary Josef Stalin had megalomaniacal tendencies that led them to dominate foreign policy decision-making, overrule political and military experts, and deny opinions and information at odds with their views. This led them both to undertake irrational decisions, such as Hitler's decision to declare war against the United States after Pearl Harbor "without consultation with his military strategists . . . without anything approaching proper preparation for such a conflict, and, as [Grand Admiral Karl] Dönitz recalled, without taking cognizance of immediate logistical considerations" and Stalin's unwillingness to prepare for an impending German attack in June 1941 despite overwhelming military intelligence of such an attack.[31] More surprisingly, Canadian prime minister William Lyon Mackenzie King reached his foreign policy decisions, including his decision to enter World War II, after consulting the spirits of his dead ancestors with the help of a medium—hardly a rational decision-making procedure![32] Irrationality

28. Ole R. Holsti, "Theories of Crisis Decision-Making," in *Diplomacy: New Approaches in History, Theory, and Policy*, ed. Paul Gordon Lauren (New York: Free Press, 1979), pp. 99–136.

29. Barbara W. Tuchman, *The Guns of August* (New York: Ballantine, 1994). See also Lebow, *Between Peace and War*, pp. 115–119.

30. See, for example, Jervis, *Perception and Misperception in International Politics*, pp. 217–271; Daniel L. Byman and Kenneth M. Pollack, "Let Us Now Praise Great Men: Bringing the Statesman Back In," *International Security*, vol. 25, no. 4 (2001), pp. 107–146; and Margaret G. Hermann, Charles F. Hermann, and Joe D. Hagan, "How Decision Units Shape Foreign Policy Behavior," in *New Directions in the Study of Foreign Policy*, ed. Charles F. Hermann, Charles W., Kegley, and James N. Rosenau (Boston: Allen and Unwin, 1987), pp. 309–336.

31. On Hitler's folly, see Ian Kershaw, *Fateful Choices: Ten Decisions that Changed the World, 1940–1941* (New York: Penguin, 2007), p. 385. On Stalin's failure, see David E. Murphy, *What Stalin Knew: The Enigma of Barbarossa* (New Haven, CT: Yale University Press, 2005).

32. See, for example, C. P. Stacey, *A Very Double Life: The Private World of Mackenzie King* (Toronto: Macmillan, 1976), pp. 182–192.

of this sort is, of course, problematic for purely structural theories, which require states to respond to international imperatives in a rather automatic fashion, selecting the most appropriate policy response to meet external conditions.

iv. The Need to Mobilize State Resources

Finally, structural realism assumes that states are functionally similar, in that they all perform the same core functions (maintaining basic levels of law and order and external defense) and that they act as unitary rational actors, responding optimally to systemic pressures in a fluid manner. These assumptions ignore the fact that, because of domestic political/economic circumstances, states cannot always extract or mobilize the domestic resources required to respond "efficiently" to systemic imperatives.[33] The structural realist model of national security policy making presumes a perfectly flexible state that is able to identify systemic imperatives correctly and respond promptly as the international circumstances require. If balancing is required, the state must be able to raise revenues, mobilize resources, and enlist military manpower in a timely fashion to prevent a revisionist state from attaining hegemony. The state must be prepared to wage preventive war when faced with a certain power transition.[34]

This level of flexibility assumes that states face no domestic constraints when making national security decisions. In practical terms, however, not all states have the ability to direct policy on their own when faced with opposition from powerful domestic interest groups and societal veto players in the legislature and elsewhere.[35] For this reason, Fareed Zakaria differentiates between state power, or the resources the state actually has at its disposal, and national power, which connotes latent capabilities.[36]

---

33. Thomas J. Christensen, *Useful Adversaries: Grand Strategy, Domestic Mobilization, and Sino-American Conflict, 1947–1958* (Princeton, NJ: Princeton University Press, 1996), pp. 3–10.

34. A. F. K. Organski and Jacek Kugler, *The War Ledger* (Chicago: University of Chicago Press, 1980); Levy, "Declining Power and the Preventive Motivation for War"; Copeland, *Origins of Major War*; and Douglas Lemke, "Investigating the Preventive Motive for War," *International Interactions*, vol. 29, no. 4 (2003), pp. 273–292.

35. George Tsebelis, *Veto Players: How Political Institutions Work* (Princeton, NJ: Princeton University Press, 2002).

36. Fareed Zakaria, *From Wealth to Power: The Unusual Origins of America's World Role* (Princeton, NJ: Princeton University Press, 1999); and Jeffrey W. Taliaferro, "Neoclassical Realism and Resource Extraction: State Building for Future War," in *Neoclassical Realism, the State, and Foreign Policy*, ed. Steven E. Lobell, Norrin M. Ripsman, and Jeffrey W. Taliaferro (Cambridge: Cambridge University Press, 2009), pp. 216–217.

Despite his preference to provide greater support for Great Britain and France against Nazi Germany, for example, US president Franklin D. Roosevelt was impeded by public and congressional opposition, which initially slowed down and limited American assistance. Until the Japanese attack on Pearl Harbor in December 1941 and Hitler's subsequent declaration of war against the United States, domestic constraints prevented Roosevelt from taking the country directly into the European war.[37] Similarly, three successive French premiers who believed that German rearmament within a European Defense Community (EDC) was a strategic necessity for France nonetheless stalled the measure and prevented a ratification vote on the EDC treaty in the National Assembly because of the magnitude of legislative opposition.[38] Nor do all states have automatic access to the human, financial, and material resources they need to implement their preferred foreign security policies. Instead, less-autonomous states must frequently bargain with legislators, power brokers, and societal groups over both the policies chosen and the amount of resources to be devoted to that purpose. Thus, Michael Barnett demonstrates that the Egyptian and Israeli states had to bargain away state power in order to mobilize resources for war in 1967 and 1973, which, in turn, made them more dependent on powerful domestic actors for subsequent mobilizations.[39] Consequently, a theory of international politics and the nature of state responses to the international system must be able to differentiate between states on the basis of their unique policymaking environments.

FIXING STRUCTURAL REALISM: TYPES I AND II NEOCLASSICAL REALISM

The purpose of neoclassical realism, as we see it, is to construct an approach to foreign policy and international politics that retains the primacy of the international system that structural realists emphasize, while relaxing the constraints of external determinism to reflect the limitations discussed above. To date, this endeavor has yielded two varieties of neoclassical realist theory. The first utilizes the intervening state- and individual-level

---

37. Robert Dallek, *Franklin D. Roosevelt and American Foreign Policy, 1932–1945* (New York: Oxford University Press, 1995), pp. 199–313; and Steven Casey, *Cautious Crusade: Franklin D. Roosevelt, American Public Opinion, and the War against Nazi Germany* (Oxford: Oxford University Press, 2001), pp. 30–45.

38. Norrin M. Ripsman, "The Curious Case of German Rearmament: Democracy and Foreign Security Policy," *Security Studies*, vol. 10, no. 2 (2001), pp. 1–47.

39. Michael Barnett, *Confronting the Costs of War: Military Power, State, and Society in Egypt and Israel* (Princeton, NJ: Princeton University Press, 1992).

variables identified by critics of structural realism as explanations for suboptimal policy choices that are at odds with systemic imperatives. The second is a more ambitious enterprise, which seeks to build a comprehensive approach to foreign policy. We discuss each of these research programs in order.

i. Type I: Neoclassical Realism as a Guide to Explaining Anomalies

The first type of neoclassical realism proceeds from the empirical observation that, while states usually conform to systemic pressures over time, they occasionally respond inconsistently with systemic imperatives. Even when systemic imperatives are quite clear, such as when the growth of German power in the 1930s threatened an imminent power transition in Europe, there have been notable incidents of what Randall Schweller calls "underbalancing."[40] Significantly, Schweller cites the French failure to prepare itself for a war against rising Germany prior to World War I and British and French appeasement of a resurgent Germany in the 1930s as quintessential cases of a failure to balance appropriately. Similarly, as Jack Snyder contends, while the international system rarely rewards expansionism and usually punishes it, and while most states avoid expansionism for that reason, history offers us many high-profile cases of states that ignore these constraints at their own peril.[41] Thus, Imperial Germany, Nazi Germany, and Imperial Japan all sought imperial expansion, which proved self-destructive in the long run. As Jeffrey Taliaferro observes, states often engage in costly interventions in regions peripheral to their core interests and, moreover, frequently persist in failing interventions.[42] Classic cases include US interventions in the Korean and the Vietnam wars in the 1950s and 1960s and the Soviet Union's war in Afghanistan in the 1980s. Finally, although Geoffrey Blainey observes that it would be logical for weaker powers to avoid disastrous wars through compromise, which is also consistent with the bargaining model of war, states occasionally initiate wars against stronger adversaries, or fail to make

40. Randall L. Schweller, "Unanswered Threats: A Neoclassical Realist Theory of Underbalancing," *International Security*, vol. 29, no. 2 (2004), pp. 159–201; and idem., *Unanswered Threats: Political Constraints on the Balance of Power* (Princeton, NJ: Princeton University Press, 2006).

41. Jack L. Snyder, *Myths of Empire: Domestic Politics and International Ambition* (Ithaca, NY: Cornell University Press, 1991).

42. Jeffrey W. Taliaferro, *Balancing Risks: Great Power Intervention in the Periphery* (Ithaca, NY: Cornell University Press, 2004).

acceptable compromises to stronger adversaries in order to avoid war.[43] Thus, for example, Japan initiated hostilities against the United States in 1941 and Iraq defied American demands in 1990, which led to a war with a far superior power.[44] At the other extreme, Thomas Juneau argues that the Islamic Republic of Iran failed to exploit a favorable strategic environment after 2001 created by the United States' invasion and removal of hostile regimes in neighboring Iraq and Afghanistan, along with the influx of hard currency from high oil prices. Instead, Iranian leaders pursued strategies with respect to the Shiite-Sunni conflict in Iraq, the faltering Israeli-Palestinian peace negotiations, and Iran's own clandestine nuclear program, that only increased Tehran's international isolation.[45]

Schweller, Snyder, Taliaferro, and other neoclassical realists explain these surprising discrepancies from structural realist expectations in terms of domestic politics. Schweller argues that underbalancing occurs as a result of four domestic political variables: elite consensus and cohesion, which affect the state's willingness to balance; and government or regime vulnerability and social cohesion, which explain the state's ability to extract resources from society to implement a balancing strategy.[46] In other words, when the state is fragmented or weak vis-à-vis society, the state cannot respond appropriately to external threats. In similar terms, Sten Rynning argues that domestic political resistance explains the time lag between French power decline and the French elite's foreign policy adaptation.[47] Ripsman explains the long delay in equipping West German forces to participate in Western defense efforts against the Soviet Union in the late 1940s and early 1950s in terms of the lack of state autonomy in Fourth Republic France, which prevented successive French prime ministers who favored German rearmament from agreeing to it in the face of domestic opposition, despite their sense of the urgency of the Soviet threat.[48]

Taliaferro argues that to explain great power intervention in peripheral regions, we must marry a defensive structural realist theory with

43. Blainey, *Causes of War*, pp. 115–124. On the bargaining model of war, see James D. Fearon, "Rationalist Explanations for War," *International Organization*, vol. 49, no. 3 (1995), pp. 379–414; Dan Reiter, "Exploring the Bargaining Model of War," *Perspectives on Politics*, vol. 1, no. 1 (2003), pp. 27–43.

44. See Taliaferro, *Balancing Risks*, pp. 123–131.

45. Thomas Juneau, *Squandered Opportunity: Neoclassical Realism and Iranian Foreign Policy* (Stanford, CA: Stanford University Press, 2015).

46. Schweller, *Unanswered Threats*. See also Snyder, *Myths of Empire*; Taliaferro, *Balancing Risks*.

47. Sten Rynning, *Changing Military Doctrine. Presidents and Military Power in Fifth Republic France, 1958–2000* (Westport, CT: Praeger, 2002).

48. Ripsman, "Curious Case of German Rearmament."

an understanding of how leaders process information, particularly their aversion to losses and their willingness to take inordinate risks to avoid losses.[49] In comparable terms, Aaron Friedberg explains the United States' choice of balancing strategies at the dawn of the Cold War in terms of a set of bargains that were struck between the executive branch of the federal government, on the one hand, and the Congress and private industry, on the other.[50] Christopher Layne seeks to explain why, despite systemic incentives to the contrary, since World War II successive administrations in the United States have pursued grand strategies of extra-regional hegemony (thwarting the rise of other great powers) as a function of a dominant domestic coalition of liberal internationalists.[51] Snyder explains pathological overextension as a consequence of the nature of domestic political regimes. Unlike most states, those led by imperialistic cartelized regimes and militaristic general staffs are more likely to pursue irrational and self-defeating policies resulting in overexpansion, over-extension, and self-encirclement.[52]

Type I neoclassical realists maintain that the international system sends clear signals to states, but that these signals must inform national policy responses only after passing through the often imperfect transmissions belts of leader perception and domestic politics.[53] In rare cases, either the signals are misunderstood or national leaders are prevented from responding properly by domestic political constraints. This face of neoclassical realism, therefore, is a theory of sub-optimality or pathology to explain what are only understood to be infrequent deviations from structural realist expectations.[54] In other words, this group of neoclassical realists contends that balancing is rather fluid and automatic most of the time; only in unusual circumstances do flawed perceptions or domestic

49. Taliaferro, *Balancing Risks*, pp. 51–52.

50. Aaron L. Friedberg, *In the Shadow of the Garrison State: America's Anti-Statism and Its Cold War Grand Strategy* (Princeton, NJ: Princeton University Press, 2000). See also Mark R. Brawley, *Political Economy and Grand Strategy: A Neoclassical Realist View* (New York: Routledge, 2009).

51. Christopher Layne, *The Peace of Illusions: American Grand Strategy from 1940 to the Present* (Ithaca, NY: Cornell University Press, 2006); Melvyn P. Leffler, *A Preponderance of Power: National Security, the Truman Administration, and the Cold War* (Stanford, CA: Stanford University Press, 1992). Layne's neoclassical realist theory of "extra-regional hegemony" draws heavily upon the Wisconsin School in the historiography of US foreign relations. See William Appleman Williams, *The Tragedy of American Diplomacy*, rev. and enlarged ed. (New York: Dell, 1962).

52. Snyder, *Myths of Empire*.

53. Gideon Rose, "Neoclassical Realism and Theories of Foreign Policy," *World Politics* vol. 51, no. 1 (1998), pp. 144–172.

54. Fareed Zakaria, "Realism and Domestic Politics: A Review Essay," *International Security*, vol. 17, no. 1 (1992), pp. 190–191.

political realities interfere with rational security responses. To explain foreign policy choices in an anarchic international environment, they judge, most of the time a structural realist model will be sufficient. Neoclassical realist theories are useful only to accommodate and explain rare and surprising cases of deviance from structural realist expectations.

ii. Type II: Neoclassical Realism as a Theoretical Approach to Explaining Foreign Policy

The second type of neoclassical realism proceeds from the assumption that the approach can do more than explain anomalies; it can also explain a broader range of foreign policy choices and grand strategic adjustment. To be sure, they would agree that, when states are faced with clear and imminent threats and little policy choice, states usually behave as structural realists would expect and neoclassical realism can only explain behavior at odds with systemic imperatives. Nonetheless, states are rarely faced with such stark choices. In the more common circumstances, when the international environment does not present a clear and imminent threat, states often have a range of policy options to choose from, rather than a clearly optimal policy dictated by international circumstances.[55] The actual choices states make under these circumstances may have far more to do with the worldviews of leaders, the strategic cultures of the states they lead, the nature of the domestic coalitions they represent, and domestic political constraints on their ability to enact and implement various policy alternatives. When French, Russian, German, American, and Japanese contenders rose in power to present potential challengers to British hegemony in the late nineteenth century, for example, it was not clear a priori how British grand strategy should respond. Instead, as Steven Lobell argues, domestic political coalitions competed to determine what degree of threat each challenger posed and whether that threat should be met with cooperative or competitive policy responses.[56] Similarly, William Wohlforth maintains that nothing in the pre–World

---

55. Norrin M. Ripsman, Jeffrey W. Taliaferro, and Steven E. Lobell, "The Future of Neoclassical Realism," in *Neoclassical Realism, the State, and Foreign Policy*, ed. Steven E. Lobell, Norrin M. Ripsman, and Jeffrey W. Taliaferro (Cambridge: Cambridge University Press, 2009), pp. 280–299.

56. Lobell, *Challenge of Hegemony*, pp. 43–85. See also Mark R. Brawley, *Liberal Leadership: Great Powers and Their Challengers in Peace and War* (Ithaca, NY: Cornell University Press, 1993), pp. 115–137; and Aaron L. Friedberg, *The Weary Titan: Britain and the Experience of Relative Decline, 1895–1905* (Princeton, NJ: Princeton University Press, 1988), pp. 135–208.

War I international system required Germany to wage war against Great Britain, its leading trading partner and the great power that threatened it least. Instead, he argues, the roots of war had their foundations in the preferences of German leaders and their concerns for relative status, which interacted with a multipolar balance of power to favor war.[57]

Sometimes, the range of choice is very limited, with the broad outlines determined primarily by external considerations, leaving domestic political considerations to affect only the style of the policy response or its timing. In this manner, Dueck contends that US military interventions in Korea and Vietnam were necessitated by Cold War exigencies, but their timing and style were affected by concerns about domestic political opposition.[58] In other circumstances, however, the range of choice is quite wide, giving the state and key societal actors greater scope to bargain over policy; consequently, policy is more likely to be tailored to suit domestic political circumstances. Thus, for example, Mark Brawley argues that British, French, and Soviet foreign policies in the 1920s were all predicated on the threat of a resurgent Germany, but given the remoteness of the threat in that decade, they were able to adopt considerably different policy responses that reflected the uniqueness of both their strategic situations and their domestic political constraints.[59]

A broad range of the emerging neoclassical realist literature is, therefore, more about foreign policy choices than pathologies. Jason W. Davidson, for example, argues that the fundamental orientation of a state as a defender of the international status quo or as a revisionist challenger is determined not only by its relative power and position within the system, but also by the degree of influence that nationalists and the military have within the domestic political coalition.[60] Colin Dueck explains patterns of US grand strategic adjustment since World War I in terms not only of its strategic position, but also the cultural values of the country's

---

57. William C. Wohlforth, "Unipolarity, Status Competition, and Great Power War," *World Politics*, vol. 61, no. 1 (2009), p. 32.

58. Colin Dueck, "Neoclassical Realism and the National Interest: Presidents, Domestic Politics, and Major Military Interventions," in *Neoclassical Realism, the State, and Foreign Policy*, ed. Steven E. Lobell, Norrin M. Ripsman, and Jeffrey W. Taliaferro (Cambridge: Cambridge University Press, 2009), pp. 139–169.

59. Mark R. Brawley, "Neoclassical Realism and Strategic Calculations: Explaining Divergent British, French, and Soviet Strategies Toward Germany between the World Wars (1919–1939)," in *Neoclassical Realism, the State, and Foreign Policy*, ed. Steven E. Lobell, Norrin M. Ripsman, and Jeffrey W. Taliaferro (Cambridge: Cambridge University Press, 2009), pp. 75–98, at pp. 81–89; and idem., *Political Economy and Grand Strategy*, pp. 93–116.

60. Jason W. Davidson, *Revisionist and Status Quo States* (New York: Palgrave Macmillan, 2006).

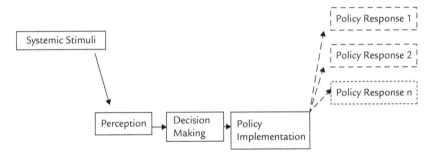

Figure 1.2
The Types I and II Neoclassical Realist Model of Foreign Policy

liberal internationalist elites.[61] Similarly, Nicholas Kitchen contends that neoclassical realism explains how grand strategy is the product of both an empirical assessment of international systemic pressures and competition among strategic ideas within a state's foreign policy executive.[62] In other words, this face of neoclassical realism is a theory of foreign policy in its own right, rather than merely a corrective to explain anomalies for structural realism.

CONCLUSION: NEOCLASSICAL REALISM ADDING EXPLANATORY POWER

The overall mission of Type I and Type II neoclassical realism, therefore, is to add explanatory power to a structural realist skeleton by incorporating domestic political and perceptual intervening processes that can more fully and accurately account for state choices. As illustrated in Figure 1.2, the essence of neoclassical realism to date has been to improve upon the external determinist core of neorealism by "bringing the state back in" to a realist analysis. Policy choices are no longer conceived of as a direct product of systemic stimuli; instead, they pass through the prism of the state, which perceives them and responds to them within the institutional constraints of its unique domestic circumstances. To understand foreign policy, therefore, it becomes essential to study the unique processes of perception, decision making, and policy implementation in individual

61. Colin Dueck, *Reluctant Crusaders: Power, Culture and Change in American Grand Strategy* (Princeton, NJ: Princeton University Press, 2008).
62. Nicholas Kitchen, "Systemic Pressures and Domestic Ideas: A Neoclassical Realist Model of Grand Strategy Formation," *Review of International Studies*, vol. 36, no. 1 (2010), pp. 117–143.

countries, which will lead them to enact different policy responses to similar challenges.

Yet, the conception of neoclassical realism presented in Figure 1.2, which encompasses Types I and II, is incomplete. It provides little information on both the nature of systemic stimuli that have causal importance (the independent variable) and the domestic political factors that can affect the intervening processes of perception, decision making, and policy implementation (the intervening variables). Moreover, it restricts the explanatory scope (the dependent variables) to the policy choices made by states, without considering that these choices might have consequential importance for broader interstate phenomena, such as international outcomes and structural change in the international system.

With this in mind, we will push the boundaries of neoclassical realist theory in the next three chapters to lay the foundation for Type III neoclassical realism: neoclassical realist theory of international politics. Chapter 2 addresses the independent variable. In it, we delineate the neoclassical realist conception of the international system and the constraints and opportunities it presents states. In Chapter 3, we break down the black box of the state and both analyze and organize the cluster of intervening unit-level ideational and institutional variables that neoclassical realists posit can affect the manner in which states respond to systemic constraints and opportunities. In addition, Chapter 4 will probe the range of phenomena that neoclassical realism can reasonably be used to explain, making the case that this research program has much to say about international politics, rather than simply foreign policy.

CHAPTER 2

The Neoclassical Realist Research Paradigm and Its Independent Variable

B oth varieties of neoclassical realism discussed in the previous chapter—theories that purport to explain only foreign policy anomalies or deviations from structural realist baselines (Type I) and theories that purport to offer general models of foreign policy behavior (Type II)— depart from structural realism in that they identify a broad range of unit and sub-unit variables that can intervene between systemic stimuli and foreign policy responses. While they agree with structural realists that policy ought to fit the international strategic environment, neoclassical realists observe that states cannot always tailor their policies to the external environment due to faulty perceptions of systemic stimuli, decision-making procedures that fall short of the rationality standard, or obstacles to policy implementation caused by a failure to mobilize societal resources. Moreover, given that a range of foreign policy choices may be appropriate responses to a given external environment, which policy is selected from among different acceptable policy options depends upon the state's domestic political arena, which can affect a foreign policy executive's perception of the international environment, its decision-making procedures and its ability to implement the policies it selects.

In particular, as illustrated in Figure 2.1, while policymakers construct policy to fit systemic stimuli, policy selection is often influenced by domestic-level intervening variables, including: leader images that interfere with accurate perceptions; strategic culture, which shapes all aspects of state responses; state-society relations, which affect the state's ability to enact and implement decisions; and domestic political institutions,

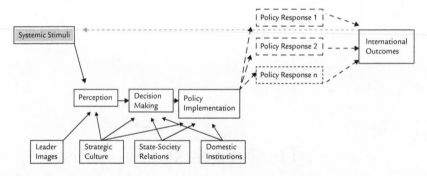

Figure 2.1
Type III Neoclassical Realist Model

which can either enable or constrain state leaders when they face societal opposition to policy selection or implementation. As a result, this more complex domestic decision-making environment implies that states do not necessarily select the optimal policy response to satisfy systemic constraints; instead, they choose from a range of policy alternatives to navigate between systemic constraints and domestic political imperatives. In this chapter, we will begin our discussion of the structural realist approach with a consideration of the independent variable that neoclassical realists employ (highlighted in Figure 2.1). In particular, we detail our conception of the international system. We discuss the intervening and dependent variables in Chapters 3 and 4.

THE INTERNATIONAL SYSTEM

The starting point for neoclassical realist theory is the international system. As Gideon Rose wrote in his 1998 review article in *World Politics,* neoclassical realists "argue that the scope and ambition of a country's foreign policy is driven first and foremost by its place in the international system and specifically by its relative material power capabilities."[1] This conception of the international system raises several definitional questions: What constitutes an international system? Who are the main actors within the international system? What are the underlying dynamics of the system? What is the scope—both temporal and geographic—of the international system? Should we speak of a single international system or a plurality (or succession) of international

---

1. Gideon Rose, "Neoclassical Realism and Theories of Foreign Policy," *World Politics,* vol. 51, no. 1 (1998), p. 146.

systems?[2] The answers to these questions have implications for the development of neoclassical realist theory.

Various definitions of the term "international system" abound in the theoretical literature.[3] While the term "interstate system" or "interstate political system" might be more descriptive for these reasons, we nonetheless chose to retain the familiar term "international system."[4] Neoclassical realism posits that territorial states are the primary units in the international system. While we do not deny the importance of a range of actors of different sizes and compositions that currently operate in the international arena—such as, but not limited to, individual firms, economic sectors, epistemic communities, multinational corporations, international organizations and institutions, terrorist networks, transnational criminal organizations, and international nongovernmental organizations (INGOs)—our conception of the international system is largely state-centric, since states—particularly the great powers—remain the most politically consequential actors. Each of these other actors in the international system can achieve important objectives internationally only when they enlist the support of powerful states. Thus, for example, the United Nations (UN) often founders in resolving interstate and intrastate conflicts when the veto-holding permanent members of the Security Council disagree. Similarly, intense INGO pressure has failed to secure ratification of the Kyoto Protocol when faced with a reluctant United States.

In this volume, when we speak of the "international system," we mainly refer to the interstate system that emerged in Western Europe during the sixteenth and the seventeenth centuries and that by the late nineteenth and early twentieth centuries—through the mechanism of European colonialism and technological diffusion—had grown into a single global international system subsuming previously autonomous systems in East Asia, sub-Saharan Africa, Central Asia, the Indian subcontinent, and the Americas.[5]

2. See, for example, Stephen Hobden, *International Relations and Historical Sociology: Breaking down Boundaries* (New York: Routledge, 2006), p. 33.

3. See for example, Inis L. Claude, *Power and International Relations* (New York: Random House, 1962), p. 42; Richard N. Rosecrance, *Action and Reaction in World Politics* (Boston: Little, 1963), pp. 224–230; Raymond Aron, *Peace and War: A Theory of International Relations*, trans. Rémy Inglis Hall, abridged ed. (Garden City, NY: Anchor, 1973), pp. 94–99; Stanley Hoffmann, "International Systems and International Law," in *The State of War: Essays on the Theory and Practice of International Politics*, ed. Stanley Hoffmann (New York: Praeger, 1961); Morton A. Kaplan, *System and Process in International Politics* (New York: Wiley, 1967), p. 96; Hedley Bull, *The Anarchical Society: A Study of Order in World Politics* (New York: Columbia University Press, 1977), pp. 8–16; and Robert Gilpin, *War and Change in World Politics* (Cambridge: Cambridge University Press, 1981), pp. 25–39.

4. Barry Buzan, Charles Jones, and Richard Little, eds., *The Logic of Anarchy: Neorealism to Structural Realism* (New York: Columbia University Press, 1993), pp. 29–30.

5. Barry Buzan and Ole Wæver, *Regions and Powers: The Structure of International Security* (Cambridge and New York: Cambridge University Press, 2003); and David B. Ralston,

Kenneth Waltz defines an international system as comprising only a structure and the interacting units:

> International-political systems, like economic markets, are formed by the coaction of self-regarding units. International structures are defined in terms of the primary political units of an era, be they city-states, empires, or nations. Structure emerges from the coexistence of states. No state intends to participate in the formation of a structure by which it and others will be constrained. International-political systems, like economic markets are individualist in origin, spontaneously generated, and unintended.[6]

Waltz argues that the chief characteristics of any political system are: (1) its ordering principle (the "first tier" or "deep structure"), that is, how the units stand in relation to one another; (2) the degree of differentiation, or lack thereof, among the units (the "second tier"); and (3) the distribution of capabilities among the units (the "third tier" or "surface structure").[7] An international political system, once in existence, constrains and shapes the behavior of the units (or states) through the reinforcing mechanisms of socialization and competition. Over time, states "learn" because they see the misfortune of others who chose not to conform to the dictates of the system.[8]

Waltz's conception of system and structure is spare. Nevertheless, it does capture two insights upon which neoclassical realism builds. The first is that while the structure of the system imposes constraints by delimiting a range of possible strategic responses and bargaining outcomes, the system itself cannot dictate the behavior of individual units. David Dessler uses the metaphor of an office building to illustrate this point. The building's external walls and the configuration of the internal spaces generate broad behavioral patterns for the workers ("units") within them. Dessler writes, "we do not find people attempting to walk through walls, crawl through air conditioning ducts, or leave via upper story windows." The actual paths that workers take to get from point A to point B will be determined by the nature of their jobs, the requirements of interoffice communication, and so on, which Dessler notes, are shaped by the attributes of the individual units (or workers).[9]

Importing the European Army: The Introduction of European Military Techniques and Institutions into the Extra-European World, 1600–1914 (Chicago: University of Chicago Press, 1990).

6. Kenneth N. Waltz, *Theory of International Politics* (Reading, MA: Addison-Wesley 1979), p. 71.

7. John Gerard Ruggie, "Continuity and Transformation in the World Polity: Toward a Neorealist Synthesis," in *Neorealism and Its Critics*, ed. Robert O. Keohane (New York: Columbia University Press, 1986), pp. 135–136.

8. Waltz, *Theory of International Politics*, pp. 76, 128.

9. David Dessler, "What's at Stake in the Agent-Structure Debate?" *International Organization*, vol. 43, no. 3 (1989), p. 466.

The second insight is that the system's anarchic ordering principle generates pervasive uncertainty among the units. To return to Dessler's building metaphor, Jennifer Sterling-Folker asks us to imagine that the office building contains hidden trapdoors on every floor. The workers may know the trapdoors exist and that the consequence of falling through one is severe injury or death, but they have no knowledge or control over the placement of these traps. Nor do they have any means to remove those traps.[10] It is not simply that anarchy leaves states unregulated and unsupervised so that war may break out any time, but as Sterling-Folker observes, "It is instead that the anarchic environment allows death to occur in the first place while providing no guidance for how to avoid it in the short-term and ultimately no means of doing so in the long-term."[11] This lack of guidance from an overarching authority renders an anarchic system a self-help environment. As we noted in the introduction of our earlier work, it also suggests that systemic incentives and threats that arise within a system, at least in the short run, are rarely unambiguous. Seldom is there a single optimal response to systemic constraints and opportunities.[12]

By emphasizing how structure imposes constraints on the units, Waltz captures the "vertical" dimension of an international system. That vertical dimension, however, is incomplete. Robert Jervis provides a somewhat fuller definition of a system: "We are dealing with a system when (a) a set of units or elements is so interconnected that changes in some elements or their relations produce changes in other parts of the system, and (b) the entire system exhibits properties and behaviors that are different from those of the parts."[13] According to Jervis, "systems often display nonlinear relationships, outcomes cannot be understood by adding together the units or their relations, and many of the results are unintended."[14] This captures the "horizontal" dimensions of an international system. In other words, just as the causal chain linking systemic variables—chiefly the relative distribution of material capabilities and anticipated power trends—to the likely external behavior of the units is complex and indirect

---

10. Jennifer Sterling-Folker, *Theories of International Cooperation and the Primacy of Anarchy: Explaining U.S. International Monetary Policy-Making after Bretton Woods* (Albany: State University of New York Press, 2002), pp. 71–72.

11. Ibid., p. 73.

12. Jeffrey W. Taliaferro, Steven E. Lobell, and Norrin M. Ripsman, "Introduction: Neoclassical Realism, the State, and Foreign Policy," in *Neoclassical Realism, the State, and Foreign Policy*, ed. Steven E. Lobell, Norrin M. Ripsman, and Jeffrey W. Taliaferro (Cambridge: Cambridge University Press, 2009), pp. 28–29.

13. Robert Jervis, *System Effects: Complexity in Political and Social Life* (Princeton, NJ: Princeton University Press, 1997), p. 6.

14. Ibid.

(as discussed below), so too are the causal chains linking the aggregate outcomes of one unit's strategies to another and to the dynamics of the system as a whole (as discussed in Chapter 4).

SYSTEM STRUCTURE AND STRUCTURAL MODIFIERS

Waltz's conception of structure is the starting point for the fuller neoclassical realist treatment of structure we lay out below. He writes, "The concept of structure is based on the fact that units differentially juxtaposed and combined behave differently and interacting produce different outcomes."[15] Furthermore, Waltz insists the definition of structure must abstract from the characteristics of the units, their behaviors, and their interactions.

According to Waltz, there are two, and only two, possible ordering principles among the units in any political system: hierarchy and anarchy.[16] Units are either arranged hierarchically, as in a world government or an empire where all units are completely subordinate to a single unit which acts as the central authority, or they are considered to be anarchic. Since Waltz maintains that the ordering principle of any international political system is by definition anarchic, the units cannot risk participating in a division of labor; therefore, they cannot afford to specialize. They must perform the same core set of tasks.[17] Waltz summarizes pithily, "In anarchic realms, like units co-act. In hierarchic realms, unlike units interact."[18]

Since the ordering principle and differentiation of functions among the units are effectively constant, at least in the modern international system, only the third element of structure—the relative distribution of capabilities among the units (the "third tier" or "surface structure")—is a causal variable in Waltz's balance-of-power theory. Furthermore, it is the polarity of the system—that is, the number of great powers—that does almost all of the causal work in Waltz's theory. Accordingly, his theory generates two probabilistic predictions: first, that across different types of international systems (bipolarity and multipolarity), balances of power will recurrently form; and second, that states will emulate the successful practices of others.[19]

---

15. Waltz, *Theory of International Politics*, p. 81.
16. Ibid., pp. 81–82 and 88–99.
17. Jack Donnelly, *Realism and International Relations* (Cambridge: Cambridge University Press, 2000), p. 84.
18. Waltz, *Theory of International Politics*, p. 104.
19. Ibid., pp. 123–128, 161–163. See also João Resende-Santos, *Neorealism, States, and the Modern Mass Army* (New York: Cambridge University Press, 2007).

Waltz's treatment of international structure has generated numerous criticisms on a variety of ontological, theoretical, and empirical grounds.[20] Some of those criticisms are well taken. At present, however, we focus on just one line of objection to Waltz's conception of structure: namely, that it ignores important variables that are located at either the unit or the systemic level of analysis.[21] As even Waltz admits, "Structures condition behaviors and outcomes, yet explanations of behaviors and outcomes are indeterminate because both unit-level and structural causes are in play."[22]

Our understanding of system structure is broader than that of Waltz. Building upon Barry Buzan's work, we submit that there are broad systemic, but not structural, factors that "not only affect the ability and the willingness of units to interact, but also determine what types of levels of interaction are both possible and desired." These factors are "systemic even though they clearly fall outside the meaning of structure."[23] Buzan calls these factors "interaction capacity" and identifies only two of them: the continual evolution (and diffusion) of technological capabilities and shared international norms and organization. While these factors are not part of the structure, they are clearly systemic and "profoundly condition the significance of structure and the meaning of the term system itself."[24] He contends that interaction capacity, too, should be considered along with structure as a "shoving and shaping" force on the units of the system, elevating it to a middle level of analysis between the structure and the unit in his reformulation of structural realism.[25]

20. See, for example, Barry Buzan and Richard Little, "Reconceptualizing Anarchy: Structural Realism Meets World History," *European Journal of International Relations*, vol. 2, no. 4 (1996), pp. 403–438; Barry Buzan and Richard Little, "Waltz and World History: The Paradox of Parsimony," *International Relations*, vol. 23, no. 3 (2009), pp. 446–463; Ruggie, "Continuity and Transformation in the World Polity," pp. 131–157; Richard Little, "Structural Realism and World History," in *The Logic of Anarchy: Neorealism to Structural Realism*, ed. Barry Buzan, Charles Jones, and Richard Little (New York: Columbia University Press, 1993), pp. 85–101; Alexander Wendt, "Anarchy Is What States Make of It: The Social Construction of Power Politics," *International Organization*, vol. 46, no. 2 (1992), pp. 391–425; and David A. Lake, *Hierarchy in International Relations* (Ithaca, NY: Cornell University Press, 2009).

21. Jervis, *System Effects*, pp. 109–110; Barry Buzan, Charles A. Jones, and Richard Little, *The Logic of Anarchy: Neorealism to Structural Realism* (New York: Columbia University Press, 1993), pp. 51–53; and Glenn H. Snyder, "Process Variables in Neorealist Theory," in *Realism: Restatement and Renewal*, ed. Benjamin Frankel (London: Frank Cass, 1996), pp. 173–193.

22. Waltz, "Reflections on Theory of International Politics," p. 343.

23. Barry Buzan, "Beyond Neorealism: Interaction Capacity," in *The Logic of Anarchy: Neorealism to Structural Realism*, ed. Barry Buzan, Charles Jones, and Richard Little (New York: Columbia University Press, 1993), p. 69.

24. Ibid., p. 72.

25. Ibid., p. 77, fig. 4.1.

Glenn Snyder coined the more descriptive term "structural modifiers" in reference to systemic variables that "modify the effects of the more basic structural elements on the interaction process, but they are not interaction itself."[26] For Snyder, these structural modifiers are external and systemic, as they affect all units in a similar manner, but they are distinct from the number of units and the distribution of capabilities that Waltz defines as structure. Military technology, for example, is a structural modifier because technological change affects all great powers, at least potentially; hence, technological diffusion is inherently a systemic variable, not a unit attribute.[27]

Similarly, Stephen Van Evera argues that the "fine-grained structure of power," which he defines as the distribution of particular types of (military) power, has a greater impact on the likelihood of interstate conflict than does the aggregate structure of power or polarity. The fine-grained structure of power encompasses the offense-defense balance, the size and frequency of power fluctuations (and resultant windows of opportunity and vulnerability), the magnitude of first-move advantages, and the cumulativity of resources (that is, the degree to which states can parlay territorial conquests into further gains). Each of these can affect the intensity of the security dilemma, and consequently, the likelihood of inadvertent conflict among states.[28]

We prefer the term "structural modifiers" to the term "interaction capacity." However, our treatment parts company with the work of Buzan, Snyder, and Van Evera in two respects. First, unlike Buzan, who identifies norms and (international) institutions as one of two components of interaction capacity, we restrict the term "structural modifier" to a class of material variables at the level of the international system or a regional subsystem, but which are not structural. Structural modifiers would include geography, the rates of technological diffusion, and the offense-defense balance in military technologies. These various factors can modify the effect of the system's structure—namely, its anarchic ordering principle and the relative distribution of capabilities—on the parameters of strategic interactions and the likely external behaviors of individual units.

Second, unlike Snyder and Van Evera, we do not hold that structural modifiers affect the behavior of all states in the system more or less evenly.

26. Snyder, "Process Variables in Neorealist Theory," p. 169.
27. Ibid., pp. 169–170.
28. Stephen Van Evera, *Causes of War: Power and the Roots of Conflict* (Ithaca, NY: Cornell University Press, 1999), pp. 7–10. Van Evera refers to these systemic variables as Type III Realism ("fine-grained structural realism"), distinct from the Type II Realism of Kenneth Waltz and John Mearsheimer.

Some structural modifiers do indeed have a uniform impact on the likely behavior of all units within the system, but there are others whose impacts are limited to particular sectors or regions within the system, categories of units (for example, the great powers as opposed to weaker states), or pairs of units. For example, Snyder writes that nuclear weapons, specifically the second-strike arsenals the United States and the Soviet Union maintained from the early 1960s until the end of the Cold War, might be considered a structural modifier in the sense that they "mollify the effects of anarchy by inhibiting aggression and ameliorating the 'security dilemma,' but they do not change the structural effect of anarchy."[29] While nuclear deterrence decreased the likelihood of an intended military confrontation between the superpowers and their principal allies and client states in Europe, East Asia, and the Middle East, the effects of nuclear weapons on the behavior of states in sub-Saharan Africa and South America (regions where, arguably, the superpowers had fewer strategic interests) were, at best, indirect.[30] Relatedly, we submit that it makes little sense to conceive of the offense-defense balance in military technology as pertaining to the international system as a whole. Instead, the offense-defense balance pertains to the balance of military technologies and therefore the intensity of the security dilemma, only between particular pairs or groups of states (units) or within specific geographic regions.[31] Thus, leaving aside the considerable debates over definition and measurement, the offense-defense balance between France and Germany and between Germany and the Soviet Union might be characterized as "offense-dominance" in 1940–1941, but it would be inaccurate to characterize the international system as a whole during that period as being "offense dominant." After all, the prevailing military technologies of 1940, along with geographic distance, made the continental United States immune from conquest by another great power.[32]

Similarly, geography is a structural modifier because it can create constraints and provide opportunities for some units and for patterns of strategic interaction within the given structure of the system.[33] However,

29. Snyder, "Process Variables in Neorealist Theory," p. 171; See also Robert Jervis, "Cooperation under the Security Dilemma," *World Politics*, vol. 30, no. 2 (1978), pp. 167–214.

30. Benjamin Miller, *When Opponents Cooperate: Great Power Conflict and Collaboration in World Politics*, 1st pbk. ed. (Ann Arbor: University of Michigan Press, 2002), pp. 64–67.

31. Jeffrey W. Taliaferro, "Security Seeking under Anarchy: Defensive Realism Revisited," *International Security*, vol. 25, no. 3 (2000), pp. 135–138.

32. See, for example, James W. Davis Jr. et al., "Correspondence: Taking Offense at Offense-Defense Theory," *International Security*, vol. 23, no. 3 (1999), pp. 179–206.

33. See John J. Mearsheimer, *The Tragedy of Great Power Politics* (New York: W. W. Norton, 2001), pp. 83–84, 114–128; Jack S. Levy and William R. Thompson, "Balancing on Land

the constraints and opportunities rarely pertain to the system as a whole. Physical distance (and consequently, the loss-of-strength gradient), strategic depth, and topographical barriers, or the lack thereof, can have an effect on the security environment in which states operate, a point on which a variety of classical realists, structural realists, and neoclassical realists would readily agree.[34] Thus, until the development of long-range bombers and eventually ballistic missiles, the continental United States was largely immune from attack by a Eurasian great power. The English Channel and the North Sea provided a similar "security buffer" for Great Britain until the advent of long-range aviation in the mid-twentieth century. Conversely, a lack of strategic depth and indefensible borders has been a perennial dilemma for many great powers (for example, Prussia/ Germany) and non-great powers (for example, Denmark, Israel, Pakistan, and Singapore) alike.[35]

To return to Dessler's office building metaphor, if the building's external walls and the configuration of the internal walls are analogous to the system structure, then structural modifiers are akin to wall partitions and cubicles on particular floors.[36] Those partitions and cubicles further delimit the possible movements for workers on a particular floor, but they generally do not affect the flow of movement within the building as a whole. Furthermore, the workers themselves may be able to move or work around some of those partitions or cubicles. In certain instances, the workers may succeed in erecting new partitions or rendering existing ones obsolete. For example, states cannot change their geography and factor endowments, except occasionally through military conquest. Nonetheless, the development and the diffusion of new technologies, such as air power, nuclear weapons, ballistic missiles, and more recently,

and at Sea: Do States Ally against the Leading Global Power?," *International Security*, vol. 35, no. 1 (2010), pp. 7–43; A. T. Mahan, *The Influence of Sea Power Upon History, 1660–1783* (Boston: Little, Brown and Company, 1890); and Halford John Mackinder, *Britain and the British Seas* (New York: Haskell House, 1969).

34. On the loss-of-strength gradient, see Kenneth E. Boulding, *Conflict and Defense: A General Theory* (New York: Harper, 1962), pp. 260–262 and 268–269.

35. See Hans Mouritzen and Mikkel Runge Olesen, "The Interplay of Geopolitics and Historical Lessons in Foreign Policy: Denmark Facing German Post-War Rearmament," *Cooperation and Conflict*, vol. 45, no. 4 (2010), pp. 406–427; Hans Mouritzen, "Past versus Present Geopolitics: Cautiously Opening the Realist Door to the Past," in *Rethinking Realism in International Relations: Between Tradition and Innovation*, ed. Annette Freyberg-Inan, Ewan Harrison, and Patrick James (Baltimore: Johns Hopkins University Press, 2009), pp. 164–190.

36. Dessler writes, "in configuring structure as an environment, [Waltz's theory] is unable to conceptualize accurately those features of the system that are the means to action rather than the setting in which action takes place." Dessler, "What's at Stake in the Agent-Structure Debate?" p. 468.

computers and the Internet, can reduce or increase effective geographic distance between states.

THE RELATIVE DISTRIBUTION OF POWER AND POLARITY

Like classical realism and structural realism, neoclassical realism views international politics as a never-ending struggle among states for power and influence in a world of finite resources and uncertainty about each other's intentions and capabilities.[37] The structure of the international system and structural modifiers shape the broad parameters of possible strategies that states can pursue, as well as the range of possible bargaining outcomes among those states. Neoclassical realist theory sees "anarchy as a permissive condition rather than an independent causal force."[38] The relative distribution of power and power trends are the explanatory variables in neoclassical realist theory and are conditioned by structural modifiers such as technology and geography. As Brian Schmidt and Thomas Juneau note, however, this raises several questions about the conception of power in international relations theories.[39]

Power, like many other important concepts in international relations, is hotly contested. There appears to be little consensus among the different theoretical schools over what constitutes power, let alone over power's casual importance relative to other variables of interest, such as democracy, international institutions, norms, and identities. Even among the three main branches of modern realist theories—classical realism, structural realism, and neoclassical realism—there are disagreements over how best to define and measure power.[40] As Schmidt and Juneau write, "the debate gets more contentious when scholars attempt to distinguish power from a host of closely related concepts such as influence, force and control."[41]

37. Benjamin Frankel, "Restating the Realist Case: An Introduction," in *Realism: Restatements and Renewal*, ed. Benjamin Frankel (London: Frank Cass, 1996), pp. ix–xx.

38. Stephen M. Walt, "The Enduring Relevance of the Realist Tradition," in *Political Science: The State of the Discipline*, ed. Ira Katznelson and Helen V. Milner (New York: W. W. Norton, 2002), p. 211.

39. Brian C. Schmidt and Thomas Juneau, "Neoclassical Realism and Power," in *Neoclassical Realism in European Politics: Bringing Power Back In*, ed. Alse Toje and Barbara Kunz (Manchester: Manchester University Press, 2012), p. 61; See also Brian C. Schmidt, "Competing Realist Conceptions of Power," *Millennium: Journal of International Studies*, vol. 33, no. 3 (2005), p. 525.

40. Schmidt, "Competing Realist Conceptions of Power," p. 528; and Schmidt and Juneau, "Neoclassical Realism and Power," p. 61.

41. Schmidt and Juneau, "Neoclassical Realism and Power," p. 62. For analysis of the debates about power among and within the different schools of international relations

David Baldwin identifies two dominant approaches to power in the international relations literature: "the relational power approach," which depicts power as an actual or potential relationship between actors, and the elements of national power approach, which treats power as resources.[42] Following other neoclassical realists, we adopt the "elements of national power approach," which sees power as a means to an end, not an end unto itself, and which separates "power" from "influence."[43]

Neoclassical realists, like structural realists and some classical realists, use various measurements or indicators of a state's material capabilities. The usual measures include a state's gross domestic product (GDP); level of annual defense spending (in absolute terms, as a percentage of GDP, or as a percentage of government expenditures); the size and the composition of the armed forces; military research and development; the size of the population, as well as demographic trends within the population; natural resource endowments; and the size of territory.[44] Like Hans Morgenthau and others, they also include various intangible resources, such as national morale and the quality of leadership and diplomacy, as elements of national power.[45] The essential point, according to Schmidt and Juneau, is that researchers can combine the more important material resources at a state's disposal into some measure of overall national power.[46] Of course, such indicators of aggregate power are not without their empirical limitations or immune from criticism.[47] Nevertheless, the elements of national power approach and resulting efforts to develop some qualitative and quantitative indicators of material capabilities (however inexact) are consistent with the soft-positivist epistemology underlying neoclassical realism, which we discuss at greater length in Chapter 5.

theories, see Felix Berenskoetter and Michael J. Williams, eds., *Power in World Politics* (London and New York: Routledge, 2007).

42. David A. Baldwin, "Power and International Relations," in *Handbook of International Relations*, ed. Walter Carlsnaes, Thomas Risse-Kappen, and Beth A. Simmons (London and Thousand Oaks, CA: Sage, 2002), p. 185.

43. See, for example, William Curti Wohlforth, *The Elusive Balance: Power and Perceptions during the Cold War* (Ithaca, NY: Cornell University Press, 1993), pp. 6–7; and Randall L. Schweller, *Deadly Imbalances: Tripolarity and Hitler's Strategy for World Conquest* (New York: Columbia University Press, 1997), pp. 17–18.

44. For example, Schweller relies upon the Correlates of War (COW) project's capability index to measure the relative capabilities of the great powers during the interwar period. See Schweller, *Deadly Imbalances*, pp. 26–31; and Waltz, *Theory of International Politics*, p. 131.

45. Hans J. Morgenthau, *Politics among Nations: The Struggle for Power and Peace*, 3rd ed. (New York: Alfred A Knopf, 1963), pp. 110–148.

46. Schmidt and Juneau, "Neoclassical Realism and Power," p. 62.

47. See, for example, Stefano Guzzini, "The Concept of Power: A Constructivist Analysis," *Millennium: Journal of International Studies*, vol. 33, no. 3 (2004), pp. 495–521; and Stefano Guzzini, *Power, Realism, and Constructivism* (New York: Routledge, 2013).

Like structural realism, neoclassical realism uses the term polarity to denote the number of great powers or major states in existence within a system at a given time, depending on their control over sufficient material components of power as well as the political and bureaucratic means to extract and mobilize these resources when necessary.[48] Scholars use the term unipolarity to denote a system in which only one state meets all the above criteria, as opposed to systems in which two states (bipolarity) or three or more states (multipolarity) meet those criteria.[49] Polarity is a function of the relative distribution of capabilities among the major states in the system, rather than the dominant patterns of alignment or alliance blocs among the great powers. In this regard, neoclassical realists part company with some twentieth-century classical realists, notably Raymond Aron and John Herz, among others, who largely conceive of polarity in behavioral terms.[50]

As John Ikenberry, Michael Mastanduno, and William Wohlforth observe, however, multipolarity, bipolarity, and unipolarity are simply "ideal types" of power configurations. The international system at any given point in time can only approximate one of these ideal types.[51] It is sometimes easier for scholars and policymakers to determine whether a system has made the transition from multipolarity to bipolarity (or vice versa) or from bipolarity to unipolarity (or vice versa), with several years of hindsight. For example, while international relations theorists now see World War II as marking the decisive shift from a multipolar system of six great powers (Great Britain, France, Germany, Japan, the United States, and the Soviet Union) to a bipolar system of two superpowers (the United States and the Soviet Union), it actually took several years for the victors to recognize it. According to Wohlforth, World War II did not provide states with clear information on power relations, and consequently, US and Soviet

---

48. This definition of a pole builds upon the discussion in Waltz, *Theory of International Politics*, pp. 131; William C. Wohlforth, "The Stability of a Unipolar World," *International Security*, vol. 24, no. 1 (1999), pp. 9–13; and Stephen G. Brooks and William C. Wohlforth, *World Out of Balance: International Relations and the Challenge of American Primacy* (Princeton, NJ: Princeton University Press, 2008), p. 12.

49. Wohlforth, "Stability of a Unipolar World," pp. 9–22. For a critique of Waltz's treatment of bipolarity, see R. Harrison Wagner, "What Was Bipolarity?" *International Organization*, vol. 47, no. 1 (1993), pp. 77–106.

50. See, for example, Aron, *Peace and War*, p. 159; and John H. Herz, *International Politics in the Atomic Age* (New York: Columbia University Press, 1959), pp. 155–156.

51. See G. John Ikenberry, Michael Mastanduno, and William C. Wohlforth, "Introduction: Unipolarity, State Behavior, and Systemic Consequences," in *International Relations Theory and the Consequences of Unipolarity*, ed. G. John Ikenberry, Michael Mastanduno, and William C. Wohlforth (Cambridge: Cambridge University Press, 2011), pp. 1–32, at p. 6.

leaders disagreed about which was of greater significance, American economic superiority or the Soviet Union's advantage in conventional forces.[52] Similarly, James McAllister contends that the early postwar international system was not unambiguously bipolar; instead, officials in Washington and Moscow perceived it as a latent tripolar system until the mid-1950s, as American and Soviet leaders both anticipated the reemergence of Germany as a European great power.[53]

CLARITY

A key systemic variable that we identify as central to neoclassical realist theory, and which distinguishes neoclassical realism from structural realism, is the clarity of signals and information the international system presents to states.[54] Essentially, clarity has three components: (1) the degree to which threats and opportunities are readily discernable; (2) whether the system provides information on the time horizons of threats and opportunities; and (3) whether optimal policy options stand out or not.

In terms of the first element of clarity, drawing on Stephen Walt and John Lewis Gaddis' analysis of George Kennan, we understand clear threats as other states (or, under certain conditions, quasi-state actors) that possess three attributes: (1) revisionism or expressed hostility to harm the state's territorial integrity or core interests; (2) the economic and military capability to inflict harm on the state, which in turn depends on geography and technology; and (3) a sense of imminence (i.e., expectations that it will use its capability to inflict harm in short order).[55] In this regard, prior to World War II the United States lacked any clear threats both because no other state showed evidence of hostile intentions and because existing technology did not permit adequate power projection across the barriers

---

52. Wohlforth, *Elusive Balance*, pp. 129–137; and idem., "The Stability of a Unipolar World," p. 22.

53. James McAllister, *No Exit: America and the German Problem, 1943–1954* (Ithaca, NY: Cornell University Press, 2002), pp. 10–11.

54. Norrin M. Ripsman, Jeffrey W. Taliaferro, and Steven E. Lobell, "Conclusion: The State of Neoclassical Realism," in *Neoclassical Realism, the State, and Foreign Policy*, ed. Steven E. Lobell, Norrin M. Ripsman, and Jeffrey W. Taliaferro (Cambridge: Cambridge University Press, 2009), pp. 282–287.

55. John Lewis Gaddis, *Strategies of Containment: A Critical Appraisal of Postwar American National Security Policy* (Oxford: Oxford University Press, 1982), p. 60; Stephen M. Walt, *The Origins of Alliances* (Ithaca, NY: Cornell University Press, 1987), pp. 22–28; idem., *Revolution and War* (Ithaca, NY: Cornell University Press, 1996), pp. 21–26. Quasi-state actors, such as ISIL/ISIS, Hezbollah, and Boko Haram, which have territorial bases and military power and which seek state capacity can also be consequential threats, at least to non-great powers in the international system.

provided by the Atlantic and Pacific Oceans. After World War II, however, the aircraft carrier and the development of long-range aircraft and missile technology made it possible for the Soviet Union to pose a significant threat to the United States. Together with increasing evidence of Soviet hostility to the United States, Washington thus faced a clear threat from Moscow. While the threat may not have appeared imminent during much of the Cold War, during key crises, in which the Soviet Union appeared poised to act imminently against US interests, greater clarity of threats existed. Thus, for example, in October 1962, when the Kennedy administration found evidence of Soviet deployment of medium-range ballistic missiles and strategic nuclear warheads in Cuba, the United States faced a clear threat to its strategic interests.

Clear opportunities require evidence of a state's improving balance of capabilities vis-à-vis other states, yielding it an unchecked advantage in a specific theater. This can occur inter alia due to the rapid improvement of the state's economic and military capabilities, the deterioration or collapse of the capabilities of one or more of its adversaries, or a combination of the two. In general, clear opportunities involve three components: (1) evidence that relative capabilities favor the state in question; (2) evidence that other consequential parties lack the political resolve to resist the state's moves in the theater in question; and (3) evidence that a favorable balance of capabilities and resolve will not persist indefinitely, making it important to act as soon as possible.[56] For example, the Iraqi invasion of Kuwait in 1990 was the result of a clear opportunity. First, Iraq, with its million-man army, possessed a favorable balance of power vis-à-vis Saudi Arabia, Iran, and other regional actors. Second, following a meeting with US ambassador April Glaspie, Iraqi president Saddam Hussein could reasonably have been assured that Washington would not resist an Iraqi move toward Kuwait. Finally, given impending Iraqi financial collapse due to the combination of high war-debt payments to Kuwait to finance the 1980–1988 Iran-Iraq War and declining oil revenue due to Kuwait's over-production of oil, there was every reason to expect that Saddam's window of opportunity would not remain open indefinitely.[57]

56. Our thinking on opportunities is influenced by Van Evera, *Causes of War*, pp. 74–75.

57. See, for example, Charles A. Duelfer, and Stephen Benedict Dyson, "Chronic Misperception and International Conflict: The U.S.-Iraq Experience," *International Security*, vol. 36, no. 1 (2011), pp. 73–100; and John Mearsheimer and Stephen Walt, "An Unnecessary War," *Foreign Policy*, no. 134 (January–February 2003), p. 54.

The second element of clarity is time horizons. Time horizons are often difficult for leaders to estimate, as they require an accurate knowledge of both adversary capabilities and intentions. To the extent that adversary behavior signals either an imminent attack or an indefinite withdrawal, however, it eases the strategic dilemmas a state faces. For example, the repeated British attempts to accommodate German challenges to the status quo in 1935–1936 (allowing German rearmament, negotiating an Anglo-German Naval Agreement in violation of the Versailles Treaty's demilitarization clauses, and refraining from an aggressive response to the remilitarization of the Rhineland) indicated that, at the beginning of a slow British rearmament program, the British were unwilling to engage Germany militarily. This presented Hitler with a clear extended opportunity to challenge more of the post–World War I order.[58] The introduction of Soviet medium-range and intermediate-range nuclear ballistic missiles to Cuba in autumn 1962, which would change the strategic balance in a matter of weeks, once they became operational, presented Kennedy with a clear short-term threat, which required him to react quickly.

The third element of clarity, clarity of options, is relatively rare in international politics. While the international system constrains states and often limits the available options that states have at their disposal, it rarely provides clarity about the optimal policy responses in a given situation. Exceptions include the situation Israel faced in 2007 when presented with evidence of an undeclared Syrian nuclear reactor in al-Kibar. Given that the development of Syrian nuclear weapons would have seriously undermined Israeli security, the Syrian regime was diplomatically isolated (as was North Korea, which aided in the design of the facility), the George W. Bush administration was supportive of independent Israeli action, and the reactor was an easy target, as it was above ground and poorly defended, the option of some form of preventive strike on the reactor was the only logical policy option at Israel's disposal.[59]

To illustrate how the system can provide different levels of these three elements of clarity, compare the following situations. In the 1880s and 1890s, Britain faced Germany, the United States, Russia, France, and Japan rising at different rates and challenging its spheres of influence in different locales. London engaged in naval building programs against France and Russia, opposed the Scramble for Empire in China, clashed

58. James P. Levy, *Appeasement and Rearmament: Britain, 1936–1939* (New York: Rowman and Littlefield, 2006); and Peter Neville, *Hitler and Appeasement: The British Attempt to Prevent the Second World War* (New York: Hambledon Continuum, 2006).

59. Yaakov Katz and Yoav Hendel, *Israel vs. Iran: The Shadow of War* (Dulles, VA: Potomac, 2012), pp. 61–84.

with the United States in North and South America, and engaged Russia in the Great Game in Central Asia. However, until 1906–1908, when Germany accelerated its battleship construction program, Britain faced no clear and present danger and thus had little clarity about threats and opportunities.[60]

After Hitler's accession to power in the 1930s, it was clear to British leaders that Germany represented the "ultimate enemy" and the most serious threat to British interests.[61] Moreover, given the state of the German rearmament program, it became clear that the time frame of the German threat to Great Britain in the mid-1930s appeared to be a few years off, most likely in 1939 or 1940.[62] Yet, while it was clear that some form of British rearmament was in order, there was room for appeasers and anti-appeasers to debate the optimal pace of rearmament and the wisdom of appeasement as a policy response.

Finally, the threat that Egypt posed to Israel in June 1967 provided clarity on all three dimensions. Gamal Abdel Nasser's constant hostile rhetoric coupled with its status as the most powerful Arab state made it clear that Egypt was Israel's greatest threat, especially if Cairo were to act with the support of Syria and Jordan. Given that Nasser had blockaded the Straits of Tiran, secured the removal of UN peacekeeping forces in the Sinai, and mobilized Egyptian forces all along the border, it was also clear that the time frame for this threat was only a matter of days or weeks. Given these constraints, Israeli decision makers had few available options available, and the option of a preventive attack was unrivaled in its optimality.[63]

We argue that clarity is a critical systemic variable for neoclassical realist analyses. With a greater degree of clarity about the nature of threats and opportunities that states face, the time frame in which they are expected to materialize, and the optimal policy responses, variance in policy choices across states and across societal coalitions within states should

60. Arthur J. Marder, *The Anatomy of British Sea Power: A History of British Naval Policy in the Pre-Dreadnought Era, 1880–1905* (New York: Alfred A. A. Knopf, 1940); and Jon T. Sumida, *In Defence of Naval Supremacy: Finance, Technology and British Naval Policy, 1889–1914* (Boston: Unwin Hyman, 1989), Table 21.

61. Wesley K. Wark, *The Ultimate Enemy: British Intelligence and Nazi Germany, 1933–1939* (Ithaca, NY: Cornell University Press, 1985).

62. British intelligence estimates consistently concluded (correctly) that, given the German need to rearm, the Germans would most likely not be prepared to contemplate war with Great Britain until about 1940. See Norrin M. Ripsman and Jack S. Levy, "Wishful Thinking or Buying Time? The Logic of British Appeasement in the 1930s," *International Security*, vol. 33, no. 2 (2008), pp. 148–181.

63. Michael Oren, *Six Days of War: June 1967 and the Making of the Modern Middle East* (Oxford: Oxford University Press, 2002).

be low. Conversely, the less clarity there is, the greater room there is for particular leaders, parties, and states to pursue unique solutions based on their preferences, parochial interests, or strategic cultures—intervening variables discussed in the next chapter.[64]

Some will no doubt argue that, despite the foregoing discussion, it will be difficult to provide a precise a priori operationalization of the concept or measure clarity; it can only be done ex post facto. We do not fully agree. We acknowledge that clarity is easier to investigate retrospectively, with the aid of primary source research, than it is prospectively. In particular, to the degree that multiple actors understood the threats and opportunities that the state faced in similar terms, as expressed by government documents and memoirs, the greater we can say the clarity of the international system was at the time. Nonetheless, the preceding discussion lays out guide points for an a priori assessment of clarity based on relative capabilities, expressed intentions, and the time horizon, as well as the salience of optimal policy responses. While this is not a precise formula, it is a good start.

Moreover, we would argue that many useful concepts of international politics are difficult to define and operationalize, yet they still advance our understanding of the field. For realists, the concept of a pole is relatively clear, but it is not as clear how to measure great power status. How, specifically, can we determine a priori whether a state has attained or lost great power status? What is the threshold for polarity?[65] These methodological hurdles do not undermine the utility of the concept as an explanatory tool of international politics and state behavior. Similarly, while the concept of international norms developed by constructivists is a useful innovation in the study of international relations, they would be hard-pressed to operationalize norms except ex post facto.[66] Thus, even if the precise measurement of clarity cannot be conclusively resolved here, we maintain that clarity is a useful and an innovative concept that can help us further our understanding of national foreign policy choices and, by extension, international outcomes. To paraphrase Justice Potter Stewart's comments

64. Norrin M. Ripsman, "Neoclassical Realism and Domestic Interest Groups," in *Neoclassical Realism, the State, and Foreign Policy,* ed. Steven E. Lobell, Norrin M. Ripsman, and Jeffrey W. Taliaferro (Cambridge: Cambridge University Press, 2009), pp. 170–193.

65. See, for example, Waltz, *Theory of International Politics,* pp. 129–132; Jack S. Levy, *War in the Modern Great Power System, 1495–1975* (Lexington: University Press of Kentucky, 1983), pp. 17–18; Schweller, *Deadly Imbalances,* pp. 16–19; Brooks and Wohlforth, *World out of Balance,* pp. 12–13; and Nuno P. Monteiro, *Theory of Unipolar Politics* (New York: Cambridge University Press, 2014), pp. 42–43.

66. Michael C. Desch, "Culture Clash: Assessing the Importance of Ideas in Security Studies," *International Security,* vol. 23, no. 1 (1998), pp. 141–170, esp. 150–152.

on obscenity, we may not come up with a precise operationalization of clarity, but we know it when we see it.[67] In the final analysis therefore even if the best neoclassical realist researchers will be able to come up with is an imprecise operationalization of clarity, we do not believe that will constitute a fatal flaw for the research agenda.

Because the international system is rarely crystal clear, states typically face some degree of uncertainty in their calculations of the balance of power, the intentions of other states, and the time horizons they face. For this reason, uncertainty is an inherent property of an anarchic international system, although it is compounded by the unit level factors we discuss in Chapter 3. Nonetheless, though neoclassical realists agree with structural realists and others that uncertainty is inherent in international politics, our view of the sources of that uncertainty differ.[68]

Whereas structural realism conceives of uncertainty as a central feature of the international system itself, neoclassical realism conceives of uncertainty as a product of both agency and structure. In her study of grand strategic adjustment and military doctrinal change in peacetime, Emily Goldman observes that "systems and structure are not uncertain; rather agents are," because of insufficient information and complex security environments.[69] Moreover, different states face varying degrees of complexity and uncertainty.[70] Following Goldman, we submit that the clarity of each states' external environment varies across time, with systemic and sub-systemic (or regional) dynamics revealing different amounts of information about the strength and conditionality of constraints and opportunities, as well as about the range of "optimal" strategic responses.

Uncertainty also results from the unit-level intervening variables discussed in Chapter 3—particularly leaders' worldviews and strategic culture—which can affect the perception of individual states and agents. Consequently, uncertainty results from the interaction of imperfect agents with an international system that is imperfectly clear. In essence, the lack of perfect clarity in the international system makes uncertainty

---

67. Justice Potter Stewart, Concurring, *Jacobellis v. Ohio*, 378 U.S. 184 (1964).

68. For a discussion of how different schools of IR theories treat uncertainty, see Brian C. Rathbun, "Uncertain About Uncertainty: Understanding the Multiple Meanings of a Crucial Concept in International Relations Theory," *International Studies Quarterly*, vol. 51, no. 3 (2007), pp. 533–557. For an argument that political and economic actors operate under conditions of both risk and uncertainty, see Stephen C. Nelson and Peter J. Katzenstein, "Uncertainty, Risk, and the Financial Crisis of 2008," *International Organization*, vol. 68, no. 2 (2014), pp. 361–392.

69. Emily O. Goldman, *Power in Uncertain Times: Strategy in the Fog of Peace* (Stanford, CA: Stanford University Press, 2011), p. 14.

70. Ibid., p. 14.

inherent to international politics; yet even with perfect clarity, because of the unit-level intervening variables neoclassical realists identify, some actors in some states might still experience uncertainty.

PERMISSIVE/RESTRICTIVE STRATEGIC ENVIRONMENTS

In addition to the relative levels of clarity and uncertainty, another key variable for neoclassical realist theory is the nature of a state's strategic environment. Whereas clarity and uncertainty pertain to the scope of information that the system provides, the strategic environment pertains to the content of that information. In our previous work, we introduced the concept of permissive and restrictive strategic environments. The distinction between permissive and restrictive strategic environments relates to the imminence and the magnitude of threats and opportunities that states face.[71] All things being equal, the more imminent the threat or opportunity and the more dangerous the threat (or the more enticing the opportunity) the more restrictive the state's strategic environment is. Conversely, the more remote the threat or opportunity and the less intense the threat or opportunity, the more permissive the strategic environment is. Restrictive and permissive strategic environments thus exist along a continuum with the former entailing relatively less complexity than the latter because there are fewer viable alternatives to redress threats or exploit opportunities.[72] Thus, for example, as we have argued before, when faced with clear signals of an impending Egyptian attack (Egypt had asked the UN Secretary-General to withdraw peacekeepers from the border, had blockaded the Straits of Tiran, and was mobilizing on the Israeli border), Israel had few available policy alternatives to pre-emption in June 1967.[73] Similarly, British foreign policy in the years immediately after World War II was so heavily constrained by greatly

71. As we will clarify later, "imminence" here is not simply a restatement of the time horizons component of clarity. Clarity of time horizons refers to the ability to distinguish short-term from long-term threats and opportunities. Imminence refers to a clear and present threat or opportunity. It is conceivable that a state could objectively face an imminent threat without its leaders being able to perceive or assess its imminence or a threat that may take a long time to develop, which it may fear will emerge more quickly. See, for example, Uri Bar-Joseph and Jack S. Levy, "Conscious Action and Intelligence Failure," *Political Science Quarterly*, vol. 124, no. 3 (2009), pp. 461–488.

72. In restrictive environments, therefore, domestic politics matters less. See Ripsman, "Neoclassical Realism and Domestic Interest Groups."

73. Ripsman, Taliaferro, and Lobell, "Conclusion," pp. 282–283. See also Oren, *Six Days of War*.

diminished British power, a large Soviet conventional force advantage in Europe, and the rise of American power that, regardless of who governed in Whitehall, it was clear that Britain would have to align with the United States to contain the Soviet Union. For this reason, despite his fears that incoming foreign secretary Ernest Bevin—a trade union leader—might cause irreparable damage to British foreign policy, after the fact, the patrician Sir Anthony Eden acknowledged that Bevin's policies did not deviate at all from what Eden himself would have done.[74]

Both Britain in the late 1940s and Israel in June 1967 confronted strategic environments characterized by relatively low levels of complexity and very high levels of actual danger to their respective physical survival, political autonomy, and interests. The high levels of actual danger that Britain and Israel faced were a function of geographic proximity and relative power. In June 1967, after all, Israel faced an imminent threat of invasion by Egypt, Jordan, and Syria. In the case of Britain, given the depth of the United Kingdom's relative economic decline and the magnitude of Soviet threat to Greece and Turkey (and the rest of Western Europe), the time frame for response was short. More often, states face strategic environments with less intense threats and opportunities and more time for the foreign policy executive to select a policy response. Consequently, unit-level intervening variables can play a greater role in shaping a state's response to systemic pressures, as we discuss in greater depth in Chapter 3.

The permissiveness or restrictiveness of the strategic environment is not merely an artifact of the polarity of the international system; all possible distributions of power can be either permissive or restrictive for states (See Table 2.1). The Cold War superpower rivalry, for example, was not static. As the actual distribution of capabilities became clearer after World War II, the United States and the Soviet Union each came to recognize that the other was the single overarching threat in a bipolar international system. Yet, the imminence and magnitude of the external threats and opportunities each superpower faced varied over time. The United States enjoyed a numerical advantage in long-range bombers and strategic nuclear weapons over the USSR, even after the end of the US atomic monopoly in August 1949.[75] A Soviet nuclear attack on North America was highly unlikely for much of the 1950s.[76] The Soviet launch

74. Anthony Eden, *Full Circle: The Memoirs of Anthony Eden* (London: Cassell, 1960), p. 5.

75. Marc Trachtenberg, "A 'Wasting Asset': American Strategy and the Shifting Nuclear Balance, 1949–1954," *International Security*, vol. 13, no. 3 (1988), pp. 5–49; and idem., "Preventive War and U.S. Foreign Policy," *Security Studies*, vol. 16, no. 1 (2007), pp. 1–31.

76. Marc Trachtenberg, *A Constructed Peace: The Making of the European Settlement, 1945–1963* (Princeton, NJ: Princeton University Press, 1999), pp. 146–200.

Table 2.1. EXAMPLES OF POLARITY AND THE NATURE OF STRATEGIC
ENVIRONMENTS

		Nature of Strategic Environment (Permissive to Restrictive)	
		Permissive Strategic Environment	Restrictive Strategic Environment
Polarity (Number of Great Powers)	Multipolarity	Britain, Russia, Austria, and Prussia after Napoleonic Wars (1815–1854)	Britain, Russia, France, and Austria-Hungary after Wars of German Unification (1871–1892)
	Bipolarity	United States in early Cold War (1945–1963)	United States in later Cold War (1963–1989)

of the first intercontinental ballistic missile in 1957, however, increased the imminence and magnitude of threat to the Western Hemisphere, despite the fact the United States retained a numerical advantage in strategic nuclear weapons and all delivery systems until the late 1960s.[77] The United States therefore confronted a more restrictive strategic environment in the 1960s than it had previously confronted in the 1950s. The strategic environment officials in Washington confronted had changed, even though the overall balance of power still overwhelmingly favored the United States and the international system remained bipolar.

Likewise, in a multipolar system, the imminence and the magnitude of external threats and opportunities that different states face also vary over time. A comparison of European great-power politics after the Napoleonic Wars (1801–1815) and after the Wars of German Unification (1862–1871) is illustrative. Napoleon's final defeat at Waterloo ended the immediate threat of a French bid for continental hegemony. The leaders of the victorious great powers—Britain, Russia, Austria, and Prussia—were aware of the latent threat of France, but they also recognized it was not imminent. This gave Austrian foreign minister Klemens von Metternich, British foreign secretary Viscount Castlereagh, and Tsar Alexander I great latitude in designing the 1815 Vienna settlement, which allowed them to

77. Historian Francis Gavin notes that changes in US nuclear doctrine and conventional force levels in Europe between the Eisenhower administration and the Kennedy administration were not as sharp as the conventional wisdom holds. Francis J. Gavin, *Nuclear Statecraft: History and Strategy in America's Atomic Age* (Ithaca, NY: Cornell University Press, 2012), pp. 30–56.

Table 2.2. EXAMPLES OF SYSTEMIC CLARITY AND THE NATURE
OF STRATEGIC ENVIRONMENTS

		Nature of Strategic Environment (Permissive to Restrictive)	
		Permissive Strategic Environment	Restrictive Strategic Environment
Degree of Systemic Clarity (High to Low)	High Clarity	United States (1945–1947)	Great Britain (1936–1939)
	Low Clarity	United States (1990–2001)	Great Britain (1933–1934)

reintegrate France (under the restored Bourbon king Louis XVIII) into the great-power club.[78]

Now consider the strategic environments the European powers confronted after 1871. German unification eliminated the central European buffer zone created by the Congress of Vienna. The Franco-Prussian War demonstrated the effectiveness of the Prussian army's offensive military doctrine, artillery, and railways.[79] The annexation of Alsace and Lorraine precluded any possibility of rapprochement between Paris and Berlin. Chancellor Otto von Bismarck's new German empire had the destabilizing mixture of shared borders with France and Russia, a considerable advantage in military potential and economic capabilities, and the strongest army in Europe. The German problem would become the central strategic dilemma in European statecraft for the next century. The imminence and the magnitude of the threat posed by German economic and military capabilities were greater and the range of options available to officials in Paris, St. Petersburg, Vienna, and London to redress it became narrower after 1871.

Similarly, the permissiveness or restrictiveness of the strategic environment is not merely a proxy for the clarity of the international system. The system could provide very clear signals about the nature of threats and opportunities, time horizons, and/or policy options in both permissive and restrictive environments (see Table 2.2). Yet it can also provide insufficient information in both permissive and restrictive environments. Consider the experience of the United States. In the immediate aftermath

78. On the 1815 settlement, see Henry Kissinger, *A World Restored: Metternich, Castlereagh and the Problems of Peace, 1812–22* (Boston: Houghton Mifflin, 1957).

79. Thomas J. Christensen, "Perceptions and Alliances in Europe, 1865–1940," *International Organization*, vol. 51, no. 1 (1997), pp. 65–97.

of World War II, the United States faced a relatively permissive environment, as it was by far the dominant global economic power, it possessed the world's only arsenal of atomic weapons, and no power had the capacity to inflict harm on its homeland, separated as it was by two ocean barriers. In this environment, however, it received clear signals that the Soviet Union was a growing threat that had to be contained. Yet, after the Cold War, facing an even more permissive environment—since US power was far greater than any other state—there is far less clarity over whether China represents an imminent threat to be contained or a state to be engaged and coopted.

Restrictive environments similarly can provide more or less clarity. In the 1930s, for example, Great Britain faced a restrictive environment, facing challenges in Europe from Nazi Germany, in the Mediterranean from Fascist Italy, and the Far East from Imperial Japan. Yet, in 1933–1934, the British security cabinet could debate whether Germany or Japan was the principal threat, since the system did not yet provide sufficient clarity on that point. Only a few years later, after the Rhineland remilitarization and the *Anschluss* of Austria and Germany, British war planners faced much more clarity that Germany was the greatest threat, and thereby restored its continental commitment.

Clarity and the nature of a state's strategic environment thus constitute two key systemic variables unique to neoclassical realism's understanding of the international system.

CONCLUSION: INTERNATIONAL SYSTEMS AND SYSTEMIC STIMULI

Neoclassical realist theories begin with this supposition: every state's external behavior is shaped first and foremost by its power and position in the international system and, specifically, by its relative share of material capabilities. In this chapter, we set forth the neoclassical realist conception of the international system. After defining the international system and identifying the principal actors within it, we explicated the concepts of system structure and structural modifiers. Structure and structural modifiers set the parameters for the likely strategic choices of the principal actors—states—as well as the range of possible international outcomes. We then introduced the important systemic variable of clarity—about the nature of threats, the time frame of these threats, and the optimal policy responses to them—that we utilize in a neoclassical realist theory of foreign policy and international politics. Finally, we have discussed the relative permissiveness or restrictiveness of states' strategic environments as an additional explanatory variable for neoclassical realists. Having thus discussed the independent variables of neoclassical realism, in the next chapter we will discuss the range of domestic-level intervening variables that can complicate national foreign policy responses to these external pressures.

CHAPTER 3

Neoclassical Realist
Intervening Variables

In the previous chapter, we developed our neoclassical realist conception of the international system and the constraints and opportunities
it presents to states. We now turn our attention to the defining feature
and one of the primary contributions of neoclassical realist theory: the
unit- and sub-unit-level intervening variables (highlighted in Figure 3.1).
As Gideon Rose indicates, neoclassical realism differs from structural
realism due to its incorporation of domestic intervening variables that
condition whether and how states respond to the international systemic
pressures that all realists assume underlie foreign policy, grand strategy, and international politics.[1] To date, Type I and Type II neoclassical
realist theories employ a wide range of intervening variables, including
domestic politics, leader perceptions, state extraction capacity, state
structure, and state strength to explain pathological behavior and foreign policy choices.

The purpose of this chapter is to provide a clearer and better-organized
set of intervening variables than neoclassical realists have hitherto articulated. In the following sections: (1) we address the criticism that neoclassical realist scholars have selected these intervening variables in an ad hoc
manner to explain a particular state's foreign policy or policymaking in a
particular issue area; and (2) we organize the intervening variables into
four general categories, based on how they are used in the field of international relations and how they operate.

---

1. Gideon Rose, "Neoclassical Realism and Theories of Foreign Policy," *World Politics*, vol.
51, no. 1 (1998), pp. 144–177.

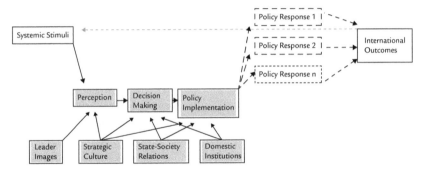

Figure 3.1
The Neoclassical Realist Model of Foreign Policy

THE INTERVENING VARIABLES EMPLOYED BY NEOCLASSICAL REALIST THEORIES

The four broad categories of intervening unit-level variables that we discuss in this chapter are the images and perceptions of state leaders, strategic culture, state-society relations, and domestic institutional arrangements.[2] These variables include psychological, bureaucratic/organizational, societal, and institutional models, which reflect alternative approaches to foreign policy analysis.[3] They reflect the various constraints on the central actors, the interactions within and between decision makers and society as a whole, and the processes and mechanisms by which foreign policy is formulated, each of which can affect the manner in which states respond to external stimuli.[4] In particular, by organizing these variables into four categories rather than continuing the eclecticism which characterizes the current state of Types I and II neoclassical realism, we argue they

2. This represents an improvement on Kunz and Saltzman, who consider only two broad categories: "perceptions in filtering systemic constraints" and "domestic constraints on foreign policy." Barbara Kunz and Ilai Z. Saltzman, "External and Domestic Determinants of State Behaviour," in *Neoclassical Realism in European Politics: Bringing Power Back In*, ed. Asle Toje and Barbara Kunz (Manchester: Manchester University Press, 2012), pp. 96–116. Instead, our classification is influenced more directly by Norrin M. Ripsman, "Neoclassical Realism," in *The International Studies Compendium Project*, ed. Robert Denemark et al. (Oxford: Wiley-Blackwell, 2011).

3. Ole R. Holsti, "Models of International Relations and Foreign Policy," *Diplomatic History*, vol. 13, no. 1 (1989), pp. 15–43; Jack S. Levy and William R. Thompson, *Causes of War* (Malden, MA: Wiley-Blackwell, 2010), pp. 83–185; Walter Carlsnaes, "Foreign Policy," in *Handbook of International Relations*, ed. Walter Carlsnaes, Thomas Risse, and Beth A. Simmons (London: Sage, 2013), pp. 331–349; Valerie M. Hudson, *Foreign Policy Analysis: Classic and Contemporary Theory* (Lanham, MD: Rowman and Littlefield, 2013).

4. As we indicate in the Introduction, many of these variables are also utilized as independent variables by scholars other than neoclassical realists. Neoclassical realists use them as intervening variables in the systematic manner described in this chapter.

represent the central intervening variables that can affect a state's foreign policy responses, especially under the conditions of a permissive strategic environment, as we discussed in Chapter 2. However, as we indicated in Figure I.1, even in the most restrictive environment these intervening variables can influence the policy selection process from a narrow range of policy alternatives, as well as policy implementation.[5]

One criticism that has been leveled against neoclassical realism is that its intervening variables have been chosen in an ad hoc manner and they can only account for specific foreign policy decisions. For instance, Stephen Walt argues that "neoclassical realism tends to incorporate domestic variables in an ad hoc manner, and its proponents have yet to identify when these variables will exert greater or lesser effects."[6] Moreover, critics have argued that neoclassical realists utilize too wide a range of unrelated intervening variables, amounting to no more than a laundry list, and that the incorporation of such unit-level variables is inconsistent with the core assumptions of realism, is degenerating, and undermines its predictive power.[7] In this chapter, we explain systematically how we categorized the intervening variables that are used in neoclassical realist theory, and when they can influence foreign policy, international outcomes, and structural change. In particular, we link our four categories of intervening variables discussed in this chapter directly to the three domestic processes we identified in Chapter 1 as potentially distorting national foreign policy responses to international systemic stimuli: perception, decision making, and policy implementation. As we indicate in Figure 3.1, the four clusters of intervening variables we identify all have a direct bearing on one or more of these processes. Perception is affected not only by international factors, but also by leader images and strategic culture. Both decision making and policy implementation are conditioned domestically by strategic culture, state-society relations, and domestic political institutions. Thus, rather than being ad hoc, we have organized the relevant domestic variables that are germane to neoclassical realist theory as unit level intervening variables based on their respective pathways to political significance, as outlined in Figure 3.1.

5. Yuen Foong Khong, "Foreign Policy Analysis and the International Relations of Asia," in *The Oxford Handbook of the International Relations of Asia*, ed. Saadia Pekkanen, John Ravenhill, and Rosemary Foot (New York: Oxford University Press, 2014), pp. 81–99; Michael Roskin, "From Pearl Harbor to Vietnam: Shifting Generational Paradigms and Foreign Policy," *Political Science Quarterly*, vol. 89, no. 3 (1974), pp. 563–588.

6. Stephen M. Walt, "The Enduring Relevance of Realist Tradition," in *Political Science: State of the Discipline*, ed. Ira Katznelson and Helen V. Milner (New York: W. W. Norton, 2002), p. 211.

7. Jeffrey W. Legro and Andrew Moravcsik, "Is Anybody Still a Realist?" *International Security*, vol. 24, no. 2 (1999), pp. 28–41; and Colin Elman, "Horses for Courses: Why Not Neorealist Theories of Foreign Policy?" *Security Studies*, vol. 6, no. 1 (1996), pp. 38–42.

Finally, as elaborated in Chapter 4, and addressing the critics of neoclassical realism, we clarify when the different intervening variables can influence the dependent variable to different degrees over time. For instance, leader perceptions will have significant influence in the short run on foreign policy decision making during crisis situations. Our rationale is that, when facing time constraints, the foreign policy executive is usually separated from the "body" of the bureaucracy and from society and domestic institutions as a whole. The combination of time constraints, secrecy, and pressures given the high stakes involved in crisis decision making, means that the other intervening variables such as state-society relations and possibly even domestic institutions, will have fewer opportunities to influence the processes and mechanisms through which decision making occurs. Alternatively, strategic culture, and especially state-society relations and domestic institutions are about domestic process. These variables address what the process looks like, including the autonomy of leaders and the constraints under which they operate, their socialization, domestic distributional competition, and the mechanisms through which differences are resolved. These process variables are likely to have more influence in the short-to-medium and the medium-to-long term, when culture, society, and institutions shape and constrain the formulation of policy planning and grand strategy.[8] Thus, as discussed in greater length in Chapter 4, these process variables demonstrate that neoclassical realism is much more than simply accounting for instances of pathological foreign policy and the problems that leaders face in assessing and adapting to systemic shifts and changes.

i. Leader Images

One important set of intervening variables concerns the beliefs or images of individual decision makers who sit at the helm of the state. We label these individuals the foreign policy executive (FPE); they include the president, prime minister, or dictator, and key cabinet members, ministers, and advisors charged with the conduct of foreign and defense policies. The FPE often possesses private information and has a monopoly on intelligence about foreign countries; therefore, it is the most important

---

8. Jennifer Sterling-Folker, "Realist Environment, Liberal Process, and Domestic-Level Variables," *International Studies Quarterly*, vol. 41, no. 1 (1997), pp. 1–25; and Randall L. Schweller, "The Progressiveness of Neoclassical Realism," in *Progress in International Relations Theory: Appraising the Field*, ed. Colin Elman and Miriam Fendius Elman (Cambridge, MA: MIT Press, 2003), pp. 311–348, at p. 319.

actor to focus on when seeking to explain foreign policy and grand strategic adjustment. Leader images are significant because they can affect the
first of the three critical intervening processes—perception of the incoming systemic stimuli.

Psychological models identify a wide range of cognitive constraints
on how decision makers process information in crisis situations when
information tends to be incomplete, overwhelming, and/or contradictory. These models emphasize cognitive explanations such as operational
codes, the fundamental attribution error, lessons from history, the role of
personality, group dynamics and group think, and the beliefs and images
of leaders.

To begin with, all people possess a set of core values, beliefs, and images
that guide their interaction with the outside world and their understanding of it. These "images" are highly personalized, as they are informed
by the individual's prior experiences and values. Moreover, to the extent
that they represent core beliefs, they are not easily altered. Once formed,
they act as cognitive filters that inform how leaders process information—what they pay attention to; what they ignore; and how they understand signals, information, and events. All incoming information about
the outside world passes through these cognitive filters, which personal-
ize and bias the leader's perception of the external stimuli.[9] As a result,
leaders will react differently to international challenges and opportunities depending on the content of their images. Thus, for example, General
Secretary Mikhail Gorbachev responded to the Soviet Union's relative
decline in the early to mid-1980s in a different manner from the ailing
Leonid Brezhnev, preferring internal reform and a relaxation of international tensions to his predecessors' internal repression and international
risk-taking.[10] Likewise, the defense and arms control policies pursued by
the Reagan administration during its first term (January 1981 to January

---

9. See for example, Robert Jervis, *Perception and Misperception in International Politics*
(Princeton, NJ: Princeton University Press, 1976); Yuen Foong Khong, *Analogies at War:
Korea, Munich, Dien Bien Phu, and the Vietnam Decisions of 1965* (Princeton, NJ: Princeton
University Press, 1992); Deborah Welch Larson, *Origins of Containment: A Psychological
Explanation* (Princeton, NJ: Princeton University Press, 1985); Stanley Allen Renshon
and Deborah Welch Larson, *Good Judgment in Foreign Policy: Theory and Application*
(Lanham, MD: Rowman and Littlefield, 2003); and Barbara Farnham, *Roosevelt and the
Munich Crisis: A Study of Political Decision-Making* (Princeton, NJ: Princeton University
Press, 1997).

10. For arguments that cognitive factors played an important role in Soviet policy change,
see Jeff Checkel, "Ideas, Institutions, and the Gorbachev Foreign Policy Revolution,"
World Politics, vol. 45, no. 2 (1993), pp. 271–300; Janice Gross Stein, "Political Learning
By Doing: Gorbachev as Uncommitted Thinker and Motivated Learner," *International
Organization*, vol. 48, no. 2 (1994), pp. 155–183; and Deborah Welch Larson and Alexei

1985) reflected President Ronald Reagan's longstanding beliefs about the illegitimacy and expansionist nature of the Soviet Union, the inadequacy (indeed, the immorality) of Mutually Assured Destruction, and the notion that past nuclear arms treaties diminished US national security. Consequently, the Reagan administration initially did not follow the course of the Nixon, Ford, and Carter administrations in pursuing strategic arms control negotiations with the Soviet Union.[11]

Among other cognitive factors, a leader's personality and character can also influence a state's response to external stimuli. Daniel L. Byman and Kenneth M. Pollack, for example, maintain that some powerful leaders, such as Otto von Bismarck, Kaiser Wilhelm II, Adolf Hitler, and Saddam Hussein have had a dramatic impact on the strategic choices their states made.[12] Studies have shown that some individuals are more prone to risk taking, while others are risk averse.[13] Philip B. K. Potter has found that the age and experience of leaders can also impact their willingness to initiate crises.[14] Consequently, to understand a state's foreign policy choices it is useful to investigate the character and psychological make-up of its political leaders, which are critical intervening variables that can influence the way they respond to systemic pressures. In this regard, Alexander L. George and Juliette George explain President Woodrow Wilson's rigid negotiating stance at the 1919 Paris Peace Conference and his later inability to build the domestic coalition needed to win Senate ratification of the Treaty of Versailles and with it the United States' membership in the League of Nations in terms of his childhood and, in particular, his relationship with his perfectionist father.[15] Similarly, Doris Kearns explains

Shevchenko, "Shortcut to Greatness: The New Thinking and the Revolution in Soviet Foreign Policy," *International Organization*, vol. 57, no. 1 (2003), pp. 77–109.

11. Rose McDermott, "Arms Control and the First Reagan Administration: Belief-Systems and Policy Choices," *Journal of Cold War Studies*, vol. 4, no. 4 (2002), pp. 29–59.

12. Daniel L. Byman and Kenneth M. Pollack, "Let Us Now Praise Great Men: Bringing the Statesman Back in," *International Security*, vol. 25, no. 4 (2001), pp. 107–146. See also Margaret G. Hermann and Joe D. Hagan, "International Decision Making: Leadership Matters," *Foreign Policy*, no. 110 (Spring 1998), pp. 124–137; and Jerrold M. Post, *The Psychological Assessment of Political Leaders: With Profiles of Saddam Hussein and Bill Clinton* (Ann Arbor: University of Michigan Press, 2003).

13. Paul A. Kowert and Margaret G. Hermann, "Who Takes Risks? Daring and Caution in Foreign Policy Making," *Journal of Conflict Resolution*, vol. 41, no. 5 (1997), pp. 611–637.

14. Philip B. K. Potter, "Does Experience Matter? American Presidential Experience, Age, and International Conflict," *Journal of Conflict Resolution*, vol. 51, no. 3 (2007), pp. 351–378.

15. George and George advance the hypothesis that "the dynamics of Wilson's political behavior is that power was for him a compensatory value, a means of restoring self-esteem damaged in childhood [by his demanding and perfectionist father] . . . his desire for power was mitigated by a simultaneous need for approval, for respect, and, especially, for feeling virtuous." Alexander L. George and Juliette L. George, *Woodrow Wilson and Colonel House: A Personality Study* (New York: J. Day, 1956), p. 320. George and George's

Lyndon Johnson's Vietnam policy, particularly his unwillingness to accept defeat, in terms of his character, which stemmed from his upbringing and his relationship to his parents.[16]

A leader's "operational codes" can also affect national foreign policy responses. As Nathan Leites, Alexander George, and Ole Holsti argue, each leader has an operational code comprising a set of "master beliefs" that help the leader understand incoming information and guide him or her in making decisions. Leaders hold onto these master beliefs rather tenaciously and are very reluctant to change them. Three types of cognitions play a special role in shaping these master beliefs: philosophical beliefs about politics, instrumental beliefs about which strategies are best to achieve one's interests, and images of one's enemy and oneself.[17] Scholars have employed the operational code to explain the decisions of multiple leaders, including US presidents Lyndon B. Johnson and Bill Clinton, secretaries of state John Foster Dulles and Henry Kissinger, and British prime minister Tony Blair.[18] These operational codes could also affect how systemic stimuli are processed.

psychoanalytic hypothesis was later challenged by other scholars who posit that Wilson's intransigence at the Paris Peace Conference and later during the ratification fight for the Versailles Treaty resulted from physical illness, specifically the debilitating strokes he suffered in 1918–1919. See Jerrold M. Post, "Woodrow Wilson Re-Examined: The Mind-Body Controversy Redux and Other Disputations," *Political Psychology*, vol. 4, no. 2 (1983), pp. 289–306; and Juliette L. George and Alexander L. George, "Comments On 'Woodrow Wilson Re-Examined: The Mind-Body Controversy Redux and Other Disputations,'" *Political Psychology*, vol. 4, no. 2 (1983), pp. 307–312. For more recent studies see Rose McDermott, *Presidential Leadership, Illness, and Decision Making* (New York: Cambridge University Press, 2008).

16. Doris Kearns, "Lyndon Johnson's Political Personality," *Political Science Quarterly*, vol. 91, no. 3 (1976), pp. 385–409.

17. Nathan Leites, *The Operational Code of the Politburo* (Santa Monica, CA: Rand Corporation, 1951); Alexander L. George, "The 'Operational Code': A Neglected Approach to the Study of Political Leaders and Decision-Making," *International Studies Quarterly*, vol. 13, no. 2 (1969), pp. 190–222; Ole R. Holsti, "Cognitive Dynamics and Images of the Enemy," *Journal of International Affairs*, vol 21, no. 1 (1967), pp. 16–39; and Jack S. Levy, "Psychology and Foreign Policy Decision-Making," in *The Oxford Handbook of Political Psychology*, ed. Leonie Huddy, David O. Sears, and Jack S. Levy, 2nd ed. (New York: Oxford University Press, 2013), p. 307.

18. Levy, "Psychology and Foreign Policy Decision-Making," p. 307. See also Ole R. Holsti, "The 'Operational Code' Approach to the Study of Political Leaders: John Foster Dulles' Philosophical and Instrumental Beliefs," *Canadian Journal of Political Science*, vol. 3, no. 1 (1970), pp. 123–157; Stephen G. Walker, "The Interface between Beliefs and Behavior: Henry Kissinger's Operational Code and the Vietnam War," *Journal of Conflict Resolution*, vol. 21, no. 1 (1977), pp. 129–168; Stephen G. Walker and Lawrence S. Falkowski, "The Operational Codes of US Presidents and Secretaries of State: Motivational Foundations and Behavioral Consequences," *Political Psychology*, vol. 5, no. 2 (1984), pp. 237–266; and Stephen G. Walker and Mark Schafer, "The Political Universe of Lyndon B. Johnson and His Advisors: Diagnostic and Strategic Propensities in Their Operational Codes," *Political*

A good deal of neoclassical realist scholarship has utilized perceptual intervening variables, which affect how leaders assess the balance of power and anticipated power trends. Neoclassical realists distinguish between the actual or real distribution of power and elites' perceptions of the balance of power in various times and places. For instance, William Wohlforth examines the role of elite perceptions of power and the impact it had on the nature of the Soviet-American competition during the Cold War. Given the difficulty political elites have in measuring aggregate power, Wohlforth maintains that leaders disaggregate or unpack the concept of power into the four aspects of power: "the elements of power" (what people think power is), "the distribution of power" (how the state compares to other great powers), "the mechanics of power" (the operation of the balance of power), and "prestige" (the state's relative status and influence over international politics).[19] Wohlforth finds that while Soviet leaders emphasized military capabilities, their American counterparts stressed, among other factors, both economic and organizational resources.

Jeffrey Taliaferro also examines how leaders think about power. He finds that leaders do not accept losses in their state's relative power, status, or prestige as sunk costs. Instead, Taliaferro maintains that leaders often continue to invest and even doubledown in failed foreign interventions in an attempt to recoup past losses. In adopting risk-acceptant strategies due to loss aversion, the result can be self-defeating military and diplomatic engagement in inconsequential locales.[20] Like Wohlforth and Taliaferro, Aaron Friedberg, examines how senior officials measure power and adjust to shifts in the distribution of power. Friedberg, like other neoclassical realists, questions the materially driven determinism of structural realism and the "explanatory and predictive power of theories that move directly from international structure to state behavior."[21] The import of his argument is that adaptation to shifts in power is often

Psychology, vol. 21, no. 3 (2000), pp. 529–543. More recently, see Gerald M. Post, ed., The Psychological Assessment of Political Leaders: With Profiles of Saddam Hussein and Bill Clinton (Ann Arbor: University of Michigan Press, 2005). On the fundamental attribution error, see Ole R. Holsti, The Belief System and National Images: John Foster Dulles and the Soviet Union (Stanford, CA: Stanford University Press, 1962). For a review of this literature, see Alexander L. George, Presidential Decisionmaking in Foreign Policy: The Effective Use of Information and Advice (Boulder, CO: Westview, 1980).

19. William C. Wohlforth, The Elusive Balance: Power and Perceptions during the Cold War (Ithaca, NY: Cornell University Press 1993), pp. 26–28. Also see idem., "The Perception of Power: Russia in the Pre-1914 Balance," World Politics, vol. 39, no. 3 (1987), pp. 353–381.

20. Jeffrey W. Taliaferro, Balancing Risks: Great Power Intervention in the Periphery (Ithaca, NY: Cornell University Press, 2004).

21. Aaron L. Friedberg, The Weary Titan: Britain and the Experience of Relative Decline, 1895–1905 (Princeton, NJ: Princeton University Press, 1988), p. 7.

"delayed" and come in the form of "discrete chunks" rather than contin-uous adaptation and updating.[22] Finally, Melvyn Leffler examines the so-called Wise Men in the Truman Administration, and how they defined American national security during the initial years of the Cold War.[23] For Leffler, like the previous authors, it is the perceptions of American policymakers of Soviet power that mattered rather than the real or actual distribution of power. Specifically, senior officials understood Soviet weaknesses and vulnerabilities, the importance of German and Japanese revival, and the significance of the Eurasian landmass and keeping it out of the control of any prospective great power adversary. However, these same officials also saw Europe fraught with more peril than was dictated by structural imperatives and exaggerated the leverage of the Kremlin. In this manner, as Hal Brands argues, in formulating the United States' Cold War grand strategy, contradictory information was either ignored or twisted to fit existing explanations.[24]

ii. Strategic Culture

The second set of core intervening variables concerns a country's strate-gic culture, which can influence the way the state perceives and adapts to systemic stimuli and structural shifts in material capability. Scholars who examine strategic culture differentiate between organizational culture, such as that of the military as a bureaucratic organization, and a broader notion of strategic culture such as entrenched beliefs, worldviews, and shared expectations of a society as a whole.[25]

In the former category, scholars such as Jeffrey Legro and Elizabeth Kier, who treat the military as a bureaucratic organization, study the effect of military culture on the formation of national security policy. According

---

22. Ibid., p. 17.

23. Melvyn P. Leffler, *A Preponderance of Power: National Security, the Truman Administration, and the Cold War* (Palo Alto, CA: Stanford University Press, 1992). See also idem., "The American Conception of National Security and the Beginning of the Cold War, 1945–48," *American Historical Review*, vol. 89, no. 2 (1984), pp. 346–381.

24. Hal Brands, *What Good Is Grand Strategy? Power and Purpose in American Statecraft from Harry S. Truman to George W. Bush* (Ithaca, NY: Cornell University Press, 2014), pp. 17–58.

25. Judith Goldstein and Robert O. Keohane, eds., *Ideas and Foreign Policy: Beliefs, Institutions, and Political Change* (Ithaca, NY: Cornell University Press, 1993). Also see Jack Snyder, *Myths of Empire: Domestic Politics and International Ambition* (Ithaca, NY: Cornell University Press, 1991); Charles Kupchan, *The Vulnerability of Empire* (Ithaca, NY: Cornell University Press, 1994), pp. 27–29; and Asle Toje, *America, the EU, and Strategic Culture: Renegotiating the Transatlantic Bargain* (New York: Routledge, 2008).

to Legro, the military's organizational culture and the attitudes of military professionals explain why the restriction on the use of chemical weapons was not breached on the battlefield during World War II.[26] Kier challenges the assumption that the military as a bureaucracy prefers offensive strategies, arguing instead that, during the interwar period, the French army's organizational culture favored the adoption of a defensive doctrine regardless of the external circumstances it faced. In her view, the French army favored a defensive doctrine not because of the external threat of German military power, but because of the battles between the Left and the Right over the domestic distribution of political power. Specifically, the ruling Left and Republican forces opposed a professional army, fearing that it would act on behalf of the reactionary Right. By enacting short-term conscription, Kier argues that the military high command could not conceptually move beyond a defensive doctrine.[27] In contrast, Charles Kupchan develops a broader understanding of strategic culture. For Kupchan, strategic culture—or deeply embedded conceptions and notions of national security—take root among elites and the general public.[28]

In both instances, ideational models of strategic culture include a set of inter-related beliefs, norms, and assumptions. Strategic culture or collective expectations shape the strategic understanding of political leaders, societal elites, and even the general public. Through socialization and institutionalization (in rules and norms), these collective assumptions and expectations become deeply entrenched and constrain a state's behavior and freedom of action by defining what are acceptable and unacceptable strategic choices, even in an anarchic self-help environment. Theories of the role of strategic culture focus on norms, such as moral restraint on the use of military power, non-use of weapons of mass destruction, and humanitarian intervention.[29] For instance, democratic transnational norms and culture are the causal mechanisms of one of the central explanations for the democratic peace or special peace among

---

26. Jeffrey Legro, *Cooperation under Fire: Anglo-German Restraint during World War II* (Ithaca, NY: Cornell University Press, 1995).

27. Elizabeth Kier, *Imagining War: French and British Doctrine between the Wars* (Princeton, NJ: Princeton University Press, 1999).

28. Kupchan, *Vulnerability of Empire.*

29. Ronald L. Jepperson, Alexander Wendt, and Peter J. Katzenstein, "Norms, Identity and Culture in National Security," in *The Culture of National Security: Norms and Identity in World Politics*, ed. Peter J. Katzenstein (New York: Columbia University Press, 1996), pp. 33–75; Nina Tannenwald, "The Nuclear Taboo: The United States and the Normative Basis of Nuclear Non-Use," *International Organization*, vol. 53, no. 3 (1999), pp. 433–446. See also T. V. Paul, *The Tradition of Non-Use of Nuclear Weapons* (Stanford, CA: Stanford Security Studies, 2009).

liberal democratic states since 1815 (rather than democratic structure and institutional constraints, which are discussed in section four of this chapter). Scholars contend that the same democratic norms of conflict resolution used to defuse domestic disputes become externalized among liberal democracies. Thus, when two democracies have a dispute, both draw upon these entrenched norms and practices of conflict resolution to resolve their differences without the expectation or fear of the use of violence or force.[30] These same cultural restraints and expectations do not exist in dyadic relations among democratic and non-democratic states or among non-democratic states.

Moreover, national strategic culture can, in exceptional circumstances, be constructed and reconstructed over time, due either to the conscious agency of national governments, the impact of major historical events, or the imposition by foreign occupiers. The impact of governments seeking to engineer cultural change can be seen in Peter the Great's modernization plan in Russia in the early eighteenth century, the efforts by Itō Hirobumi, Yamagata Aritomo, and other Meiji oligarchs to build a modern Japanese state in the late nineteenth century, Lee Kuan Yew's integrative social and economic policies, and Kemal Atatürk's secularization plan in Turkey in the early twentieth century, all of which had a transformative effect on their respective strategic cultures.[31] The causal effect of historical experience is evident in the cumulative impact of three consecutive military defeats at German hands on French insecurity after the two world wars.[32] The experience of western Germany and Japan after World War II illustrates the impact of victorious powers. While both countries had excessively militaristic strategic cultures, their catastrophic defeat in World War II and American-led state and social engineering in

30. Bruce Russett, *Grasping the Democratic Peace* (Princeton, NJ: Princeton University Press, 1993); and John M. Owen IV, *The Clash of Ideas in World Politics: Transnational Networks, States, and Regime Change* (Princeton, NJ: Princeton University Press, 2010), pp. 202–239. Also see, G. John Ikenberry, *After Victory: Institutions, Strategic Restraint, and the Rebuilding of Order after Major Wars* (Princeton, NJ: Princeton University Press, 2001). Ikenberry discusses constitutional orders and contrasts them to balance of power and hegemonic orders.

31. Richard J. Samuels, *Machiavelli's Children: Leaders and Their Legacies in Italy and Japan* (Ithaca, NY: Cornell University Press, 2003); Michael D. Barr and Zlatko Skrbis, *Constructing Singapore: Elitism, Ethnicity and the Nation-Building Project* (Copenhagen: Nordic Institute of Asian Studies Press, 2008), pp. 112–126; James Cracraft, *The Revolution of Peter the Great* (Cambridge, MA: Harvard University Press, 2006), pp. 75–113; and Yücel Bozdağlıoğlu, *Turkish Foreign Policy and Turkish Identity: A Constructivist Approach* (London and New York: Routledge, 2003), pp. 46–50.

32. See Norrin M. Ripsman, "Domestic Practices and Balancing: Integrating Practice into Neoclassical Realism," in *International Practices*, ed. Vincent Pouliot and Emanuel Adler (Cambridge: Cambridge University Press, 2010), pp. 200–228, at pp. 207–208.

the war's aftermath completely remade postwar Japan and the Federal Republic of Germany and their strategic cultures. Consequently, the newly entrenched norm of antimilitarism has made it difficult for their governments to adopt assertive foreign policies.[33]

We would also include dominant ideologies, which can affect the state's attitudes toward international affairs and willingness to use force, and degrees of nationalism as important components of strategic culture. After all, the Soviet ideology, which presumed capitalist encirclement, increased the likelihood that Lenin and Stalin would view Western acts as threatening and made it more difficult for them to cooperate with Western states.[34] In this regard, Mark Haas argues that ideological distance is an important determinant of international alignment patterns.[35] A nationalist culture, which promotes personal sacrifices in support of the state, can aid in resource mobilization in support of national security policy.[36] Thus, for example, Randall Schweller argues that fascism was ideally suited to the demands of an anarchic environment in the era of total warfare because it eased war mobilization for Germany, Italy, and Japan on the eve of World War II.[37]

Strategic culture can place severe constraints on the ability of elites to undertake strategic adjustment to systemic changes. Specifically, as Kupchan observes, decision-making elites can become trapped by strategic culture, which can prevent them from reorienting grand strategy to meet international imperatives and avoid self-defeating behavior. In extreme cases, as Kupchan suggests, the result is a pathological foreign policy characterized by strategic exposure, self-encirclement, or overextension. In each instance, the state is left pursuing policies that jeopardize

33. Thomas U. Berger, "Norms, Identity, and National Security in Germany and Japan," in *The Culture of National Security: Norms and Identity in World Politics*, ed. Peter J. Katzenstein (New York: Columbia University Press, 1996), pp. 317–356. Also see Jennifer Lind, "Apologies in International Politics," *Security Studies*, vol. 18, no. 3 (2009), pp. 517–556; David M. Edelstein, *Occupational Hazards: Success and Failure in Military Occupation* (Ithaca, NY: Cornell University Press, 2008), pp. 28–39 and 122–135.

34. William Curti Wohlforth, *The Elusive Balance: Power and Perceptions During the Cold War* (Ithaca, NY: Cornell University Press, 1993), pp. 32–58.

35. Mark L. Haas, *The Ideological Origins of Great Power Politics, 1789–1989* (Ithaca, NY, and London: Cornell University Press, 2005).

36. Zoltan I. Buzas, "How Nationalism Helps Internal Balancing but Hurts External Balancing: The Case of East Asia," paper presented at the Center for International Peace and Security Studies, McGill University, September 19, 2014.

37. Randall Schweller, "Neoclassical Realism and State Mobilization: Expansionist Ideology in the Age of Mass Politics," in *Neoclassical Realism, the State, and Foreign Policy*, ed. Steven E. Lobell, Norrin M. Ripsman, and Jeffrey W. Taliaferro (Cambridge: Cambridge University Press, 2009), pp. 227–250.

its primary security interests because strategic culture prevents the state from responding fluidly to external challenges and opportunities.[38] Even in less extreme circumstances, when states face a more permissive external environment, strategic culture might limit and shape national policy choices.

Among Type I and Type II neoclassical realists, Nicholas Kitchen, Colin Dueck, and Victor Cha use strategic culture and ideas as an intervening variable between the distribution of capabilities and foreign policy behavior. For Kitchen, "prevailing ideas influence the type of foreign policy response to structural imperatives."[39] Ideas can intervene through several different means including state leaders, institutions (including epistemic communities, and formal rules and procedures) and the broader cultural preferences of a state. For Dueck, the international environment sets the broad parameters on state behavior; changes in the distribution of power will encourage strategic adjustment in the form of a more or less expansive grand strategy. However, strategic culture conditions the specific patterns of change and continuity. In particular, Dueck argues that policy makers will choose to frame, adjust, and modify strategic choices to reflect culturally acceptable preferences to maintain domestic political support. Moreover, due to strategic culture, leaders might be unwilling or unable to generate support since some strategic ideas will simply resonate better with the general public both culturally and ideationally than other choices.[40] Finally, for Victor Cha, a combination of external threats, history, and culture play a critical role in alliance dynamics. In examining quasi-alliances or instances in which two unaligned states share a great power patron, he finds that historical animosity between Japan and Korea shaped their alliance dynamics with the United States.[41]

iii.   State-Society Relations

The third cluster of intervening variables encompasses state-society relations, which we define as the character of interactions between the central

38. Kupchan, *Vulnerability of Empire*, chapter 2.

39. Nicholas Kitchen, "Systemic Pressures and Domestic Ideas: A Neoclassical Realist Model of Grand Strategy Formation," *Review of International Studies*, vol. 36, no. 1 (2010), p. 132.

40. Colin Dueck, *Reluctant Crusaders: Power, Culture, and Change in American Grand Strategy* (Princeton, NJ: Princeton University Press, 2006).

41. Victor D. Cha, *Alignment Despite Antagonism: The United States-Korea-Japan Security Triangle* (Stanford, CA: Stanford University Press, 1999); and idem., "Powerplay: Origins of the U.S. Alliance System in Asia," *International Security*, vol. 34, no. 3 (2010), pp. 158–196.

institutions of the state and various economic and or societal groups. Key questions relate to the degree of harmony between the state and society, the degree to which society defers to state leaders on foreign policy matters in the event of disagreements, distributional competition among societal coalitions to capture the state and its associated spoils, the level of political and social cohesion within the state, and public support for general foreign policy and national security objectives. These factors can affect whether state leaders have the power to extract, mobilize, and harness the nation's power.[42] Of particular importance are the nature of state-society interactions, the processes and mechanisms to resolve state-society differences and disputes, and the impact of these interactions and mechanisms on policy formulation and implementation.

A related issue, which we discuss in the next section, is the degree to which political institutions allow the state to reach decisions autonomously from society. To the extent that political institutions insulate the FPE in the making of foreign policy, policy is more likely to conform to state preferences and the demands of the external environment. The effect of state-society harmony, however, is less straightforward. If good relations between the FPE and key societal interests or the public at large are indicative of high levels of societal respect for and trust of the state, then that should serve to reinforce policy making consistently with the structural realist model, since the state will have a relatively free hand to enact policy as it sees fit. In contrast, if harmony implies extensive consultation during the policy-making process and the participation of societal actors in policy formulation, it could result in policy that satisfies domestic interests, rather than exclusively international ones (or even at the expense of international ones).

Policymaking is complicated to a greater degree in the event of state-society discord—unless political institutions insulate the executive—as the FPE must struggle with and seek to overcome domestic opposition or bargain with its opponents over the content of policy.[43] As far as policy implementation is concerned, if society is suspicious of the state and resists what it considers to be state incursions upon societal rights and resources, it will be difficult to carry out foreign policy decisions. After all, foreign policy and grand strategy require immense human, material, and monetary resources. If key societal groups that possess these resources—or the public at large—withhold them from the state, the state apparatus will have to

---

42. See Fareed Zakaria, *From Wealth to Power: The Unusual Origins of America's World Role* (Princeton, NJ: Princeton University Press, 1998).

43. Michael N. Barnett, *Confronting the Costs of War: Military Power, State, and Society in Egypt and Israel* (Princeton, NJ: Princeton University Press, 1992).

devote considerable revenue collection, policing and internal security, and propaganda resources in order to extract them, which will undermine the efficiency of national policy.[44] Moreover, pursuing unpopular policies in such an environment could even threaten the security of both the regime and the state itself, as the leaders of Tsarist Russia learned when the hardships of war in 1905 and 1917 led to revolutionary acts against the regime. Not only did the 1917 revolution lead to the overthrow of Tsar Nicholas II, but it also brought about military defeat at German and Ottoman hands while the Russian military effort ground to a halt.[45] Similarly, the 1625 decision by King Philip IV of Spain's chief minister, the Count-Duke Olivares, requiring all territories of the Spanish Crown to furnish a reserve army for Spain inspired Catalonia to rebel and Portugal to declare its independence from Spain.[46] Thus, war mobilization clearly came at a political price.

A further state-society consideration relates to the dynamics of coalition politics in the state. To the extent that a particular socio-economic interest group, economic sector, or coalition of interests captures the state, it may be unable to enact policies that diverge from the preferences of that underlying coalition. This can occur either because the leaders are drawn from that political coalition and therefore view international affairs through the prism of their parochial interests, or because they recognize that they can maintain their power positions only by satisfying their support base's demands. In this regard, scholars who take a political economy approach to the state assume that states captured by inward-oriented nationalist coalitions will pursue policies of protectionism and military competition, whereas those whose dominant coalition is comprised of outward-oriented internationalists will pursue grand strategies of freer trade and international cooperation.[47] Thus, unless the state possesses

44. See Rosella Cappella Zielinski, *How States Pay for Wars* (Ithaca, NY: Cornell University Press, 2016), chapter 2.

45. Aviel Roshwald, *Ethnic Nationalism and the Fall of Empires: Ethnic Europe, Russia, and the Middle East, 1914–1923* (New York: Routledge, 2001), p. 90; and Arthur Mendel, "On Interpreting the Fate of Imperial Russia," in *Russia Under the Last Tsar*, ed. Theofanis G. Stavrou (Minneapolis: University of Minnesota Press, 1971), pp. 13–41, at p. 36.

46. Geoffrey Parker, *Europe in Crisis, 1598–1648* (Ithaca, NY: Cornell University Press, 1979); and J. H. Elliott, *Spain and Its World, 1500–1700* (New Haven, CT: Yale University Press, 1989).

47. Etel Solingen, *Scientists and the State: Domestic Structures and the International Context* (Ann Arbor: University of Michigan Press, 1994); Jeffry A. Frieden, *Debt, Development, and Democracy: Modern Political Economy and Latin America, 1965–1985* (Princeton, NJ: Princeton University Press, 1991); Peter Trubowitz, *Defining the National Interest: Conflict and Change in American Foreign Policy* (Chicago: University of Chicago Press, 1998); Benjamin O. Fordham, *Building the Cold War Consensus: The Political Economy of U.S. National Security Policy, 1949–51* (Ann Arbor: University of Michigan Press, 1998); Steven E. Lobell, *The Challenge of Hegemony: Grand Strategy, Trade, and Domestic Politics*

sufficient institutional autonomy to shield it from domestic pressures, the composition of the dominant coalition and its relationship with the state can affect the state's policy preference's and its willingness to make and implement particular grand strategic choices.[48]

The nature of civil-military relations captures a final element of state-society interaction. Civil-military relations involve matters related to the interaction between civil society, political elites, and the military as an institution. The military has specialized and technical expertise in the use of force and is tasked with protecting the nation-state. The central issue is how to strike a balance between civilian control over the military and ensuring a strong and effective military, which has its own narrow parochial interests. This balance is further complicated in democracies. Samuel Huntington, in responding to allegations that the United States was becoming too militarized and a garrison state, warned of the danger of responding by undermining the military's war-fighting capability.[49] Huntington's solution was the objective, rather than the intrusive, civilian control over military affairs. Under this model, the professional officer corps would be entrusted with the conduct of military operations (subject to civilian oversight) but remain insulated from the political process. From this perspective, the American war effort in Vietnam was a failure due to the Johnson administration's tendency to micro-manage the conflict.[50] In challenging Huntington's military professionalism based model, Peter Feaver adopts a rationalist principal-agent framework to understand the dynamics of civil-military relations.[51] The problem of civilian (principal) oversight of the military (agent) is that although the

(Ann Arbor: University of Michigan Press, 2003); and Kevin Narizny, *The Political Economy of Grand Strategy* (Ithaca, NY: Cornell University Press, 2007).

48. One problem with some of this literature is that parochial groups have too narrow a base to capture the state. Jack Snyder argues that groups join with other pro-imperial interests to form a powerful logrolled coalition. Such logrolled coalitions have the greatest opportunity to capture state policy where power is highly centralized—in cartelized political systems such as Germany and Japan in the 1930s. The consequence is overexpansion or more expansion than any single parochial group desired, since each group will get elements of the policy or program of expansion that it most prefers. However, multiple expansions can result in strategic over-commitment and self-encirclement. In the long run, even the pro-imperial parochial groups are harmed by the counterproductive expansion. Jack Snyder, *Myths of Empire: Domestic Politics and International Ambition* (Ithaca, NY: Cornell University Press, 1993).

49. Samuel P. Huntington, *The Soldier and the State: The Theory and Politics of Civil-Military Relations* (Cambridge, MA: Harvard University Press, 1981), pp. 190–192. See also Morris Janowitz, *The Professional Soldier: A Social and Political Portrait* (New York: Free Press, 1971).

50. Eliot Cohen, *Supreme Command: Soldiers, Statesmen, and Leadership in Wartime* (New York: Free Press, 2002).

51. Peter D. Feaver, *Armed Servants: Agency Oversight and Civil-Military Relations* (Cambridge, MA: Harvard University Press, 2003).

latter is subordinate in the relationship, the military agents have specialized knowledge and are responsible for carrying out civilian orders. For
Feaver, the military's willingness to comply or challenge civilian agency
depends less on its professionalism than on its strategic calculations of
whether shirking behavior will be caught and punished. Therefore, civil-
military relations as a manifestation of state-society relations influence
the strategies that states are able to pursue abroad.

For neoclassical realists, the nature of state-society relations can have a
significant impact on the strategic behavior of states. Indeed, as Schweller
argues, underbalancing—when the state does not balance or does so inef-
ficiently in response to a dangerous aggressor—occurs for two domestic
reasons: leaders' preferences are more influenced by domestic rather than
international concerns or the potential domestic political risks and costs
from balancing behavior are deemed too high.[52] For Schweller, state-
society factors and especially the degree of consensus or fragmentation at
the elite and the societal levels can condition the occurrence of inappropriate balancing behavior. The level of elite consensus and cohesion, for
instance, will affect whether the leadership is in agreement on the nature
and extent of foreign threats, and the appropriate strategic response to
them. The level of societal cohesion reflects the degree of political and
social integration. In highly fragmented and divided states, the leadership is prone to select the lowest common denominator policies, though
they can result in underreacting to external threats. Finally, regime vulnerability and its ability to resist domestic challengers including the military, opposition parties, and interests groups will affect the government's
willingness to mobilize society and the resources necessary for timely
and appropriate balancing behavior. For Schweller, states characterized
by high levels of fragmentation and divisions among elites and societal
actors are prone to underbalancing behavior, thereby departing from the
systemic imperatives of balance of power theory.

For Steven Lobell, state-society relations, and particularly societal
competition between broad inward and outward oriented coalitions (e.g.,
economic nationalist and free trade blocs) will affect a declining hegemon's grand strategic policies.[53] A hegemon's international environment,
and especially the commercial composition of the major states, will have

---

52. Randall L. Schweller, *Unanswered Threats: Political Constraints on the Balance of Power*
(Princeton, NJ: Princeton University Press, 2006), pp. 11–13.

53. Steven E. Lobell, "Second Image Reversed Politics: Britain's Choice of Freer Trade or
Imperial Preferences, 1903–1906, 1917–1923, 1930–1932," *International Studies Quarterly*,
vol. 43, no. 4 (1999), pp. 671–694; and idem., *The Challenge of Hegemony: Grand Strategy,
Trade, and Domestic Politics* (Ann Arbor: University of Michigan Press, 2003), pp. 19–41.

the domestic effect of ratcheting up the strength of some societal actors and rolling back the strength of others; the commercial orientation of the contenders will affect the domestic balance of political and economic power. The empowered coalition will use these gains to lobby the FPE to further advance its preferred grand strategic goals and thereby capture additional distributional benefits. Any subsequent reversals in the commercial composition of the rising states can enable the opposing societal group and thereby alter the domestic balance of power. Departures from systemic imperatives occur when the erstwhile ruling faction, which is under threat of being rolled back, advances a grand strategy that will ratchet up its own relative coalitional power. Nonetheless, such strategies will erode the hegemon's long-term productive strength or undermine its security, and thereby shorten its great power tenure.

iv. Domestic Institutions

The last cluster of intervening variables for neoclassical realist theory involves state structure and domestic political institutions, which often crystallize state-society relations. Formal institutions, organizational routines and processes, and bureaucratic oversight, often established by constitutional provisions with clearly specified rules and regulations set the broad parameters within which domestic competition over policy occurs.[54] Consequently, they determine who can contribute to policy formation, at what stage of the policy process, and who can act as veto players, using their power to block policy initiatives in order to reshape governmental policies.[55] In this regard, the differing institutional structures of states can have an important impact on their ability to respond to systemic pressures.[56]

In the section on strategic culture above, we discussed the constraints of shared democratic norms and rules as one explanation for the

54. Barry R. Posen, *The Sources of Military Doctrine* (Ithaca, NY: Cornell University Press, 1984); Jack Snyder, *The Ideology of the Offensive: Military Decision Making and the Disasters of 1914* (Ithaca, NY: Cornell University Press, 1984); and Jack S. Levy, "Organizational Routines and the Causes of War," *International Studies Quarterly*, vol. 30, no. 2 (1986), pp. 193–222.

55. On veto players, see George Tsebelis, *Veto Players: How Political Institutions Work* (Princeton, NJ: Princeton University Press, 2002).

56. Graham Allison's organizational and bureaucratic politics models of foreign policy, for example, highlight the effect of domestic institutional processes, organizational routines, and internal government politics on the foreign policy making process. Graham Allison and Philip Zelikow, *Essence of Decision: Explaining the Cuban Missile Crisis*, 2nd ed. (London: Longman, 1999).

special peace among democracies. An alternative explanation for this special peace is the institutional constraints inherent in democracies.[57] According to this approach, structural impediments such as a division of powers, checks and balances, and public support serve to constrain democratic leaders and make it difficult for them to go to war. Nonetheless, democracies vary in the degree to which their institutions provide checks and balances on their FPEs; therefore, it is useful to examine their institutional differences.[58] In a democratic polity, the most important institutional rules relate to the autonomy of the executive—be it presidential, parliamentary, or mixed—and its relationship to the legislature and the bureaucracy.[59] Important institutional variables affecting the foreign policy of democracies include the degree to which power is concentrated in the executive's hands, executive-legislative relations, party systems and whether it is a two-party or multiparty system, voting rules and whether the electoral system is based on plurality voting or proportional representation, and the quality of the government and its administrative competence. These variables will affect whether state leaders can harness the nation's power, as discussed above, and whether democratic states can adjust and adapt readily to external shocks or shifts in the international distribution of power.[60] Moreover, it matters whether mechanisms and processes of legislative oversight have been established and how onerous they are, and which body—the executive or the legislature—is responsible for appointing the foreign minister and other key officials charged with making foreign policy. For instance, according to Michael Mastanduno, the checks and balances in the US Constitution have the intent of checking the authority of the presidency and ensuring that domestic power is

57. Michael W. Doyle, "Kant, Liberal Legacies, and Foreign Affairs," *Philosophy and Public Affairs*, vol. 12, no. 3 (1983), pp. 205–235; and idem., "Kant, Liberal Legacies, and Foreign Affairs, Part 2," *Philosophy and Public Affairs*, vol. 12, no. 4 (1983), pp. 323–353. Christopher Layne quickly dismisses institutional arguments by asserting that democracies should also be less war-prone. Christopher Layne, "Kant or Cant: The Myth of the Democratic Peace," *International Security*, vol. 19 (1994), pp. 5–49.

58. Norrin M. Ripsman, "Peacemaking and Democratic Peace Theory: Public Opinion as an Obstacle to Peace in Post-Conflict Situation," *Democracy and Security*, vol. 3, no. 1 (2007), pp. 89–113.

59. See Norrin M. Ripsman, *Peacemaking by Democracies: The Effect of State Autonomy on the Post-World-War Settlements* (University Park: Penn State University Press, 2002); and Kenneth Schultz, *Democracy and Coercive Diplomacy* (Cambridge: Cambridge University Press, 2001). For a discussion of the differential domestic constraints of presidential, parliamentary, and coalition governments, see David P. Auerswald and Stephen M. Saideman, *NATO in Afghanistan: Fighting Together, Fighting Alone* (Princeton, NJ: Princeton University Press, 2014), chapters 4, 5, and 6.

60. Ripsman, *Peacemaking by Democracies*. See also Peter Gourevitch, "Domestic Politics and International Relations," in *Handbook of International Relations*, ed. Walter Carlsnaes, Thomas Risse, and Beth A. Simmons (London: Sage, 2002), pp. 309–328, at p. 312.

widely shared among the citizenry. But like a large cruise ship that cannot "turn on a dime," the disadvantage of the American system is that it can hamstring the president in times when quick and decisive foreign policy is necessary.[61] This constraint on the foreign policy making process raises questions about democracies in general, in terms of whether they are less likely to be prepared for war, especially in peacetime, whether they can engage in offensive military strategies and preventive wars, and whether they make for reliable allies.[62] In non-democratic states, domestic institutions determine the leadership's scope of authority and the degree to which it must consult or respect the wishes of key societal interests, such as the military, the aristocracy, or important business elites.[63]

In addition to these formal institutions, there are less formal institutions, decision-making procedures, or political practices that also affect the ability of FPEs to enact and implement policy.[64] These refer to routinized patterns of interaction, customary practices, and unwritten rules, which although uncodified, nonetheless exert causal influence on actors' behavior. In general, these less formal institutions and practices affect the scope of action actors have within the formal institutional framework of the domestic environment. Practices, such as the use of party discipline in Great Britain and non-partisanship/bipartisanship in US foreign policy in the immediate post–World War II period, which routinize support for the executive, typically assist FPEs who command a majority of support in the legislature. In contrast, those which require the executive to consult with opposition forces or which encourage actors outside the executive to use their power to the fullest can complicate policy making and

---

61. Michael Mastanduno, "The United States Political System and International Leadership: A 'Decidedly Inferior' Form of Government?" in *American Foreign Policy: Theoretical Essays*, ed. G. John Ikenberry and Peter L. Trubowitz (Oxford: Oxford University Press, 2015), pp. 227–242.

62. See Russett, *Grasping the Democratic Peace*. Jack Snyder argues that democracies will not engage in overexpansion and Mark Brawley argues that democracies are more likely to create larger coalitions for war and are more likely to win wars. Snyder, *Myths of Empire*; and Mark R. Brawley, *Liberal Leadership: Great Powers and Their Challengers in Peace and War* (Ithaca, NY: Cornell University Press, 1994), pp. 21–22. Also see David A. Lake, "Powerful Pacifists: Democratic States and War," *American Political Science Review*, vol. 86, no. 1 (1992), pp. 24–37; and Randall L. Schweller, "Domestic Structure and Preventive War: Are Democracies More Pacific?" *World Politics*, vol. 44, no. 2 (1992), pp. 235–269.

63. In contrast to democracies, which require a wide base of domestic support, non-democratic states need a smaller winning coalition to rule, and can therefore engage in foreign economic policies that allow for rent seeking for a narrow interest group. Brawley, *Liberal Leadership*.

64. On the importance of political practices, see Emanuel Adler and Vincent Pouliot, "International Practices Introduction and Framework," in *International Practices*, ed. Vincent Pouliot and Emanuel Adler (Cambridge: Cambridge University Press, 2010), pp. 3–35; and Ripsman, "Domestic Practices and Balancing."

implementation.[65] These features will determine whether the FPE has the autonomy to conduct policy as it sees fit or whether it must make compromises with institutional veto players or logroll with others to form a winning coalition to secure a policy's adoption.[66]

Several Type I and Type II neoclassical realists include domestic institutional intervening variables in their analyses. By unpacking democratic states rather than treating them as a unitary actor, Norrin Ripsman finds that different institutional arrangements will affect how democracies formulate their foreign security policies. Some of the important distinctions include parliamentary and presidential systems, the number of political parties, the frequency of major elections, and the relations between foreign ministers and the legislature. For Ripsman, the degree of the structural autonomy of FPEs will affect their independence from both legislative and popular opposition. Strong executives can pursue their policies even when confronting strong opposition, while weak executives will have great difficulty in pursuing an autonomous foreign policy. However, Ripsman argues that even constrained democratic leaders can pursue a host of strategies to create independence from political and societal opponents.[67]

Friedberg, Schweller, and Taliaferro each posit an important intervening role for domestic institutions, regime vulnerability, and extractive capacity in shaping states' responses to changes in their external environments. According to Friedberg, the combination of weak state institutions, the material interests of various societal actors, and a deeply embedded anti-statist ideology shaped the United States' force posture and military strategy during the early Cold War. Toward that end, the Truman, Eisenhower, and Kennedy administrations pursued a de facto industrial policy whereby the Department of Defense served as a procurement agent, relying on private manufacturers for weapons systems and supporting technologies.[68] For Schweller, the likelihood that states can effectively balance against a foreign adversary or coalition is, in part, a function of the regime's or government's vulnerability to removal from office (whether through constitutional or extra-constitutional means).[69]

65. Of course, non-partisanship cuts both ways, as it also requires governments to consult with legislators. Ripsman, "Domestic Practices and Balancing."

66. On executive autonomy, see Eric A. Nordlinger, *On the Autonomy of the Democratic State* (Cambridge, MA: Harvard University Press, 1981); Hugh Heclo, *Modern Social Politics in Britain and Sweden* (New Haven, CT: Yale University Press, 1974); and Ripsman, *Peacemaking by Democracies*.

67. Ripsman, *Peacemaking by Democracies*.

68. Aaron L. Friedberg, *In the Shadow of the Garrison State: America's Anti-Statism and Its Cold War Grand Strategy* (Princeton, NJ: Princeton University Press, 2000), pp. 245–295.

69. Schweller, *Unanswered Threats*, pp. 46–68.

Finally, Taliaferro contends that the extractive capacity of state institutions vis-à-vis society, the degree of state-sponsored nationalism, and embedded statist (or anti-statist) ideology shape whether states respond to external vulnerability by emulating the military practices of more powerful states, trying to offset an enemy's perceived advantage through military innovation, or persisting in existing strategies.[70]

CONCLUSION

In this chapter, we identified four broad categories of intervening unit-level variables. These categories reflect the range of intervening variables that neoclassical realist scholars have identified, in a deductively organized manner, specifying the impact they are likely to have on how states process and respond to systemic pressures. This represents a significant contribution, which will help dispel the charge leveled by some critics that neoclassical realists introduce intervening variables in an ad hoc manner. In Chapter 4, we turn our attention to the dependent variable, which we argue is much broader than hitherto acknowledged by Type I and II neoclassical realists. By expanding the explanatory range of the dependent variable, we make our case more fully for neoclassical realist theory of international politics in Chapter 4.

---

70. Jeffrey W. Taliaferro, "Neoclassical Realism and Resource Extraction: State Building for Future War," in *Neoclassical Realism, the State, and Foreign Policy*, ed. Steven E. Lobell, Norrin M. Ripsman, and Jeffrey W. Taliaferro (Cambridge: Cambridge University Press, 2009), pp. 215–222.

The Scope and Domain of Neoclassical Realism

The Dependent Variables

Having delineated the independent and intervening variables employed by neoclassical realists in Chapters 2 and 3, we now turn our attention to our dependent variables (highlighted in Figure 4.1). As we will argue in this chapter, these encompass not only states' foreign policy choices (the dependent variable of Types I and II neoclassical realism), but also international outcomes that the interaction of these policy choices produces and the systemic structure itself, which is occasionally affected by international outcomes. We term this Type III neoclassical realism or neoclassical realist theory of international politics.

RETHINKING THE DICHOTOMY BETWEEN THEORIES OF INTERNATIONAL POLITICS AND FOREIGN POLICY

In our previous work, we argued that neoclassical realism was an approach to the study of foreign policy and grand strategy, but not to international politics.[1] In particular, we argued that neoclassical realism is, in essence,

---

1. Jeffrey W. Taliaferro, Steven E. Lobell, and Norrin M. Ripsman, "Introduction: Neoclassical Realism, the State, and Foreign Policy," in *Neoclassical Realism, the State, and Foreign Policy*, ed. Steven E. Lobell, Norrin M. Ripsman, and Jeffrey W. Taliaferro (Cambridge: Cambridge University Press, 2009), pp. 1–41; and Norrin M. Ripsman, Jeffrey W. Taliaferro, and Steven E. Lobell, "The Future of Neoclassical Realism," in *Neoclassical*

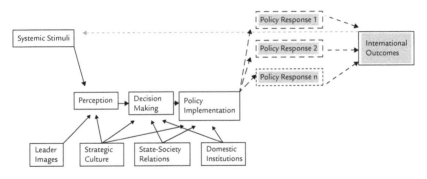

Figure 4.1
The Neoclassical Realist Model of Foreign Policy

a theory of foreign policy, in that it explains how states construct policy responses to international circumstances. In the short- to medium-term time frame, that is essentially correct. Nonetheless, the aggregate of the policies and strategies selected by the major powers of the international system, and the interaction of these policies, can have important effects on international outcomes and systemic structure over time. Therefore, over the longer run, neoclassical realism has much to say about international politics more broadly. For these reasons, we agree with James Fearon and Colin Elman that the rigid distinction between foreign policy and international politics that Kenneth Waltz made is largely overdrawn.[2]

In essence, as illustrated in Figure 4.2, we argue that the scope of the dependent variable that neoclassical realism can help explain grows over time and is broader than neoclassical realists have heretofore articulated. In the shorter term, neoclassical realism can help explain the short-term policy choices that states make to respond to the particular challenges and opportunities that the international system and other states present to them. Over the short-to-medium term, neoclassical realist theories can shed light on the processes of policy planning and grand strategic adjustment with which states attempt to navigate not only immediate crises but also expected shifts in power and future threats and opportunities. This

Realism, the State, and Foreign Policy, ed. Steven E. Lobell, Norrin M. Ripsman, and Jeffrey W. Taliaferro (Cambridge: Cambridge University Press, 2009), pp. 280–299.

2. James Fearon, "Domestic Politics, Foreign Policy, and Theories of International Relations," *Annual Review of Political Science,* no. 1 (1998), pp. 289–313; and Colin Elman, "Horses for Courses: Why *Not* Neorealist Theories of Foreign Policy?" *Security Studies,* vol. 6, no. 1 (1996), pp. 7–53. Cf. Shibley Telhami, "Kenneth Waltz, Neorealism, and Foreign Policy," *Security Studies,* vol. 11, no. 3 (2002), pp. 158–170. On Waltz's distinction between foreign policy and international relations, see Kenneth N. Waltz, *Theory of International Politics* (Reading, MA: Addison-Wesley 1979), p. 64; and idem., "International Politics Is Not Foreign Policy," *Security Studies,* vol. 6, no. 1 (1996), pp. 55–57.

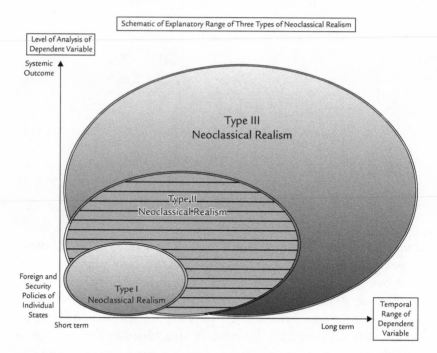

Figure 4.2
Explanatory Range of Three Types of Neoclassical Realism

is the scope of Type I and Type II neoclassical realism, including our own earlier efforts. *But it would be a mistake to say that neoclassical realism can explain only individual states' foreign policies and grand strategic adjustment.* Over the medium-to-longer term, international outcomes are affected by the interaction of the grand strategic choices of the great powers. Since these strategic choices are themselves products of not only international structure, but also domestic political arrangements within the great powers, neoclassical realism can shed more light on them than a purely systemic theory of international politics.[3] Similarly, we argue that, since over time grand strategic choices can affect relative power and international outcomes, and at times reshape the structure of the international system, neoclassical realism can also contribute to an explanation of changes in the nature of the international system. Consequently, we maintain that the dependent variable for neoclassical realists varies depending on the

3. In this regard, we are influenced by Patrick James's conception of elaborated structural realism. Patrick James, "Neorealism as a Research Enterprise: Toward Elaborated Structural Realism," *International Political Science Review*, vol. 14, no. 2 (1993), pp. 123–148, esp. pp. 135–136. Also see idem., *International Relations and Scientific Progress: Structural Realism Reconsidered* (Columbus: Ohio State University Press, 2002).

time frame. We discuss the nature of the dependent variable for each of these time frames below.

In the shorter term, defined in terms of days, weeks, and months, states navigate rather fixed international circumstances. Except in very rare circumstances, relative power is unlikely to shift within such a short time frame. Policy making, therefore, consists of navigating the given power distribution, without opportunities to augment one's own power through economic development, expansion of the military apparatus, or research and development of new military technologies—the essence of internal balancing. Nor is there time to initiate a full-scale alliance with another great power, with attendant joint military planning, training exercises, and strategic coordination. Instead, this is the realm of crisis decision-making and policy responses to unexpected events, which involves matching available national resources with readily available resources from other great powers to react to events. American decision making during the Cuban Missile Crisis, when it was clear that intermediate-range nuclear missiles the Soviet Union had secretly deployed in Cuba would be operational in a matter of weeks, presents a classic case of short-term decision making, as the Kennedy administration was constrained to match available power resources to the Soviet challenge. Similarly, European calculations during the July Crisis of 1914, when national leaders could no longer forge alliances and modernize their armed forces, but needed to make immediate calculations based on the existing balance-of-capabilities and assessments of their adversaries' short-term intentions, also fits this frame of crisis decision making and policy responses to unexpected events.[4]

As we extend the time frame slightly to the short-to-medium term— defined in terms of months and years, but not decades—policy making is more forward-looking and less responsive to fixed conditions and imperatives. Instead, policymakers engage in strategic planning, or an attempt to construct grand strategy. In US secretary of state Dean Acheson's words, strategic planning entails "to look ahead, not into the distant future, but beyond the vision of the operating officers caught in the smoke and crisis of current battle; far enough ahead to see the emerging form of things

---

4. See Dale C. Copeland, "International Relations Theory and the Three Great Puzzles of the First World War," in *The Outbreak of the First World War: Structure, Politics, and Decision-Making*, ed. Jack S. Levy and John A. Vasquez (Cambridge: Cambridge University, 2014), pp. 167–199; and Ronald P. Bobroff, "War Accepted but Unsought: Russia's Growing Militancy and the July Crisis, 1914," in *The Outbreak of the First World War: Structure, Politics, and Decision-Making*, ed. Jack S. Levy and John A. Vasquez (Cambridge: Cambridge University Press, 2014), pp. 227–251.

to come and outline what should be done to meet or anticipate them."[5] Similarly, the mission statement of the Policy Planning Staff in the State Department calls for taking "a longer term, strategic view of global trends and frame recommendations for the Secretary of State to advance US interests and American values."[6] The goal of policymakers is to formulate a national grand strategy, to help the state navigate both expected and unanticipated future crises, challenges, and opportunities, as well as likely power shifts.

As we develop elsewhere, grand strategy refers to "the organizing principle or conceptual blueprint that animates all of a state's relations with the outside world. . . It is a future-oriented enterprise involving considerations of external threats and opportunities, as well as the specific material, political, and ideological objectives of the state."[7] This level of planning gives policymakers more flexibility in terms of the means and resources that states can utilize to promote policy ends.[8] The longer time frame means they can not only draw upon existing resources available to the state but also make plans to expand upon them over time by promoting economic growth, providing more extensive training to the armed forces, or engaging in research and development of new weapons systems. In addition, they have time to enter into more extensive arrangements with foreign powers, such as full-scale alliances with joint planning and efforts to promote interoperability of the different armed forces.

Neoclassical realism can help explain the grand strategic choices of states as determined in the first instance by the power of the state, both actual and potential, and the expected international distribution of power. Yet, a state's specific goals within a given power distribution and its strategies for pursuing them will also depend on unit level factors, such as its ideological priorities, societal pressures, and the state's ability to enact policy and

5. Quoted in Daniel W. Drezner, "The Challenging Future of Strategic Planning in Foreign Policy," in *Avoiding Trivia: The Role of Strategic Planning in American Foreign Policy*, ed. Daniel W. Drezner (Washington, DC: Brookings, 2009), p. 4.

6. US Department of State, Policy Planning Staff, "Mission Statement," http://www.state.gov/s/p/, accessed April 20, 2015.

7. Steven E. Lobell, Jeffrey W. Taliaferro, and Norrin M. Ripsman, "Introduction: Grand Strategy between the World Wars," in *The Challenge of Grand Strategy: The Great Powers and the Broken Balance between the World Wars*, ed. Jeffrey W. Taliaferro, Norrin M. Ripsman, and Steven E. Lobell (Cambridge: Cambridge University Press, 2012), pp. 1–36, at p. 15. See also John Lewis Gaddis, "What is Grand Strategy?" in *Conference on American Grand Strategy after War* (Durham, NC: Triangle Institute for Security Studies and Duke University Program in American Grand Strategy, Duke University, 2009), pp. 1–17, http://tiss-nc.org/wp-content/uploads/2015/01/KEYNOTE.Gaddis50thAniv2009.pdf, accessed December 5, 2015.

8. See, for example, Barry Posen, *The Sources of Military Doctrine: France, Britain, and Germany between the World Wars* (Ithaca, NY: Cornell University Press, 1984), p. 13.

extract resources to implement it. For instance, German battleship construction provoked the Anglo-German naval race (1906–1912). However, the pace of British construction was affected by competition between the Liberal government's supporters (in the City of London and the Bank of England) and the Conservative opposition. Consequently, in response to further German naval construction after 1907–1908, the Liberals took a middle ground, building four dreadnoughts immediately—less than the eight the Conservatives had demanded, but more than commercial interests, seeking to manage the competition, had advocated—and pursuing a naval arms limitation agreement with Berlin, under the threat of building four more if Germany continued its construction.[9]

Extending the time frame further to the medium-to-longer term, defined in termed of years and decades, allows the strategic choices of the different great powers to interact and to have an impact on international systemic outcomes. By "systemic outcomes" we mean observable political phenomena resulting from the coaction and interactions of the strategies pursued by two or more actors in the international arena. Thus, whether there will be great power war or peace will depend not merely upon the distribution of power in the international system, but also upon the strategic choices that several states pursue. The outbreak of World War II provides a vivid illustration of this. As historian Ian Kershaw observes, it was the decisions made by the leaders of Germany, Great Britain, the Soviet Union, the United States, Japan, and Italy between May 1940 and December 1941 that "transformed the two separate wars in different continents into one truly global conflagration, a colossal conflict with genocide and unprecedented barbarism at its centre."[10]

Overextension by some states might lead to systemic war, as other states are left with no alternative but to balance aggressively, whereas more prudent strategies would have led to relative systemic stability.[11] Strategies of reassurance by strong powers might inspire other status quo powers to respond to power shifts with restraint, leading to stability.[12] Conversely, pursuing strategies of underbalancing when faced with a rising revisionist power might unnecessarily lead to outcomes of empire or

9. Steven E. Lobell, *The Challenge of Hegemony: Grand Strategy, Trade, and Domestic Politics* (Ann Arbor: University of Michigan Press, 2003), pp. 53–68.

10. Ian Kershaw, *Fateful Choices: Ten Decisions That Changed the World, 1940–1941* (New York: Penguin, 2007), p. 5.

11. Jack Snyder, *Myths of Empire* (Ithaca, NY: Cornell University Press, 1991).

12. On reassurance signaling, see Andrew Kydd, "Trust, Reassurance, and Cooperation," *International Organization*, vol. 54, no. 2 (2000), pp. 325–357; and Evan Montgomery, "Breaking out of the Security Dilemma: Realism, Reassurance, and the Problem of Uncertainty," *International Security*, vol. 31, no. 2 (2006), pp. 151–185.

systemic war.[13] Similarly, whether the international economy will be an open system characterized by interdependence or a closed system characterized by the pursuit of autarky will depend not simply upon structural considerations, but also upon the balance of domestic interests in the leading powers, and whether their respective governing coalitions expect to gain more through free trade or protectionism.[14] In each of these cases, the systemic outcome cannot simply be inferred or predicted from international structure. Structure interacts with the grand strategies of the great powers—which themselves are influenced by the unit-level factors outlined in Chapter 3—to produce outcomes. In this regard, a neoclassical realist approach should provide better explanations for and predictions of international outcomes than a purely systemic theory.

Finally, we argue that over the longer term, defined in terms of decades, international outcomes and the policies and grand strategies of the principal units themselves can help reshape international structure. This is akin to Jervis's notion of delayed and often indirect feedback.[15] Clearly, systemic outcomes can alter systemic structure by weakening existing great powers and/or generating new ones. This dynamic is clearly apparent in the event of major power wars, which can exhaust some great powers and empower others at their expense. In this manner, World War II led to the collapse of Great Britain, France, Germany, and Japan as great powers and the meteoric rise of the United States and the Soviet Union. As a result, the war ended the longstanding multipolar international system and ushered in bipolarity in its place. To the extent that the strategic choices of states influence systemic outcomes, therefore, they also can contribute to structural changes.

Yet, the link between grand strategy and changes in system structure is not only indirect. As avid structural theorists, such as Robert Gilpin and Kenneth Waltz, acknowledge, the underlying sources of change in the international system are the differential growth rates of the great powers.[16] These growth rates are largely determined by strategic economic and

---

13. On underbalancing, see Randall L. Schweller, "Unanswered Threats: A Neoclassical Realist Theory of Underbalancing," *International Security*, vol. 29, no. 2 (2004), pp. 159–201; and idem., *Unanswered Threats: Political Constraints on the Balance of Power* (Princeton, NJ: University Press, 2006).

14. See, for example, Ronald Rogowski, *Commerce and Coalitions* (Princeton, NJ: Princeton University Press, 1989); and Mark R. Brawley, "Factoral or Sectoral Conflict? Partially Mobile Factors and the Politics of Trade in Imperial Germany," *International Studies Quarterly*, vol. 41, no. 4 (1997), pp. 633–654.

15. Robert Jervis, *System Effects: Complexity in Political and Social Life* (Princeton, NJ: Princeton University Press, 1997), pp. 5 and 127–128.

16. Robert Gilpin, *War and Change in World Politics* (Cambridge: Cambridge University, 1981) and Waltz, *Theory of International Politics*.

political choices these states make over time as part of their foreign policy and grand strategic planning. Consequently, structural change has its roots in the individual investment decisions of the great powers, their decisions to pursue a grand strategy of restraint or one of overextension, and the particular domestic constraints and opportunities of particular great powers. In this regard, the source of China's ascent to great power status in the post–Cold War era can be traced back to Deng Xiaoping's decision in the late 1970s and early 1980s to modernize and restructure the Chinese economy.[17] A theory of international politics that does not take into consideration the grand strategies of the great powers and the sources thereof would be static. Such a theory would not be able to account for structural change. In contrast, a neoclassical realist approach that starts with structure but considers how structure interacts with the strategic choices and domestic political constraints of the principal units of the international system holds out far more promise as a dynamic approach to explaining international politics.

This is the great irony of structural theory. Waltz eschews reductionism and claims that a purely structural theory is sufficient to explain systemic outcomes, such as the recurrence of interstate (and especially great power) warfare. Yet, in reality a purely structural theory, not augmented by unit-level intervening variables, explains very little. It is insufficient to explain why any particular war occurs, why a particular peace treaty is signed, why some periods are characterized by open trading regimes whereas others are more restrictive, and a range of other international outcomes. Moreover, it is insufficient to explain structural change. Consider, for example, the relatively peaceful end of the Cold War and transition from a bipolar to a unipolar international system between 1985 and 1991. Structural realism, especially balance-of-power theory, came under intense criticism from scholars working in various research traditions for its failure to predict the end of the Cold War a priori or even offer a compelling post-hoc explanation for why the Soviet Union made unilateral concessions to the United States in nuclear and conventional force levels, abandoned its empire in Eastern Europe, acquiesced to the reunification of Germany within the North Atlantic Treaty Organization (NATO), and ultimately dissolved itself.[18] We contend, therefore, that, at

17. See Ezra F. Vogel, *Deng Xiaoping and the Transformation of China* (Cambridge, MA: Belknap Press of Harvard University Press, 2011), especially pp. 423–476 and 693ff.

18. The literature debating the failure of structural realism, in general, and Waltz's balance-of-power theory in particular, to predict or adequately explain the end of the Cold War is voluminous. Some major works that address this debate include Richard Ned Lebow and Thomas Risse-Kappen, eds., *International Relations Theory and the End of the Cold War* (New York: Columbia University Press, 1995); William C. Wohlforth, "The Stability of a Unipolar World," *International Security*, vol. 24, no. 1 (1999), pp. 5–41; Stephen

best, structural realism may explain recurring patterns of international politics. It cannot even fully explain these, however, since it is static and does not account for the interactive behaviors of the great powers, subject to the structural modifiers and internal constraints we discussed in Chapters 2 and 3.

We do not reject structural theory. Only by marrying the insights of structural theory to a more contextual approach, however, taking into account the grand strategies of the great powers and their domestic political and economic constraints, can we truly explain international phenomena. In this regard, neoclassical realism fully unleashes the explanatory power of structural realism by getting over Waltz's misguided fear of reductionism. We, thus, have a much broader and richer conception of the utility of neoclassical realism than its original proponents.[19] Rather than accepting that structural realism explains most of international politics and that neoclassical realism is useful only to explain rare anomalies, we assert that neoclassical realism is a better overall theory of international politics than structural realism is and can explain far more than a purely structural theory can.

As illustrated in Figure 4.2, therefore, the scope of neoclassical realism's focus expands with time. In the short-to-medium term, neoclassical realism is an approach to the study of foreign policy and grand strategy. Over the medium-to-long term, however, it becomes an approach to the study of international politics. This makes intuitive sense, since, as discussed, it takes time for the grand strategic choices of one or more great powers to affect the grand strategies of others and more time for the interaction of great power grand strategies to help determine systemic outcomes. It takes even more time for systemic outcomes determined in this manner to reshape international structure. Therefore, the temporal link between unit-level variables having an impact on the structure of the international system is quite extended. Nonetheless, in rare circumstances, such as in the event of a systemic war, the time line may contract considerably.

Consider, for example, the logic of preventive war.[20] In the event that the grand strategy of a rising great power leads a great power in relative

G. Brooks and William C. Wohlforth, "Power, Globalization, and the End of the Cold War: Reevaluating a Landmark Case for Ideas," *International Security*, vol. 25, no. 3 (2000), pp. 5–53; and Randall L. Schweller and William C. Wohlforth, "Power Test: Evaluating Realism in Response to the End of the Cold War," *Security Studies*, vol. 9, no. 3 (2000), pp. 60–107.

19. See the literature reviewed by Gideon Rose, "Neoclassical Realism and Theories of Foreign Policy," *World Politics*, vol. 51, no. 1 (1998), pp. 144–172.

20. Jack S. Levy, "Declining Power and the Preventive Motivation for War," *World Politics*, vol. 40, no. 1 (1987), pp. 82–107.

decline to fear an eventual power transition, the declining power may conclude that immediate war while it is still ascendant would be less damaging than an eventual war once the power transition is completed. Under these circumstances, it might respond with force well before war might ordinarily have broken out. Furthermore, that war might hasten international structural change by strengthening or weakening some of the great power participants. In this regard, those who view World War I as a preventive war by Germany to forestall the ongoing Russian strategic forces modernization that threatened to allow Russia to overtake Germany by 1917 believe, in essence, that war was hastened by a German strategic response to the Russian grand strategy of modernization.[21] Although it was World War II that completed these trends, World War I then hastened the relative decline of the European great powers and the rise of the United States to global primacy, at least in terms of aggregate power. Thus, if this reading of history is correct, the links between grand strategy, international outcomes, and structural effects in this case occurred over a relatively short time frame.

By providing the timeline that we do in Figure 4.2 and operationalizing these time frames as we do above, then, we are asserting what we believe is the typical pace of events in international politics. This is not intended as a hard-and-fast rule, however, and we acknowledge that at times, when events proceed at a faster pace, neoclassical realism may have more to say about international outcomes and structural change in the nearer term.

Whatever the time frame, the essence of the causal logic that we have developed over the past three chapters remains realist, as it continues to give causal primacy to the international system. International structures have the dominant influence over the range of systemic outcomes that are possible. What outcomes will obtain, however, will depend upon the character of the units and the foreign policies and grand strategies they select. Thus, for example, as we argue in Chapter 6, we can elucidate the debate between Waltz and Gilpin over the consequences of unipolarity with attention to the nature of the hegemon and its domestic structure. Waltz and Gilpin both assert that international structure solely determines international outcomes; however they disagree on what that outcome will be. Waltz expects unipolarity to be competitive because the hegemon has every incentive to behave in a predatory manner and other

---

21. See Dale Copeland, *The Origins of Major War* (Ithaca, NY: Cornell University Press, 2000); Stephen Van Evera, *Causes of War: Power and the Roots of Conflict* (Ithaca, NY: Cornell University Press, 1999); Jack S. Levy, "Preferences, Constraints, and Choices in July 1914," *International Security*, vol. 15, no. 3 (1990–1991), pp. 151–186; and Fritz Fischer, *Germany's Aims in the First World War* (New York: W. W. Norton, 1967).

states, fearing predation, will seek to balance against the unipole.[22] In contrast, Gilpin argues that unipolarity will engender greater stability and cooperation, as the hegemon can set rules of international politics that benefit it, and then coerces others and provides selective incentives for them to cooperate.[23] A neoclassical realist approach would suggest that the nature and character of the hegemon could affect whether unipolarity leads to greater systemic cooperation or competition.[24] A domestically constrained hegemon—one whose power to determine its own policy choices and mobilize domestic resources in support of foreign policy and grand strategy is limited by domestic political institutions and state-society relations—is less likely to engage in predatory behavior internationally. Moreover, other states are less likely to view such a constrained hegemon as threatening. Consequently, they are less like to balance against it and are more likely to cooperate without fear. In contrast, a domestically unconstrained hegemon should be better able to act aggressively and, thus, will inspire greater fear and competition internationally. In this regard, neoclassical realism is not merely a theory of foreign policy, but also can help explain international outcomes.

We do not argue, however, that states themselves determine the structure of the international system through the foreign policies and grand strategies they select. Certainly, over the longer term, they do have an impact on international structure—and even Waltz and Gilpin agree that they do. Structural realists agree that the distribution of power over time is determined by the differential growth rates of states, which in turn is affected by domestic political and economic choices and dynamics of the particular units. In the short-to-medium term (the scope of Type I and II neoclassical realism), however, states must act within a given international structure, which constrains their foreign policy and grand strategic choice, as well as the range of likely international systemic outcomes, such as patterns of conflict and cooperation, the stability of the international system, etc. In the short-to-medium term, therefore, states must navigate within a given international structure, which limits their freedom of action and constrains their foreign policy choices. In the next section, we illustrate how these independent, intervening, and dependent variables interact in this manner.

22. Kenneth N. Waltz, "The Emerging Structure of International Politics," *International Security*, vol. 18, no. 2 (1993), pp. 44–79.

23. Robert Gilpin, *War and Change in World Politics* (Cambridge: Cambridge University, 1981).

24. See, for example, Norrin M. Ripsman, "Domestic Practices and Balancing: Integrating Practice into Neoclassical Realism," in *International Practices*, ed. Vincent Pouliot and Emanuel Adler (Cambridge: Cambridge University Press, 2011), pp. 200–228.

LINKING OUR INDEPENDENT, INTERVENING, AND DEPENDENT VARIABLES

Because the scope of the dependent variable expands over time, we should expect each of the intervening variables (IVV) described in Chapter 3 to vary slightly in their influence over specific aspects of the dependent variable (DV) at specific times. For example, leader images should matter most in the short term. When secrecy and a quick decision are required, as in a crisis, a leader has his/her greatest potential impact on policy, since other actors tend to be excluded from the process.[25] Consequently, the leader's psychological make-up, worldview, and attitudes toward international affairs and other states should be most consequential in affecting foreign policy and crisis decision-making. As decision time increases, however, an individual leader's control over policy decreases, as more actors—decision makers, legislatures, bureaucracies, key interest groups, and society at large—have opportunities to contribute to defining problems and devising policy solutions. Consequently, leader images will be less relevant to explaining strategic planning and grand strategic adjustment than some of the other IVVs we discuss.

Consider, for example, the Kargil War between nuclear-armed adversaries India and Pakistan from early May to mid-July 1999. While leader images—specifically the calculations and misperceptions of Pakistani prime minister Nawaz Sharif and chief of army staff General Pervez Musharraf about the local balance of forces in the divided region of Kashmir and Indian leaders' resolve—are useful in explaining the planned infiltration operation in the Kargil sector across the Line of Control, once the Indian army responded to that incursion in force in early May, other categories of IVVs, such as state-society relations or domestic institutions (especially civil-military relations), become more useful in explaining how Pakistan conducted itself during the conflict.[26]

Strategic culture should influence both short-term foreign policy decision-making and longer-term planning. During a crisis or day-to-day

25. Daniel L. Byman and Kenneth M. Pollack, "Let Us Now Praise Great Men: Bringing the Statesman Back In," *International Security*, vol. 25, no. 4 (2001), pp. 107–146; and Eugene R. Wittkopf and Christopher M. Jones with Charles W. Kegley Jr., *American Foreign Policy: Pattern and Process*, 7th ed. (Belmont: Thomson Wadsworth, 2008), pp. 489–518.

26. S. Paul Kapur, "Nuclear Proliferation, the Kargil Conflict, and South Asian Security," *Security Studies*, vol. 13, no. 1 (2003), pp. 79–105; idem., *Dangerous Deterrent: Nuclear Weapons Proliferation and Conflict in South Asia* (Stanford, CA: Stanford University Press, 2007), pp. 117–131; and Sumit Ganguly and Devin T. Hagerty, *Fearful Symmetry: India-Pakistan Crises in the Shadow of Nuclear Weapons* (Seattle: University of Washington Press, 2005), pp. 143–166.

situation, when a quick decision is called for, strategic culture—particularly national attitudes toward the use of force and other policy options—may guide or constrain the choices of national leaders and key officials charged with policy making. In general, over the shorter term, strategic culture can affect how top policymakers discuss and interpret international events.[27]

Over the longer term, as the foreign policy executive (FPE) and its associated bureaucracy draft plans for grand strategic adjustment, we would expect that national values, attitudes toward force, and cultural preferences should all be of significance. Leaders are less likely to select policy options that are at odds with domestic values for three reasons. First, having been themselves inculcated with national attitudes, leaders and policy officials are likely to buy into many of these cultural attitudes toward national security. Second, leaders may expect greater opposition from societal groups, domestic political institutions, and the country as a whole that may interfere with the enactment and implementation of a grand strategy at odds with the country's strategic values. Third, flouting domestic attitudes toward national security could even jeopardize the leader's hold on power, if it generated significant political opposition. Thus, unless national attitudes change, it would be difficult to imagine a Japanese government pursuing security by internal balancing, by ramping up defense spending well beyond 1 percent of gross domestic product, rather than with a strategy of external balancing relying on its alliance with the United States.[28] Similarly, barring major changes to national attitudes, one would not expect Germany to pursue security through the development of nuclear weapons, which is anathema for most Germans.[29]

Finally, state-society relations and domestic institutions should have very little influence on short-term policy responses, but a significant effect

27. Judith Goldstein and Robert O. Keohane, "Ideas and Foreign Policy: An Analytical Framework," in *Ideas and Foreign Policy: Beliefs, Institutions, and Political Change*, ed. Judith Goldstein and Robert O. Keohane (Ithaca, NY: Cornell University Press, 1993), pp. 3–31. Also see Colin Dueck, *Reluctant Crusaders: Power, Culture, and Change in American Grand Strategy* (Princeton, NJ: Princeton University Press, 2006).

28. Thomas U. Berger, "Norms, Identity, and National Security in Germany and Japan," in *The Culture of National Identity: Norms and Identity in World Politics*, ed. Peter J. Katzenstein (New York: Colombia University Press, 1996), pp. 317–357.

29. Thomas Risse-Kappen, "Public Opinion, Domestic Structure, and Foreign Policy in Liberal Democracies," *World Politics*, vol. 43, no. 4 (1991), pp. 506–507. That said, the German popular opposition to nuclear weapons (especially after the Cold War) does not mean that the leaders of the Federal Republic of Germany (FRG) never harbored nuclear ambitions. For an analysis of how the Adenauer government sought to acquire an independent nuclear deterrent between 1954 and 1963 and how the Erhard and Kiesinger governments sought to retain a weapons option between 1964 and 1969, but ultimately acquiesced to US nonproliferation demands, see Gene Gerzhoy, "Alliance Coercion and Nuclear Restraint: How the United States Thwarted West Germany's Nuclear Ambitions," *International Security*, vol. 39, no. 4 (2015), pp. 91–129.

on longer-range planning. In the short term, as the exigencies of a crisis or quick decision place disproportionate power in the hands of the leader to shape the national response, even strong societal groups and power-ful domestic institutions that could ordinarily constrain policy making might be sidestepped. For example, in 1914, when strategic pressures required a firm commitment to Belgian neutrality, the British Cabinet ignored the City of London's preferences for a limited liability strategy.[30] In the more time-consuming processes of altering national strategy, how-ever, key societal actors and domestic veto players would have a greater opportunity to shape, constrain, or defeat policies at odds with their pref-erences. Therefore, the degree to which state-society relations are coop-erative rather than competitive and the degree to which domestic political institutions allow the executive greater policy autonomy will be of great significance to policy planning endeavors.[31]

All four groups of intervening variables can have some impact on systemic outcomes and structural changes. After all, to the extent that national foreign policy decisions and grand strategy can contribute to systemic outcomes, such as war, peace, trading patterns, etc., all of the domestic-level influences can at least potentially be consequential to some degree.

Not only should the IVVs interact with the DVs in the manners that we describe, but the intervening variables themselves can also be influenced by our independent variables (IVs). Indeed, as Ripsman and Taliaferro have individually noted before, the development of the institutions of the national security state in the United States after World War II—and the resulting increased autonomy of the presidency and the executive branch vis-à-vis the Congress and federal courts in matters of national security—can be traced to the development of aircraft carriers and rocketry, which effectively downgraded the ocean barriers that had previously protected North America.[32] Nonetheless, the domestic environment is not merely epiphenomenal of the external environment. First, there is a time lag

---

30. Steven E. Lobell, "The Political Economy of War Mobilization: From Britain's Limited Liability to a Continental Commitment" *International Politics*, vol. 43, no. 3 (2006), pp. 283–304.

31. See Norrin M. Ripsman, *Peacemaking by Democracies: The Effect of State Autonomy on the Post-World-War Settlements* (University Park: Penn State University Press, 2002).

32. Ripsman, *Peacemaking by Democracies*, pp. 83–85; and Jeffrey W. Taliaferro, "Neoclassical Realism and Resource Extraction: State Building for Future War," in *Neoclassical Realism, the State, and Foreign Policy*, ed. Steven E. Lobell, Norrin M. Ripsman and Jeffrey W. Taliaferro (Cambridge: Cambridge University Press, 2009), pp. 216–217. See also Eric J. Hamilton, "International Politics and Domestic Institutional Change: The Rise of Executive War-Making Autonomy in the United States," PhD diss., School of International Relations, University of Southern California, 2015.

between the strategic environment and the adaptation of national institutions and practices. Second, the specific national responses of states
to international circumstances may vary as the state's strategic environment interacts with its strategic culture. Thus, while the United States and
Great Britain responded to the great insecurity of the 1930s and 1940s
by developing practices and institutions that deferred to the executive
in matters of national security, the French responded to similar external
threats with practices that obstructed the executive in security matters.[33]
Consequently, it would be a mistake to assume that the domestic political IVVs are merely epiphenomenal of the external IVs and do not do any
heavy lifting on their own.

Therefore, we would utilize the independent variables we introduced
in Chapter 2 pertaining to the clarity of the international system and
the nature of the strategic environment to determine when the specific clusters of IVVs are operative and matter most. As we indicated,
the strategic environment refers to the magnitude and imminence of
threats and opportunities that a state faces. Clarity refers to the degree
to which the international system provides information about the
nature of threats and opportunities, their time frame, and the optimal
policy choice to respond to them. As we illustrate in Table 4.1, in situations of high clarity in a restrictive environment, where states are aware
that they face high threats, short time horizons, and restricted choices,
we would not expect the FPE to have significant rounds of bargaining
with domestic interest groups. Consequently, there is little time for the
more ponderous IVVs of state-society relations and domestic institutions to affect policy. Instead, we would expect leader images and strategic culture to be the most relevant IVVs that could condition how
the leadership perceives the external environment and how it prefers to
respond to it. This is not to say that state-society relations or domestic
institutions are irrelevant in shaping states' responses in acute international crises, but rather they are less likely to have an immediate and
easily discernable impact on the FPE's selection of short-term foreign
and defense strategies.

Conversely, in permissive environments with high clarity, where states
have the luxury of time and no pressing threats or waning opportunities,
we would expect the other two categories of IVVs—domestic institutions and patterns of state-society relations—to become more prominent.
As the time frame lengthens, the FPE faces the dilemma of mobilizing
domestic support for (and defusing potential opposition to) its preferred
external strategies. We would thus expect state-society relations and

33. Ripsman, *Peacemaking by Democracies*, pp. 70–90.

Table 4.1. INTERVENING VARIABLE CLUSTERS BY THE DEGREE OF SYSTEMIC CLARITY AND THE NATURE OF STRATEGIC ENVIRONMENT

		Degree of Systemic Clarity (High to Low)	
		High Clarity	Low Clarity
Nature of Strategic	Restrictive		
Environment	Environment	*Leader images and Strategic*	*Leader images and*
(Restrictive to		*culture*	*Strategic culture*
Permissive)	Permissive		
	Environment	*Strategic culture, Domestic*	*Indeterminate—all*
		institutions, and State-	*four clusters could be*
		society relations	*relevant.*

domestic institutions to play a greater role in grand strategic adjustment, while leader images will be less relevant, as the importance of individual leaders tends to decrease the more time is involved.

When clarity is low and the environment is permissive, we would expect that all four clusters of IVVs could be relevant and, in effect, which take priority should be indeterminate, since the absence of a pressing threat or limited time opportunity will allow all domestic actors to vie for their preferred policy or grand strategy. In an unclear but restrictive environment, however, we would expect leader images and strategic culture to matter most, since the high degree of threat or the importance of the waning opportunity will both compel societal actors to the sidelines in the national interest and also encourage national leaders to ignore societal demands on strategic grounds.

Thus we do not select our IVVs in an ad hoc manner. Instead, we select IVVs that are logically connected to both our independent and our dependent variables in a well-specified and predictable manner.

WHAT CANNOT BE EXPLAINED WITH NEOCLASSICAL REALISM

Although neoclassical realism, through its inclusion of structural/ systemic and unit/sub-unit level variables, as well as its attention to different time horizons of effects, can explain a broad range of phenomena in international politics, it remains focused on the particular. Consequently, while neoclassical realist theories might help us explain why a particular state opted for war in a particular set of circumstances, why war was endemic to a particular historical period, such as the classical balance of power in Europe, or why the bipolar postwar international system was supplanted by a unipolar American-led system, its focus on the particular makes it an inefficient explanation of recurring patterns, such as why wars occur in general. This is more properly the domain of systemic theory, with no need for unit-level intervening variables.[34] Similarly, while neoclassical realists might be able to explain why Brazil and Argentina gave up the pursuit of nuclear weapons capability while North Korea and Iran did not, they have less to say than structural realists and constructivists about the development of a nuclear taboo.[35]

Furthermore, while Type III neoclassical realism can explain international outcomes and structural change more effectively than structural realism, since it incorporates more of the domestic-level drivers of change together with systemic drivers, there are still some explanatory variables of structural change, including technology, environmental patterns, demographic growth, geography, and unexpected catastrophic events, which remain exogenous. It would be unfair, however, to be too critical of neoclassical realism for this, as no theory of international politics adequately addresses and treats all of these phenomena as endogenous.

Even in the shorter term, neoclassical realism is not always superior to other approaches in explaining foreign policy and grand strategy in all circumstances. Neoclassical realism explains state choices as, in the first instance, responses to the particular international structural constraints and opportunities they face, tempered by the domestic political environment they inhabit and the salient characteristics of the decision makers themselves. In the absence of clear and salient international pressures, however, the approach—like other realist theories—would be no more useful than *Innenpolitik* theories that understand foreign policy solely as the product of domestic political coalitions or leader preferences.[36]

34. Kenneth N. Waltz, *Man, the State, and War: A Theoretical Analysis* (New York: Columbia University Press, 1959).

35. For serious theoretical approaches to the nuclear "taboo," see T. V. Paul, *The Tradition of Non-Use of Nuclear Weapons* (Palo Alto, CA: Stanford University Press, 2009); and Nina Tannenwald, *The Nuclear Taboo: The United States and the Non-Use of Nuclear Weapons Since 1945* (Cambridge: Cambridge University Press, 2007).

36. Norrin M. Ripsman, Jeffrey W. Taliaferro, and Steven E. Lobell, "Conclusion: The State of Neoclassical Realism," in *Neoclassical Realism, the State, and Foreign Policy*, ed. Steven E. Lobell, Norrin M. Ripsman, and Jeffrey W. Taliaferro (Cambridge: Cambridge University Press, 2009), pp. 282–287.

Since neoclassical realism is, like all realist theory, a state-centric approach, it has comparatively little to say about the behavior of non-state actors (NSAs), be they corporations, societal interest groups, national non-governmental organizations (NGOs), or international non-governmental organizations (INGOs). To explain the behavior of these actors, we would need theories of the motives, interests, and constraints they face, which neoclassical realism does not attempt to do. Nonetheless, neoclassical realist theory could help explain the conditions under which NSAs are more likely to influence the foreign policy behavior of states when they attempt to do so. In general, NSAs should be both more likely to implicate themselves in foreign policy debates and more likely to influence policy choices during a permissive international environment, when national security is not threatened imminently. In a more restrictive environment, however, when the costs of policy deviating from systemic imperatives could potentially be high, NSAs should be more willing to defer to the FPE, and the FPE should be less willing to allow NSA interference.[37] This explains why domestic lobby groups had more influence over US foreign policy in the immediate aftermath of the Cold War than they did during that prolonged geopolitical competition.[38] Conversely, armed NSAs (such as terrorist groups or non-state militias) may affect a state's foreign policy and grand strategy when these groups possess the capability to threaten what states value most, namely when the scale of violence it can use against states crosses a threshold making it comparable to what a state can inflict. Neoclassical realism may also shed light on circumstances under which states use armed NSAs as force multipliers.[39]

In contrast, our approach should be useful for understanding the behavior of intergovernmental organizations (IGOs), whose members are sovereign states. As realists point out, because these institutions are dependent upon their member-states to enact and adhere to organizational policies, they do not have an independent effect and are largely epiphenomenal of power relations in the international system and state policy choices within that system. Since neoclassical realism has much

37. Norrin M. Ripsman, "Neoclassical Realism and Domestic Interest Groups," in *Neoclassical Realism, the State, and Foreign Policy*, ed. Steven E. Lobell, Norrin M. Ripsman, and Jeffrey W. Taliaferro (Cambridge: Cambridge University Press, 2009), pp. 170–193.

38. James McCormick, "Interest Groups and the Media in Post-Cold War U.S. Foreign Policy," in *After the End: Making U.S. Foreign Policy in the Post-Cold War World*, ed. James M. Scott (Durham, NC: Duke University Press, 1998), pp. 170–198.

39. For analysis of how Iran has used its support for Hezbollah in Lebanon as a force multiplier, see Thomas Juneau, *Squandered Opportunity: Neoclassical Realism and Iranian Foreign Policy* (Stanford, CA: Stanford University Press, 2015), pp. 139–168; and Daniel Byman, *Deadly Connections: States that Sponsor Terrorism* (Cambridge: Cambridge University Press, 2005), pp. 79–107.

to say about national policy choices and can help explain international power relations, it can explain IGO actions more easily than it can INGO actions.

Overall, while our conception of neoclassical realist theory is subject to the limitations laid out in this section, it is far more powerful than Type I and Type II neoclassical realism, with a far greater scope. Moreover, for the reasons we outline, our Type III neoclassical realism has greater explanatory power than structural realism or any of its *Innenpolitik* competitors.

CONCLUSION: THE WIDER SCOPE OF NEOCLASSICAL REALISM

In this chapter, we have carved out a much more ambitious scope for neoclassical realism than it has previously been accorded. We acknowledge that while it is, in the first instance, an approach to explain state responses to international pressures, its explanatory power broadens over time to help explain both international outcomes and structural change. Consequently, neoclassical realist theory presents a considerable challenge to structural realism not simply in the realm of foreign policy, which the latter gladly abdicates, but even the realm of international politics. Therefore, our conception of neoclassical realist theory detailed in Chapters 2–4 should yield the most powerful and versatile approach to international relations, with greater explanatory power than structural realism, liberalism, or constructivism. In this regard, we have taken the steps at a first cut at a neoclassical realist theory by linking the intervening and dependent variables. In the next chapter, we will discuss the methodology of neoclassical realism and provide a practical guide on how to use neoclassical realist theory to shed light on all aspects of foreign policy and international politics.

CHAPTER 5

A Methodology of Neoclassical Realism

Having discussed the independent, the intervening, and the dependent variables of neoclassical realist theory in the previous three chapters, we now turn to a discussion of methodology and research design. Conducting social science research is messy, time-consuming, and complicated. No matter how careful one is in formulating the research question, identifying plausible alternative theories, specifying predictions from hypotheses derived from one's preferred theory and alternative theories, gathering data, analyzing that data, and reporting results, one's conclusions will always be subject to challenge by others and, consequently, revision. Our purpose in this chapter is to guide neoclassical realist researchers through some of the complexities of conducting qualitative research. This methodological discussion is a prelude to Chapter 6, where we illustrate the utility of neoclassical realist theory in resolving long-standing debates in the international relations literature.

We organize this chapter in the same order in which we believe a researcher should undertake a neoclassical realist project. The chapter progresses as follows: The first section addresses the identification of appropriate research questions and puzzles for neoclassical realist theories. The second section discusses the "soft" positivist approach that underlies our epistemology and methodology. In the third section, we address the practical matter of how a researcher might go about developing a neoclassical realist theory and deriving testable hypotheses from that theory. The identification of the appropriate unit-of-analysis for any neoclassical realist theory, what we call the foreign policy executive (FPE), follows in the fourth section. Historiography, process tracing, and standards of evidence are the subjects of the fifth section. Throughout this chapter, we illustrate our approach to epistemology, qualitative and multimethod methodology, and historiography with references to various works in the neoclassical realist literature.

IDENTIFYING APPROPRIATE RESEARCH QUESTIONS OR PUZZLES

The first challenge in conducting social science research entails the identification of an appropriate research question. The research question, in turn, guides the researcher in delimiting the scope of the phenomenon (or phenomena) to be explained, the level-of-analysis at which that phenomenon occurs, the unit or units of analysis to be studied, the identification of theories that might generate testable hypotheses and competing explanations, and finally, the universe of potential cases to be examined. Explaining the outcomes of individual cases is a core goal of qualitative research. As James Mahoney and Gary Goertz observe, "A central purpose of research is to identify the causes of these specific outcomes for each and every case that falls within the scope of the theory under investigation."[1]

In the international relations subfield of political science, both qualitative and quantitative scholars use terms like "research question" and "research problem" almost interchangeably with "research puzzle."[2] We draw a distinction between the two. Research questions and research puzzles both involve queries about the causes or the consequences of a particular phenomenon or phenomena. Both fall into the "causes-of-effects" approach to causation that Mahoney and Goertz identify and to which we return to later in this chapter.[3] Research questions, however, involve theoretical problems. They are categorical, and involve generalities and generalizations (e.g., How does the state of category X respond to changes in the state of category Y and why?). They are deductive in nature, abstract, and separate from empirical phenomena. They may stem from unexplored

---

1. James Mahoney and Gary Goertz, "A Tale of Two Cultures: Contrasting Quantitative and Qualitative Research," *Political Analysis*, vol. 14, no. 3 (2006), p. 230.

2. For example, King, Keohane, and Verba use the term "research question." See Gary King, Robert O. Keohane, and Sidney Verba, *Designing Social Inquiry: Scientific Inference in Qualitative Research* (Princeton, NJ: Princeton University Press, 1994), pp. 14–19. George and Bennett use the terms research "problem" or "puzzle." See Alexander L. George and Andrew Bennett, *Case Studies and Theory Development in the Social Sciences* (Cambridge, MA: MIT Press, 2005), pp. 74–79. For an earlier discussion of research puzzles see Dina A. Zinnes, "Three Puzzles in Search of a Researcher: Presidential Address," *International Studies Quarterly*, vol. 24, no. 3 (1980), pp. 315–342.

3. Gary Goertz and James Mahoney, *A Tale of Two Cultures: Qualitative and Quantitative Research in the Social Sciences* (Princeton, NJ: Princeton University Press, 2012), pp. 43–44.

areas or gaps in the existing theoretical literature or from debates between or within schools of theories.

Consider the research questions that one of us (Norrin Ripsman) poses in an earlier book: Do democratic states behave similarly in the international arena? Do the institutional, normative, and procedural differences among democratic states have a discernable effect on their ability to respond to systemic pressures and opportunities, and thus the types of foreign policies they pursue? Specifically, does the degree of structural autonomy that heads of state and/or government have from legislatures and public opinion, as well as the ability of those leaders to conceal their aims in international negotiations from domestic constituents, influence the type and the substance of peace settlements offered to defeated adversaries?[4]

The democratic peace literature suggests that states' domestic regime type is the most important determinant of their behavior in the international arena. Shared political norms and institutional restraints prevent pairs of liberal democratic states from waging war on each other. In contrast, structural realists assume the external behavior of democracies is not dissimilar from that of other types of states. Like all states, democracies are compelled either to pursue their national interests in an anarchic international system or risk putting their very survival at risk. Therefore, both democratic peace theorists and their structural realist critics effectively treat democratic states as "functionally similar," albeit for different reasons and with different implications for foreign policy and international outcomes. Ripsman's inquiry stems from the supposition that "the conventional treatment of democracies as a group of like states that behave similarly in the international area is both inappropriate and misleading."[5] His research questions unpack the category of "democracy" and the neoclassical realist theory of structural autonomy he subsequently develops purports to explain how international systemic pressures filter through different types of democratic institutions and domestic political dynamics to account for variation in the types of peacemaking strategies different democratic great powers ultimately pursue.

Research puzzles (or empirical puzzles), by contrast, involve empirical observations or empirical anomalies for existing theories (e.g., Why did country X pursue policy Y at time t, when theory A would expect policy Z at time t?). They are inductive in nature. The very existence of a

---

4. Norrin M. Ripsman, *Peacemaking by Democracies: The Effect of State Autonomy on the Post-World War Settlements* (University Park: Pennsylvania State University Press, 2002), pp. 3, 6–7.
5. Ibid., p. 4.

puzzle implies that there is one or more observable empirical phenomena that needs to be explained. Jillian Schwedler draws a useful distinction between two "ideal" types of research puzzles common in political science: "first, the kind for which no answer is readily at hand; and second, the kind for which the answers suggested by previous studies do not seem to apply."[6]

Both types of puzzles require an answer and the resulting piece of scholarship is only considered "successful" or a contribution to the literature to the extent that it provides such an answer, even if the answer is only tentative. An example of the first kind of puzzle would be a major political development for which there is little or no precedent, and thus little existing knowledge to answer the "why" question, at least not until the researcher studies the event and begins to break it down into component parts. Schwedler poses this example: "Why did the Soviet Union [*recte*: the Soviet empire in Eastern Europe] disintegrate so suddenly in 1989?" These types of unprecedented political events—the second-ranked superpower relinquishing its traditional sphere of influence, followed soon afterward by that superpower's own collapse—are rare, even by the standards of international politics.

The second kind of research puzzle, the surprising outcome or causal sequence that appears anomalous from the predictions of existing theories, is more common in international relations scholarship. Schwedler provides this example: "Why did Islamists begin to cooperate with communists and socialists in Jordan in 1993 when they had consistently refused to do so just a year earlier—and had refused to do so for decades before that, even though earlier coordination would have given them a majority bloc in parliament?"[7] This particular example of a "surprising outcome puzzle," which was central to Schwedler's book, deals with comparative politics, rather than international relations.[8] Nonetheless, the "surprising outcome or behavior" type of puzzle is frequently utilized in much of the international relations literature and a promising starting place for researchers seeking to develop and test neoclassical realist theories.

An example of the "surprising outcome or behavior" type research puzzle would be the one Thomas J. Christensen seeks to resolve in his first

6. Jillian Schwedler, "Puzzle," *Qualitative and Multi-Method Research*, vol. 11, no. 2 (2013), pp. 27–30, quote from p. 28. See also Zinnes, "Three Puzzles in Search of a Researcher," pp. 317–318.

7. Schwedler, "Puzzle," p. 28.

8. Jillian Schwedler, *Faith in Moderation: Islamist Parties in Jordan and Yemen* (Cambridge: Cambridge University Press, 2006).

book, identified as one of the foundational neoclassical realist works.[9] His empirical anomaly is the inability of the United States and the People's Republic of China to make common cause against the perceived threat of the Soviet Union from 1949 until 1972, despite underlying continuity in the relative distribution of power. The post-1972 rapprochement between Washington and Beijing, brought about by the unlikely diplomatic duo of Richard Nixon and Mao Zedong, is often seen as a triumph of balance-of-power logic over ideology and domestic politics in both countries. But, as Christensen writes, "China and the United States were each other's most active enemy in the years 1949–1972, fighting wars in Korea and Vietnam that claimed the vast majority of each country's Cold War casualties. . . . If bipolarity and common Soviet threat prescribed cooperation in 1972, why did they not push leaders in similar directions in the 1950s?"[10]

We can identify a third "ideal type" of research puzzle that revolves around political phenomena that appear to be inadequately explained by existing theories, but which might not be empirical anomalies per se. The distinction between Schwedler's "type II" puzzle and a "type III" puzzle is subtle. Whereas the former puzzle begins with observed phenomena clearly at odds with the predictions of various theories or a particular theory, the latter puzzle arises because the predictions of existing theories (or a theory) are underspecified.

Colin Dueck's book on the United States' grand strategic adjustment over the past century is an example of a neoclassical realist work that seeks to resolve a "type III" puzzle. The United States emerged from World War I, World War II, the Cold War, and the period immediately following the September 11, 2001 terrorist attacks with overwhelming power advantages over current and potential adversaries. Nevertheless, theories that privilege either the international balance-of-power or the underlying continuities in American domestic politics and strategic culture cannot explain the resulting shifts in US grand strategy. For example, there were three plausible grand strategic alternatives for the United States after World War I: participation in the League of Nations; disengagement from Europe; or a military alliance with Britain and France. As Dueck notes, "international conditions could not have predicted a return to disengagement, given America's immense power by 1918." Instead, "from a

9. Gideon Rose, "Neoclassical Realism and Theories of Foreign Policy," *World Politics*, vol. 51, no. 1 (1998), pp. 144–177.

10. Thomas J. Christensen, *Useful Adversaries: Grand Strategy, Domestic Mobilization, and Sino-American Conflict, 1947–1958* (Princeton, NJ: Princeton University Press, 1996), p. 4.

structural realist perspective any of the three options were viable, and in fact, a Western alliance would have been preferable."[11]

Typically, a research puzzle resonates with readers because it calls into question the conventional wisdom about the causes of particular phenomena or because it highlights an observable outcome that does not appear to match theoretical expectations. The research puzzle that one of us (Steven Lobell) poses in an earlier book is illustrative: "Why did Britain pursue a cooperative grand strategy prior to World War I, emphasizing free trade, reducing defense spending, signing arms limitation agreements, and retreating from empire, but then, prior to World War II, punish contenders by adopting imperial preferences and closer ties to the empire, enacting colonial quotas, and increasing defense spending?"[12]

Lobell's "type III" research puzzle is significant for several reasons. First, explaining the grand strategies of ascendant and declining great powers is a perennial subject of interest for students of international history and international politics. Second, the diametrically opposed grand strategies that Britain pursued between 1889 and 1912 and between 1932 and 1939 are truly puzzling, given the fact that in both eras the British Empire faced simultaneous and multiplying threats across several geographic regions (East Asia, the Middle East and northern Africa, the Mediterranean, central Asia, the north Atlantic, and the European continent), involving the same cast of potential great power adversaries and allies (Germany, the United States, Russia/Soviet Union, France, Italy, and Japan), and across the same range of material capabilities (naval and land-based military power, industrial output, trade, finance, etc.). In both periods, the dilemma for British policymakers was how to respond to these dangers, given limited national resources and extended global commitments.[13] Yet, the resultant grand strategic choices of British leaders were quite different and not well explained by existing theories that either privilege international (systemic) variables to the exclusion of domestic (unit-level) variables or that privilege domestic variables to the exclusion of international variables.

Research puzzles or questions are just the starting point. In the following section, we discuss the epistemology of neoclassical realism that underlies our methodological choices and theory construction.

---

11. Colin Dueck, *Reluctant Crusaders: Power, Culture, and Change in American Grand Strategy* (Princeton, NJ: Princeton University Press, 2006), p. 6.

12. Steven E. Lobell, *The Challenge of Hegemony: Grand Strategy, Trade, and Domestic Politics* (Ann Arbor: University of Michigan Press, 2003), pp. 1–2.

13. Ibid., pp. 43, 85.

SOFT POSITIVISM

Theory construction is of only limited practical utility if we are unable to test alternative theories against the empirical evidence to determine which are better guides for policymakers. After all, social science theories are not merely retrospective, seeking to explain past events; they are prospective, in that they seek to make predictions for future events of a similar class and aim to provide a guide for future action. While post-positivists and critical theorists reject theory testing as a fruitful endeavor, neoclassical realists embrace key elements of positivism and, therefore, believe that theory testing is possible and, indeed, essential. In particular, we accept the principle that there is an objective world out there and that we can gain knowledge of that world through careful experimentation or case studies. More specifically, we assume that researchers can make contingent causal inferences about observable phenomena that can be verified through careful case research that follows the process tracing method we outline later in this chapter.

Nonetheless, we recognize that there are also limits to theory testing in the social sciences, which study human behavior, that make hard positivism problematic. In the social sciences, there are problems of human subjectivity and interpretation that complicate the fact-value distinction and make it difficult to define and measure phenomena objectively. After all, while researchers can readily agree on how to measure the temperature of a metal or the volume of a liquid, usually with a standard weight or measurement and an agreed upon measuring device, it is far more complex to measure social phenomena, such as self-esteem or international norms. Social science researchers are compelled either to rely upon the subjective reports of the subjects themselves—which may be deliberately or unconsciously incorrect—or to devise indirect methods of gauging their variables of interest, which may say more about how the researcher conceptualizes the variables than the phenomenon under observation itself. For example, a researcher seeking to investigate the impact of job stress on self-esteem could avoid relying upon the subjects' evaluation of their stress levels by finding alternative indicators of stress, such as the subjects' volume of sweat or evidence of skipped heartbeats. These might, however, reflect how the researcher herself responds to stress rather idiosyncratically, rather than a general representation of how the average person responds to stress.

Furthermore, the difficulty of experimentation in the social sciences, due to practical and ethical considerations, leaves researchers with a limited set of cases (especially in international relations) and the inability to manipulate observations. Finally, the possibility of novelty, learning, and innovation in human affairs complicates the process of categorization that is necessary to cumulate findings and to make generalizations. In this regard, does it make sense to lump Athenian democracy, nineteenth-century restricted franchise democracies, and modern industrial democracies together under the category of "democracy"? Or, if leaders can learn from previous studies of problems of rationality in decision making and alter their behavior as a result, might past generalizations about, say, cognitive consistency be less applicable in the future?[14]

Despite these difficulties, which render theory testing in the social sciences more complex and less rigorous than in the natural sciences, theory testing is still an important endeavor. Without the ability to verify or dismiss particular theories, we would have no ability to choose between theories to guide our behavior and accumulate knowledge. Therefore, we subscribe to a soft positivist epistemology, where we search for law-like generalizations across cases and test these generalizations with rigorous case-study analysis based on well-selected cases.[15] The essence of this approach is that we can identify elements of comparability across at least somewhat similar cases. We can test these discernable patterns employing process-tracing analysis (which we discuss in detail below) to evaluate the causal impact of specific hypothesized independent variables (IVs) and intervening variables (IVVs) on the dependent variables (DVs). We may also generalize based on patterns that are verified through careful case-based analysis to inform predictions and generate policy relevant advice. Nonetheless, we must recognize the limitations of social science theory testing mentioned above and consequently maintain a healthy degree of skepticism in our findings.

14. Nuno Monteiro similarly observes that the possibility of learning and changes in the beliefs of leaders make a hard science of international relations inappropriate. See Nuno P. Monteiro, "We Can Never Study Merely One Thing: Reflections on Systems Thinking and IR," *Critical Review*, vol. 24, no. 3 (2012), pp. 343–366, esp. pp. 345–346.

15. According to Huw Macartney, soft positivism refers to the methodological position that shares with hard positivism the assumptions that it is possible to attain objective knowledge of the world and that theory testing and empirical analysis are the hallmarks of social scientific inquiry. Nonetheless, soft positivists do not agree with hard positivists that the same methods can be used in the social sciences as are used in the natural sciences, and they do not believe that there are regularities in the social world that can be captured effectively with inductive-statistical methods. Huw Macartney, "Variegated Neo-Liberalism: Transnationally Oriented Fractions of Capital in EU Financial Market Integration," *Review of International Studies*, vol. 35, no. 2 (2009), pp. 451–480, at p. 457n. See also Steve Smith, "Positivism and Beyond," in *International Theory: Positivism and Beyond*, ed. Steve Smith, Ken Booth, and Marysia Zalewski (Cambridge: Cambridge University Press, 1996), pp. 11–44, at pp. 15–16; and Nina Tannenwald, "Ideas and Explanation: Advancing the Theoretical Agenda," *Journal of Cold War Studies*, vol. 7, no. 2 (2005), pp. 13–42.

In addition, because the theories we develop and test in international relations are probabilistic theories, they are not falsifiable and would not be even if we could overcome the problems of social science theory testing identified above.[16] After all, a probabilistic theory seeks to explain as much of the DV's variance as possible with the IVs and IVVs it identifies but does not claim to explain 100 percent of that variance. Therefore, it posits that the theory should hold *ceteris paribus* but that other factors not enumerated in the theory may also affect outcomes. In this regard, democratic peace theory does not posit that liberal democracies will never wage war against other liberal democracies, just that, all things being equal, pairs of democracies should be far less likely to wage war against each other than any other dyad. We cannot, therefore, talk about conclusive proof or about disproving theories. A single case diverging from the theory's prediction would not disprove the theory, as that deviance may be explained not by the inadequacy of the theory or the lack of influence of the hypothesized IVs and IVVs on the DV, but by the influence of confounding variables or random error. A large number of cases that are consistent with the hypothesized relationship would also not constitute proof of the theory, since this too could, at least in principle, be an artifact of case selection. Instead, it would be more accurate to speak about confirming or disconfirming evidence.[17]

Despite the limitations of theory testing in the social sciences, then, we maintain that researchers can test theories, hypotheses, and propositions against carefully selected cases to evaluate their performance. In general, theories that pass more important tests of history, that can provide traction over even hard test cases—those which a priori appear more favorable to rival theoretical explanations—or which have confirming evidence from a broad range of observations or cases can be said to have strong empirical support.

---

16. As Lakatos notes, "no finite sample can ever disprove a universal probabilistic theory." Imre Lakatos, "Falsification and the Methodology of Scientific Research Programmes," in *Criticism and the Growth of Knowledge*, ed. Imre Lakatos and Alan Musgrave (Cambridge: Cambridge University Press, 1970), pp. 91–196, at p. 102. Even in the natural sciences, where we can test theories with greater precision and rigor, the best we can do is reject a null hypothesis only with a particular confidence level, which means that we acknowledge that there is still a chance, however small, that our findings do not represent the underlying data distribution. Thus, we can never be fully confident about having proven or disproven a theory unless we were able to observe the entire distribution of cases.

17. In fact, that is true even in the natural sciences, where standard multivariate regression equations routinely include an error term and results include confidence levels.

THEORY CONSTRUCTION

How should a researcher actually develop a neoclassical realist theory? What is an appropriate DV? What is the IV? Neoclassical realism posits four clusters of intervening variables, as discussed in Chapter 3. But, which of the various intervening variables is more appropriate, that is, more likely actually to "intervene" between the independent and the dependent variables? What are the appropriate scope conditions for a neoclassical realist theory?

In this section, we answer these questions. First, we discuss the selection of the dependent variable. As we have argued in previous chapters, neoclassical realism can explain phenomena ranging from the foreign policy behavior and grand strategic adjustment of individual states to broad patterns of international outcomes and structural change. Second, we discuss how a researcher might specify an appropriate structural realist baseline for a neoclassical realist theory. Third, we discuss how the researcher might identify the appropriate unit-level intervening variable or variables from among those discussed in Chapter 3 to include in a neoclassical realist theory. Last, we address how the researcher might establish the scope conditions for his or her neoclassical realist theory.

Selection of Dependent Variables

The principal goal of qualitative research in the social sciences is the explanation of outcomes in individual cases or the "causes-of-effects" approach to explanation. According Mahoney and Goertz, the objective "is to identify the causes of these specific outcomes for each and every case that falls within the scope of the theory under investigation."[18] This contrasts with what they call the "effects-of-causes" approach in quantitative research, in which the researcher seeks to replicate the conditions of a controlled experiment within the confines of an observational study and where the purpose is to evaluate the average effect of hypothesized causes across the universe of cases (or at least across a random sample).[19]

18. Mahoney and Goertz, "A Tale of Two Cultures," p. 232. See also Goertz and Mahoney, *A Tale of Two Cultures*, pp. 46–48; George and Bennett, *Case Studies and Theory Development in the Social Sciences*, pp. 131–135; and Andrew Bennett and Colin Elman, "Qualitative Research: Recent Developments in Case Study Methods," *Annual Review of Political Science*, vol. 9 (2006), pp. 457–458.

19. Mahoney and Goertz, "A Tale of Two Cultures," p. 230. King, Keohane, and Verba's treatise on qualitative methods adopts the "effects-of-causes" approach to causality common in quantitative methods and privileges identifying causal effects over causal mechanisms. King, Keohane, and Verba, *Designing Social Inquiry*, pp. 85–86.

Neoclassical realism falls squarely within the causes-of-effects approach. At the same time, we acknowledge that both causes-of-effects and the effects-of-causes approaches are of value in the study of international politics and that they may actually complement each other. As Mahoney and Goetz write, "Ideally, an explanation of an outcome in one or a small number of cases leads one to wonder if the same factors are at work when a broader understanding of scope is adopted, stimulating a larger-N analysis in which the goal is less to explain particular cases and more to estimate average effects."[20] While our discussion of neoclassical realist theory construction and hypothesis testing deals exclusively with qualitative methods, we would not exclude the possibility or the desirability of employing mixed-method research designs, if doing so is appropriate to resolve the research question or puzzle of interest.[21]

The selection of the dependent variable flows directly from the research question or the (empirical) puzzle the investigator identifies. Since the qualitative research process typically begins with the selection of positive cases—those in which the outcome of interest actually occurs—the following discussion of selecting appropriate dependent variables for neoclassical realist theories also touches upon case selection.[22] We argued in Chapter 4 that the potential scope of the dependent variables for Type III neoclassical realism grows over time and is much broader than previous neoclassical realists have heretofore acknowledged. As Figure 5.1 below illustrates, the range of the dependent variable can expand along two dimensions: the time frame and the level-of-analysis. The time frame refers to the temporal dimensions of the phenomena of interest either within a particular case (observation) or across the sample or even the entire population of cases: days, weeks, months, years, decades, or even centuries. The level-of-analysis pertains to the level of aggregation at which the dependent variable is observable: the external behavior of an individual state, bargaining within a dyad, bargaining outcomes among several states within a regional subsystem, or bargaining outcomes across the international system as a whole.[23] While most discussions of the

20. Mahoney and Goertz, "A Tale of Two Cultures," p. 231. Also see James Mahoney, "Toward a Unified Theory of Casuality," *Comparative Political Studies*, vol. 41, nos. 4–5 (2008), pp. 412–436; and Goertz and Mahoney, *A Tale of Two Cultures*, pp. 46–47.

21. An example of a neoclassical realist work that employs a multi-method research design is Vipin Narang, *Nuclear Strategy in the Modern Era: Regional Powers and International Conflict* (Princeton, NJ: Princeton University Press, 2014).

22. Mahoney and Goertz, "A Tale of Two Cultures," p. 239. Quite often qualitative researchers also choose "negative" cases to test their theories. See James Mahoney and Gary Goertz, "The Possibility Principle: Choosing Negative Cases in Comparative Research," *American Political Science Review*, vol. 98, no. 4 (2004), pp. 653–669.

23. The levels-of-analysis at the dependent variable level for studies of international politics do not correspond to levels of aggregation for independent variables.

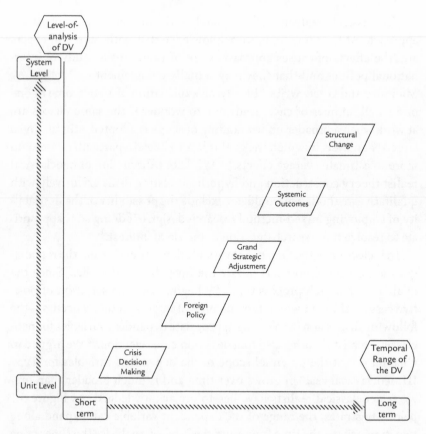

Figure 5.1
Range of Dependent Variables

levels-of-analysis problem in international relations have focused on the location of the independent variable, the levels-of-analysis problem is also relevant to dependent variables.[24]

An example of a dependent variable at the level of an individual state's external behavior and over a relatively short time-span (e.g., hours, days, or weeks) would be a study of elite decision making in a single international crisis. Neoclassical realists often undertake such studies to resolve empirical research puzzles. Consider two parallel neoclassical realist theories

24. The most explicit discussion of the levels-of-analysis problem as it pertains to dependent variables (rather than independent variables) of which we are aware remains Colin Elman, "Horses for Courses: Why *Not* Neorealist Theories of Foreign Policy?" *Security Studies*, vol. 6, no. 1 (1996), pp. 7–53. See also Kenneth N. Waltz, "International Politics Is Not Foreign Policy," *Security Studies*, vol. 6, no. 1 (1996), pp. 54–57; and Colin Elman, "Cause, Effect, and Consistency: A Response to Kenneth Waltz," *Security Studies*, vol. 6, no. 1 (1996), pp. 58–61.

of crisis decision-making in the Kosovo War of 1999. Balkan Devlen and Özgür Özdamar seek to explain why Yugoslav president Slobodan Milošević refused demands contained in the March 1999 Rambouillet Accords, which called for the restoration of Kosovo's autonomy and the deployment of a NATO peacekeeping force to enforce a cease-fire between the Serbs and the Kosovar Albanians. His recalcitrance was puzzling because of the extreme power imbalance between Serbia and NATO.[25] One of us (Jeffrey Taliaferro) seeks to explain not only why President Bill Clinton and his advisers initiated Operation Allied Force in March 1999, given the lack of any tangible threat to US security interests, but also why Clinton's national security team persisted in a 78-day bombing campaign despite abundant evidence the air strikes were producing the very outcomes officials sought to avoid, namely, large-scale ethnic cleansing, an international refugee crisis, and the fragmentation of NATO.[26]

Grand strategic adjustment, which occurs over a longer term than crisis decision-making and entails the integration (or lack thereof) of various elements of a state's foreign, security, and economic policies, is the dependent variable of many neoclassical realist theories. Consider again the research puzzle that Lobell poses in his book on adjustment to hegemonic decline.[27] His dependent variable is grand strategic adjustment by a declining hegemonic state over time. A hegemon's grand strategy can vary along a continuum between cooperation with a rising challenger and punishment. Moreover, that variation can be within a particular case (e.g., the simultaneous pursuit of cooperation and punishment in different subcomponents of a declining hegemon's grand strategy), as well as across cases (e.g., variation in the grand strategies of different declining hegemons). Lobell defines grand strategy as encompassing a state's military doctrine, diplomatic activities, foreign trade policies, and domestic resource extraction.[28] Cooperation entails trade liberalization, reductions in defense spending, participation in collective security arrangements, arms limitation, the redeployment of naval and land forces from forward positions, and territorial concessions. "Punishment involves extraction of additional resources for defense expenditure and protectionism."[29] This

25. Balkan Devlen and Özgür Özdamar, "Neoclassial Realism and Foreign Policy Crises," in *Rethinking Realism in International Relations: Between Tradition and Innovation*, ed. Annette Freyberg-Inan, Ewan Harrison, and James Patrick (Baltimore: Johns Hopkins University Press, 2009), pp. 136–163.

26. Jeffrey W. Taliaferro, "Neoclassical Realism: The Psychology of Great Power Intervention," in *Making Sense of International Relations Theory*, ed. Jennifer Sterling-Folker (Boulder, CO: Lynne Rienner, 2009), pp. 38–54.

27. Lobell, *Challenge of Hegemony*, p. 1

28. Ibid., p. 14.

29. Ibid., pp. 12–13, 19–20.

may entail trade restrictions, increased defense spending, arms buildups, the avoidance of collective security arrangements, the forward deployment of land and naval forces, and a refusal to make territorial concessions.

Lobell's choice of dependent variable guides his selection of cases. He employs a comparative case method, specifically a structured focus comparison of great powers "that have extensive global commitments and encountered contenders for leadership in different parts of their formal and/or informal empire in peacetime and wartime, rather than focusing solely on the latter."[30] The cases are Spain, 1621–1640; Britain, 1889–1912; and Britain, 1932–1939. The selected time frame reflects the period in which the hegemon first began to confront potential challengers, rather the period immediately before a major war and the collapse of the hegemon's empire. Lobell writes, "The adoption of a regionally differentiated framework of world politics means each case study consists of subcases that examine the dyadic nature of the relationship and how the hegemon responded in the specific locale."[31]

The dependent variable for Christensen's domestic mobilization model is also at the level of grand strategy. He seeks to explain variation in national security strategies pursued by the United States and the Chinese Communist Party (and after October 1949, by the People's Republic of China) toward each other between 1947 and 1958. While acknowledging that classical realists and structural realists frequently disagree about precisely which policies fall within the expectations of their theories, Christensen also acknowledges there is more agreement among them that certain types of policies are simply inconsistent with realist tenets. The dependent variable—the type of national security strategy pursued—can take one of three values along an ordinal scale: over-active (the optimal policy set plus added conflict), preferred (the optimal policy set), and underactive (a suboptimal policy set).[32] Christensen writes, "Underactive policies entail the failure to mobilize domestic power resources or to form effective balancing alliances in the face of rising international threat (e.g., interwar American and British strategies)." In contrast, "overactive policies include those that waste valuable resources on areas of peripheral value to national security (e.g., American intervention in Vietnam and the Soviet invasion of Afghanistan) and those that needlessly either increase

---

30. Ibid., p. 15. On structured focused comparison, see Alexander L. George, "Case Studies and Theory Development: The Method of Structured, Focussed Comparison," in *Diplomacy: New Approachs in History, Theory, and Policy*, ed. Paul Lauren (New York: Free Press, 1979), pp. 43–68; and George and Bennett, *Case Studies and Theory Development in the Social Sciences*, pp. 66–72.

31. Lobell, *Challenge of Hegemony*, p. 15.

32. Christensen, *Useful Adversaries*, pp. 13–14.

the number and power of one's enemies or decrease the number and strength of one's allies (e.g., Chinese foreign policy during the Cultural Revolution)."[33]

Neoclassical realism also can explain international outcomes. For example, Randall Schweller implicitly recognized this, as his balance-of-interests theory purports to explain both the alliance strategies of poles and lesser greater powers and the outbreak of World War II.[34] More recent neoclassical realist theories of alliance management and intra-alliance bargaining also implicitly address systemic-level dependent variables. Victor Cha poses this puzzle: "Why did the United States pursue a network of bilateral alliances in East Asia following the end of World War II rather than the multilateral security alliances it preferred in Europe, Southeast Asia, and the South Pacific?"[35] The dependent variables of his powerplay theory are the shifts in the diplomatic and military strategies of the Truman and Eisenhower administrations in East Asia and the security arrangements the United States ultimately contracted with Japan, the Republic of Korea (ROK), and Taiwan (namely, bilateral alliance treaties) during the first decade of the Cold War. The second is a dyadic level phenomenon—the outcome of the bargaining between the United States, Japan, ROK, and Taiwan, respectively.

One neoclassical realist theory that purports to explain dependent variables at the strategic and regional subsystemic levels appears in Vipin Narang's book on nuclear postures of regional powers: China, India, Pakistan, Israel, South Africa, and France. Narang poses two research questions: Which one of three distinct nuclear postures—catalytic, assured retaliation, or asymmetric—will a regional power select and for what reason? Does this choice of nuclear posture have any effect on the state's ability to deter conflict?[36]

The dependent variables are the nuclear postures selected by the regional powers and the impact of that choice on the likelihood of conflict. The first dependent variable, nuclear posture choice, is consistent with a causes-of-effects approach to causation.[37] The second dependent variable, the impact of this choice on deterrence, however, is more consistent with the effects-of-causes approach in quantitative research.[38]

33. Ibid., p. 14.

34. See Randall L. Schweller, *Deadly Imbalances: Tripolarity and Hitler's Strategy for World Conquest* (New York: Columbia University Press, 1997), pp. 39–58 and 59–92.

35. Victor D. Cha, "Powerplay: Origins of the U.S. Alliance System in Asia," *International Security*, vol. 34, no. 3 (2010), pp. 158–196, at 158.

36. Narang, *Nuclear Strategy in the Modern Era*, p. 23.

37. Ibid., pp. 52–54.

38. In fact, Narang does investigate this second issue with quantitative methods, whereas he investigates his first "causes-of-effects" question with case studies. Ibid., pp. 222–252;

Specifying the Appropriate Structural Realist Baseline

The specification of an appropriate structural realist baseline is a critically important aspect of neoclassical realist theory development. The baseline is, in effect, a systemic-level independent variable. Specifying a baseline directs the researcher to ask: *How much of the variance in the dependent variable could a structural realist theory explain if the intervening variables posited by a neoclassical realist theory were not present?* The value-added of any neoclassical realist theory, therefore, lies in its ability to predict and explain political behavior that a sparer structural realist theory cannot.

As we have explained earlier in this book and elsewhere, the term "structural realism" is not confined to Waltz's balance-of-power theory.[39] Rather, structural realism subsumes a variety of systemic realist theories, some of which build explicitly upon Waltz's theory and others that generate hypotheses at odds with that theory.[40] Thus, there can be a variety of structural realist baselines derived from defensive realism, offensive realism, and hegemonic and power transition theories. Determining the specific baseline is entirely up to the researcher as long as three conditions are met: (1) the researcher can clearly specify, a priori, what the baseline happens to be; (2) that the baseline can be empirically verified; and (3) that the baseline can be specified for an entire category of events (within which one can identify a universe of cases).

One approach to specifying a baseline involves identifying an empirical anomaly or set of anomalies for a particular structural realist theory. Consider the baseline that Evan Resnick proposes in his study of the United States' bargaining within so-called alliances of convenience from the early Cold War to the present. Balance-of-power theory expects that, at least on issues of interest to US policymakers and given the tremendous power imbalance between the United States and its endangered allies, Washington would generally prevail in intra-alliance bargaining.[41] Note that his baseline meets all three criteria listed above. First, he specifies, a priori, the expected range of behavior that would be consistent with

and Vipin Narang, "What Does It Take to Deter? Regional Power Nuclear Postures and International Conflict," *Journal of Conflict Resolution*, vol. 57, no. 3 (2013), pp. 478–508.

39. Jeffrey W. Taliaferro, Steven E. Lobell, and Norrin M. Ripsman, "Introduction: Neoclassical Realism, the State, and Foreign Policy," in *Neoclassical Realism, the State, and Foreign Policy*, ed. Steven E. Lobell, Norrin M. Ripsman, and Jeffrey W. Taliaferro (Cambridge: Cambridge University Press, 2009), p. 17, fn. 47.

40. George and Bennett, *Case Studies and Theory Development in the Social Sciences*, p. 161.

41. Evan N. Resnick, "Strange Bedfellows: U.S. Bargaining Behavior with Allies of Convenience," *International Security*, vol. 35, no. 3 (2010), p. 144. This is similar to Norrin M. Ripsman's baseline for bargaining outcomes between the United States and its allies in the aftermath of wars. Ripsman, *Peacemaking by Democracies*.

balance-of-power theory: since intra-alliance bargaining outcomes will match the relative distribution of power and interests, the United States ought generally to prevail in bargaining with its allies of convenience. Second, the use of within-case methods such as process tracing can reveal whether the causal mechanisms identified by balance-of-power theory are present or absent in particular cases. Third, the structural realist baseline can be specified for an entire category of events and the entire universe of cases of alliances of convenience the United States contracted since 1945.

Another approach involves identifying phenomena where a structural realist theory yields indeterminate predictions or expectations. Balance-of-power theory, for example, serves as the baseline for Randall Schweller's neoclassical realist theory of underbalancing.[42] He poses the research question: "What are the necessary conditions for the proper operations of the balance-of-power? What factors confound the logic and predictions of the theory?"[43] Schweller limits his research question to the prevalence of just one type of maladaptive strategic behavior: underbalancing, or the failure of states to respond to rising threats efficiently or in a timely manner.[44] Schweller's underbalancing theory predicts how states operating under various domestic constraints will respond to external threats.[45]

Note that the baseline for Schweller's theory is not the complete absence of balancing against powerful or aggressive states, per se. Rather, the baseline is *timely* and *efficient* balancing behavior. In other words, if the values on the four intervening variables posited by his theory of underbalancing were muted or completely absent, then one might expect the threatened state to balance in an efficient and timely manner. This particular baseline meets all three criteria stated above: (1) it can be stated a priori, (2) it can be empirically verified, and (3) it can be specified for an entire category of events and the subsidiary universe of potential cases.

Offense-defense theory, nuclear deterrence theory, and offensive realism provide the baseline for Narang's posture optimization theory. Waltz, Robert Jervis, Steven Van Evera, Charles Glaser, and John Mearsheimer,

42. For a useful distinction between theories of balancing and theories of power balances, see Daniel H. Nexon, "The Balance of Power in the Balance," *World Politics*, vol. 61, no. 2 (2009), pp. 330–359. The baselines of Schweller's, Narang's, and Resnick's respective neoclassical realist theories derive from what Nexon calls theories of balancing.

43. Randall L. Schweller, *Unanswered Threats: Political Constraints on the Balance of Power* (Princeton, NJ: Princeton University Press, 2006), p. 10.

44. Ibid. Schweller cites bandwagoning and buck-passing as the two other non-balancing strategies, whose prevalence is more widespread than neorealist balance-of-power theory would suggest. On buck passing, see ibid., p. 7.

45. Ibid., pp. 46–68.

argue that the mere possession of nuclear weapons, and especially the possession of secure-second strike forces, is sufficient to deter conventional conflict systematically, even against a far more powerful adversary.[46] Like the two superpowers during the Cold War, therefore, once a regional power acquires nuclear weapons, its leaders should eschew security guarantees from third-party patrons; learn to avoid provoking crises with neighboring states; and strive to establish robust command, control, and communications (C^3) systems for their nuclear forces.[47]

As with the previous examples, the "existential deterrence" or "nuclear acquisition" baseline gleaned from offense-defense theory, deterrence theories, and offensive realism can be stated a priori; empirically verified; and specified for an entire category of events and the subsidiary universe of potential cases. Whereas, the "existential deterrence" baseline suggests stable deterrence regardless of the nuclear posture regional powers adopt and that nuclear-armed states will eventually adopt an assured retaliatory posture, Narang's neoclassical realist theory predicts and seeks to explain *variation* in the nuclear postures adopted by regional powers over time and variation in the likelihood of conflict between those states and their neighbors.[48]

Offensive realism provides the baseline for Thomas Juneau's neoclassical realist theory of Iranian strategic adjustment between 2001 and 2009. Arguably, after 2001, the Islamic Republic of Iran faced a favorable strategic environment as a consequence of the United States' ouster of the hostile Taliban and Ba'athist regimes in neighboring Afghanistan and Iraq, along with swelling coffers from the rising price of oil. Juneau writes, "As a rising power faced with a window of opportunity and surrounded by hostile states—especially in Tehran's view, the hegemony-seeking United States—Iran should behave like an offensive realist."[49] Offensive realism

46. Narang, *Nuclear Strategy in the Modern Era*, pp. 1–12.

47. Kenneth N. Waltz, "The Spread of Nuclear Weapons: More May Be Better," in *Adelphi Papers No. 171* (London: International Institute for Strategic Studies, 1981); Robert Jervis, *The Meaning of the Nuclear Revolution: Statecraft and the Prospect of Armageddon* (Ithaca, NY: Cornell University Press, 1989); Charles L. Glaser, *Analyzing Strategic Nuclear Policy* (Princeton, NJ: Princeton University Press, 1990); Stephen Van Evera, *Causes of War: Power and the Roots of Conflict* (Ithaca, NY: Cornell University Press, 1999); John J. Mearsheimer, *Tragedy of Great Power Politics* (New York: W. W. Norton, 2001); and Scott D. Sagan and Kenneth N. Waltz, *The Spread of Nuclear Weapons: A Debate Renewed*, 2nd ed. (New York: W. W. Norton, 2003).

48. According to Narang, the adoption of a catalytic posture by a nuclear-armed or even a nuclear-capable regional power is puzzling from the standpoint of structural realism's self-help assumption. With a catalytic posture, a regional power depends upon timely diplomatic or military intervention from a third-party guarantor (generally the United States) to save it from an all-out conventional or nuclear attack from a neighbor. See Narang, *Nuclear Strategy in the Modern Era*, pp. 48–49.

49. Thomas Juneau, *Squandered Opportunity: Neoclassical Realism and Iranian Foreign Policy* (Stanford, CA: Stanford University Press, 2015), pp. 1–2, 7.

would expect Iran, by virtue of its latent power (e.g., geographic location, large and educated population, and abundant oil and natural gas reserves), to seek security by becoming the regional hegemon in the Persian Gulf and a key power broker in Middle East conflicts. The baseline for Juneau's neoclassical realist theory of Iranian grand strategic adjustment meets all three criteria outlined earlier: (1) it can be stated a priori; (2) it can be empirically verified; and (3) it can be specified for an entire category of events and the subsidiary universe of potential cases.

The examples cited above do not constitute an exhaustive list of possible structural realist baselines for the development of neoclassical realist theories. Waltz's balance-of-power theory has provided the implicit or explicit baseline for several extant neoclassical works. That said, Waltz's theory is not the sum total of structural realism and not the only source of possible baselines, as Narang's and Juneau's respective books illustrate. It is entirely possible for the researcher to derive an appropriate baseline from any number of structural realist theories, for example, hegemonic or power preponderance theories, or balance-of-threat theory, as long as such a baseline pertains to the researcher's chosen dependent variable and meets the three criteria we have outlined above.

Selection of the Appropriate Intervening Variables

The core contention of neoclassical realism is that the international system is an imperfect transmission belt because its influence on outcomes must pass through intervening domestic-level processes that can amplify, obstruct, or distort it. Those intervening variables condition whether, how, and when states respond to the international systemic pressures that all variants of realism assume underlie crisis behavior, "ordinary" foreign and security policies, longer-term patterns of grand strategic adjustment, and international political outcomes.

In Chapter 3, we organized what has heretofore been an eclectic list of intervening variables that various neoclassical realist theories posit into four general categories: (1) leaders' images; (2) strategic culture; (3) patterns of state-society relations; and (4) domestic institutions. However, in developing a neoclassical realist theory, which interning variable (or variables) should a researcher include?

We suggest two "ideal type" strategies for identifying appropriate intervening variables: deduction and induction. In the former, the researcher seeks to focus the inquiry a priori on the causal power of particular intervening variables with a logical, abstract analysis, based on extant neoclassical realist theories, existing theoretical debates, or even thought experiments or formal models. In the latter, the researcher either relies on surface-level knowledge of empirical cases to suggest possible intervening variables, or develops theoretical models following systematic qualitative or quantitative tests of competing models. We discuss each strategy in turn, although we acknowledge that, in practical terms, they cannot be separated so easily; all deductive approaches will have at least a small inductive component and all inductive approaches will be at least somewhat informed by deductive theorizing.

Deductive approaches use a minimum possible reference to cases. Instead, this approach is about the logic of which intervening variables ought to, a priori, moderate the effect of the international system on the dependent variable. A researcher may do this by puzzling in the abstract about which variables should be likely to have a causal impact on the dependent variable. Alternatively, he/she may engage in a counterfactual thought experiment, where he/she puzzles about the likely effect of changing particular parameters (i.e., the variables) of a historical case.[50] For example, the researcher could puzzle, as Richard Ned Lebow does about whether World War I would have occurred had Archduke Franz Ferdinand not been assassinated on June 28, 1914, or whether the Cold War would have ended the same way if someone other than Mikhail Gorbachev had succeeded Konstantin Chernenko as the general secretary of the Communist Party of the Soviet Union (CPSU) on March 11, 1985.[51] In each case, the researcher's answer will affect his/her assessment about whether nationalist politics or individual leaders' worldviews affect how states behave within a given international structure. This assessment, in turn, will affect the theoretical models he/she builds and tests systematically. The researcher could also construct theories deductively by constructing formal models that suggest hypotheses about how actors would be expected to react under specific structural conditions and expected payoff structures.[52]

Our own deductive strategy for determining which of the four categories of intervening variables are more likely to be operative in filtering systemic pressures would begin with our discussion of the time frame of the dependent variable in Chapter 4. As we indicated, in the shorter term, when states are responding to crises and making short-term foreign policy

---

50. See, for example, the contributions to Philip E. Tetlock and Aaron Belkin, eds., *Counterfactual Thought Experiments in World Politics: Logical, Methodological, and Psychological Perspectives* (Princeton, NJ: Princeton University Press, 1996).

51. Richard Ned Lebow, *Forbidden Fruit: Counterfactuals and International Relations* (Princeton, NJ: Princeton University Press, 2010).

52. See, for example, Charles A. Lave and James G. March, *An Introduction to Models in the Social Sciences* (Lanham, MD: University Press of America, 1993).

decisions, the role of leaders is paramount, especially since there is little time to consult societal actors. If the study seeks to explain crisis decision-making, therefore, it would make most sense to select variables from the leader image and strategic culture clusters, since the short time frame reduces the impact of the societal and institutional variables. Consider again the parallel neoclassical realist theories of crisis decision-making in the Kosovo War. Both Devlen and Özdamar, and Taliaferro posit a unit-level intervening variable from the leader images category (Milošević's operational code and the Clinton national security team's aversion to a perceived loss in US prestige and credibility vis-à-vis its NATO allies, respectively). Devlen and Özdamar, however, also posit a second intervening variable, namely Milošević's domestic prospect of political survival. Any capitulation to NATO and the Clinton administration on Kosovo without a fight would have called into question Milošević's bona fides as a Serb nationalist and possibly invite an internal challenge to his leadership.[53] Neither model, though, incorporated state-society relations or domestic institutional variables.

Scholars seeking to explain longer-term dependent variables, however, would be better advised to privilege variables from the strategic culture, state-society relations, and domestic institutions clusters, since the impact of individual leaders diminishes over time. This is how we understand Schweller's theory of underbalancing. The dependent variable, underbalancing behavior, is an aspect of strategic adjustment and thus more likely to occur over the span of several years, rather than weeks or months. Underbalancing theory posits four domestic-level variables—the degree of elite consensus, elite cohesion, societal cohesion, and regime or government vulnerability—that shape how a state responds to systemic imperatives.[54] The first two intervening variables (elite consensus and elite cohesion) fall under our leader images category, while the latter two (social cohesion and regime vulnerability) fall under state-society relations. According to Schweller, underbalancing behavior will occur according to one of four causal schemes or configurations (and sequences) of the independent and the intervening variables: the additive model, the extremely incoherent state model, the polarized democratic model, and the underbalancing through wishful thinking model.[55]

53. Devlen and Özdamar, "Neoclassial Realism and Foreign Policy Crises," pp. 142–143.
54. Schweller inconsistently refers to elite consensus, elite cohesion, social cohesion, and government/regime vulnerability as the *independent* variables of his underbalancing theory at some points in the book and as intervening variables at other points. See Schweller, *Unanswered Threats*, pp. 15, 19, 63, and 69.
55. Ibid., pp. 62–64.

Induction is a second "ideal" approach to identifying intervening variables for inclusion in a neoclassical realist theory. Induction implies beginning with insights from one or more appropriate cases, which then suggest a generalization about which intervening-level variables are likely to affect outcomes. Two inductive approaches suggest themselves. The first would entail an unsystematic, surface-level consideration of a case or cases prior to theory construction to assist the researcher in variable selection. In this manner, the researcher could, without incurring sunk costs, develop an idea of which domestic factors, if any, seemed to affect outcomes in these cases. This is a low-cost strategy of induction, although it is also fraught with risks, as the surface-level intuitions it generates may be incorrect.

A more intensive strategy for induction would be to begin the investigation by testing the structural realist baseline against a selection of cases (or with a large-N quantitative analysis) in order to determine whether its predictions fall short and why. The researcher can then utilize that information to construct a plausible alternative theory that can be tested against a wider set of cases.[56]

This is the strategy utilized by Norrin M. Ripsman and Jean-Marc F. Blanchard in their study of economic interdependence and international conflict. They began by testing commercial liberal and realist theories about the effects of economic interdependence on national decisions to run the risks of war. Their conclusion is that realist theory provides a better guide to those cases, but that, in addition to the geostrategic motivations posited by realists, decision-makers are also motivated by regime survival considerations. Consequently, they concluded inductively that the realist theory ought to be augmented by variables that captured this dynamic.[57]

In another work of this kind, Ripsman begins his research on the causes of peacemaking between regional rivals with a test of realist, liberal, and constructivist theories, using the paradigmatic case of Franco-German peacemaking after World War II. He concluded that structural realist and liberal theories each got only part of the story right. Consequently, he developed a staged theory that assumes that the transition to peace depends on realist and statist incentives, but the stability of the settlement

---

56. That quantitative studies could be used to generate insights that could be tested systematically for causal impact is suggested by Bruce N. Russett, "International Behavior Research: Case Studies and Cumulation," in *Approaches to the Study of Political Science*, ed. Michael Haas and Henry S. Kariel (Scranton, PA: Chandler, 1970), pp. 425–443.

57. Norrin M. Ripsman and Jean-Marc F. Blanchard, "Commercial Liberalism under Fire: Evidence from 1914 and 1936," *Security Studies*, vol. 6, no. 2 (1996–1997), pp. 4–50.

depends on the degree to which society is brought on board afterward through liberal mechanisms.[58]

Deductive approaches are far more common in international relations research, as the barriers to theorizing are lower. Researchers can construct testable theories without first investing time and resources to investigate particular cases or to construct and test a large-N data set. Nonetheless, it is fraught with the risk that the deductive assumptions made by the researcher are not empirically valid. Surface-level inductive approaches pose relatively low barriers to theorizing, as the researcher does not need to analyze cases systematically before making theoretical generalizations; however, there is a danger of tailoring the theory to the particular cases considered.[59] If these cases are somehow unique, they might not be generalizable and, consequently, will lead to inaccurate theoretical generalizations. Finally, beginning with careful theory testing of the structural realist baseline at the outset would present the fewest risks of inaccurate assumptions, but it would impose the highest start-up costs for theory building. Thus, the researcher should be aware of the relative advantages and disadvantages of deduction and induction before selecting a strategy that meets his/her particular needs.

Establishing Scope Conditions for a Neoclassical Realist Theory

As Mahoney and Goertz observe, qualitative researchers typically define narrow scopes for their theories, meaning that the inferences they draw cannot be generalized to the entire universe of cases.[60] While neoclassical realism can explain phenomena ranging from individual states' short-term foreign policy behavior to recurrent patterns of international outcomes, an individual neoclassical realist theory should have clear scope conditions; when formulating a theory a researcher should specify how universal the theory is. According to Goertz and Mahoney, scope conditions are "the parameters within which a given theory is expected to be valid. . . . The need for scope conditions grows out of the fact that social scientists rarely formulate universal propositions that hold across all times and

58. Norrin M. Ripsman, "Two Stages of Transition From a Region of War to a Region of Peace: Realist Transition and Liberal Endurance," *International Studies Quarterly*, vol. 49, no. 4 (December 2005), pp. 669–693.

59. Bennett and George, *Case Studies and Theory Development in the Social Sciences*, pp. 20–21, 240–244.

60. Mahoney and Goertz, "A Tale of Two Cultures," p. 237; and Goertz and Mahoney, *A Tale of Two Cultures*, pp. 46–47, 192–196.

places; rather, they formulate conditional propositions that apply to specific contexts."[61] Researchers should ask themselves what is the total range of cases that populate the explanation? What are the appropriate limits on their generalizability?

Some neoclassical realist theories are generalizable to a wider range of cases. For example, the scope conditions for Schweller's underbalancing theory are rather broad; his findings should be generalizable beyond his four cases to a range of states (great powers, major powers, and weaker states) in the modern international system. In cases where the independent variable takes on a low value and where all four intervening variables also take on low values (or are simply not present) one would not expect to observe underbalancing. Where states confront rising external threats (the independent variable), but where there is also elite consensus about the nature of threat and a high degree of elite cohesion, one would expect the outcome to approximate the standard balance-of-power model. However, in cases where states face rising external threats and where some or all of the intervening variables are present or take on high values, one should expect underbalancing to occur according to one of four causal schemes.[62]

Ripsman's theory of democratic peacemaking is generalizable (without modification) to cases where different types of liberal democratic great powers negotiate peace settlements in limited wars, rather than simply major wars (or world wars). The theory may also generate predictions in cases where liberal democratic non-great powers attempt to negotiate postwar settlements. In fact, one might expect to find the hypothesized causal pathways between the IV—the international distribution of power—and IVV—the degree of structural autonomy enjoyed by the FPE—across a wide range of cases in which states conduct international negotiations that may not necessarily involve the termination of interstate wars.[63] Likewise, the scope conditions of Christensen's domestic mobilization model extended beyond the cases of the United States and China during the first decade of the Cold War. The hypothesized causal pathways from external threat to the height of domestic mobilization hurdles confronting an FPE and the states' resulting balancing behavior is potentially generalizable to other cases of states with different regime types and relative capabilities.[64]

61. Gary Goertz and James Mahoney, "Negative Case Selection: The Possibility Principle," in *Social Science Concepts: A User's Guide*, ed. Gary Goertz (Princeton, NJ: Princeton University Press, 2006), p. 193.

62. Schweller, *Unanswered Threats*, pp. 63–68.

63. Ripsman, *Peacemaking by Democracies*.

64. Christensen, *Useful Adversaries*, pp. 248–252.

Other neoclassical realist theories have narrower scope conditions. For example, Lobell's theory is largely limited to grand strategic adjustment by a subset of great powers, namely existing hegemons that simultaneously confront relative economic decline and rising military challenges in multiple theaters. The universe of potential cases that meet those criteria is extremely small. He excludes cases where the hegemon lost its empire in a single catastrophic event, for example, Napoleonic France, which suffered a crushing defeat in the 1815 War of the Sixth Coalition, or cases where other great powers protected the territorial integrity of a declining hegemon's empire, such as the Ottoman Empire, which relied on Britain and France for protection against Russia.[65] Similarly, Narang's optimization theory purports to explain the source of and the deterrent consequences of the regional powers' nuclear strategies. His book examines the full universe of empirical cases. Excluding the former Soviet Union and the United States, only seven states have developed and maintained independent nuclear arsenals since 1945.[66]

Identifying Key Actors: The Foreign Policy Executive

A key first step in conducting empirical research from a neoclassical realist perspective is to identify the FPE of the states under observation. After all, while societal actors within a state may express many views, these views may not represent the key decision makers' attitudes or their rationale for policy decisions. Moreover, these views may not even make it to the "Cabinet table" and, consequently, might not be considered seriously by the FPE when it makes its decisions. Thus, for example, while the City of London may have been eager to avoid war for economic reasons in 1914, that should not be taken as evidence that the British government was reluctant to join the war on economic grounds.[67] Determining whose opinions were consequential involves: identifying the members and composition of the FPE; pinpointing those policymakers "who matter" in the formulation of foreign policy and where decisions are made; and determining the relative power and influence of actors within the FPE. After all, many individuals inside and outside of the government have an interest in foreign

65. Lobell, *Challenge of Hegemony*, pp. 16–17.
66. Oddly, Narang does not classify the United Kingdom as maintaining an *independent* nuclear arsenal because of the tight integration of UK and US nuclear forces since 1958. See Narang, *Nuclear Strategy in the Modern Era*, p. 3, fn. 3.
67. Paul A. Papayoanou does this in "Interdependence, Institutions, and the Balance of Power: Britain, Germany, and World War I," *International Security*, vol. 20, no. 4 (1996), pp. 42–76.

policy and make statements about policy, yet not all of these actors have meaningful input into policymaking, nor are they necessarily aware of the true rationale behind policies selected. Further complicating matters for the researcher, the composition of the FPE varies across states and within states over time. Whose statements and motivations then should the researcher concentrate on if he/she wants an accurate understanding of the government's selection of a particular policy initiative? In this section, we discuss how to identify who is meaningfully involved in a state's FPE, who is most consequential, and how to parse them. Finally, we address the additional complications of identifying the FPE in nondemocratic states, which can be particularly difficult given the lack of transparency, archival access, and ability to conduct meaningful interviews.

The first distinction a researcher must make is between the FPE and the foreign, defense, and intelligence bureaucracy (FDIB), since the secondary literature might discuss a foreign policy "team," which includes both groupings. The FPE consists of the individuals who are responsible for making the foreign policy choices, usually including the head of government and ministers—such as the minister of foreign affairs and the minister of defense—charged with foreign policy issue areas. In addition, the FPE may also include other individuals who are members of ministerial, subcommittee, or subcabinet sessions on foreign security policy, and therefore have some determinative influence over foreign policy choices.

The FDIB, in contrast, refers to the bureaucratic organizations charged with the collection and assessment of foreign intelligence or the formulation of specific policy options for consideration and selection by the FPE, as well as with the implementation of actual foreign and defense policies. The precise composition of the FDIB and the types of FDIB officials most likely to have direct contact with members of the FPE varies across different states and even within the state over time. For example, the United Kingdom and postwar Germany and Japan all have strong civil service traditions. In those states, the senior echelons of the FDIB who have direct contact with their respective FPEs are career civil servants, diplomats, intelligence analysts, and military officers. In the United States, by comparison, the senior levels of the executive departments (e.g., State, Defense, Treasury, and Homeland Security); the intelligence community (e.g., Central Intelligence Agency and the Office of the Director of National Intelligence); and various independent agencies (e.g., National Security Staff and White House Office) are presidential appointees.[68]

---

68. The United States is unusual among liberal democratic states in that the president nominates, subject to Senate confirmation, the top seven layers of the sixteen executive departments and the various independent agencies, as well as ambassadorships and major

Nevertheless, even in the United States, the members of the FPE (e.g., the president and the members of National Security Council Principals and the Deputies Committees) may have contact with intelligence analysts, uniformed military officers, career diplomats and civil servants, who are not presidential appointees.

Although the foreign policy, defense, and intelligence experts of the FDIB might be present at meetings with the FPE, they do not weigh in on the final decision but instead provide expertise on political, economic, military, or intelligence matters to the FPE, often writing background papers and making policy recommendations. The experts may provide competing and contradictory information to the FPE. Although they do present intelligence or policy advice, the FPE might not accept their recommendations. Indeed, FPE members—often seasoned politicians with extensive experience—are frequently accustomed to hearing competing explanations and making difficult decisions at odds with the advice of policy experts. Even when the FPE does pursue the policies recommended by foreign policy experts, its reasons for doing so might be very different from those advanced by the policy advisors. Therefore, it is essential to understand the decision makers' rationale, rather than that of the advisors.[69]

It is important for the researcher further to distinguish the FPE from the rest of the cabinet or government, which does not play a central role in matters of foreign affairs. In rare cases, the FPE can be as limited as a single individual such as a president, prime minister, or a dictator. Thus, for example, although other individuals, such as foreign ministers Maxim Litvinov and Vyacheslav Molotov, participated in the making of Soviet foreign policy in the 1930s, 1940s, and early 1950s, decision making clearly rested in Josef Stalin's hands.[70] More often, the FPE consists of

---

military commands. During the George W. Bush administration, a total of 3,361 executive branch positions were filled by presidential appointment. See William A. Galston and E. J. Dionne Jr., "A Half Empty Government Can't Govern: Why Everyone Wants to Fix the Appointments Process, Why It Never Happens, and How We Can Get It Done," in *Governance Studies at Brookings* (Washington, DC: Brookings Institution, 2010). In contrast, in the United Kingdom there are only 122 prime ministerial appointments: twenty-two cabinet ministers and one hundred junior ministers across twenty-four ministerial departments. See Prime Minister's Office, 10 Downing Street https://www.gov.uk/government/how-government-works, accessed August 21, 2014.

69. In the United States, for example, there is strong injunction against intelligence analysts and managers attempting to influence policy. For an overview of the analyst-policy-maker relationship in the United States, see Mark M. Lowenthal, *Intelligence: From Secrets to Policy*, 5th ed. (Los Angeles: SAGE/CQ, 2012), pp. 199–216.

70. For detailed analyses of Stalin's dominant role in formulating Soviet grand strategy and foreign policies during the interwar period, World War II, and the early Cold War, see Geoffrey Roberts, *Stalin's Wars: From World War to Cold War, 1939–1953* (New Haven, CT: Yale University Press, 2006); Geoffrey Roberts, *The Unholy Alliance: Stalin's Pact with*

a small group or inner circle of decision makers such as President John F. Kennedy's Executive Committee of the National Security Council (ExCom) during the Cuban Missile Crisis, President Lyndon Johnson's Tuesday Lunch Group, Prime Minister Golda Meir's Kitchen Cabinet, or Prime Minister Menachem Begin's Ministerial Committee on Security Affairs.[71] Begin's Ministerial Committee, for example, consisted of a subgroup of the full Cabinet, with access to secret information that was not available to the general Cabinet.[72]

The researcher should also seek to determine what hierarchy, if any, exists among the decision makers and what the decision-making dynamics with the FPE happen to be. Obviously, the head of government (president, prime minister, or dictator) may have disproportionate influence over foreign policy decisions. But it is also useful to investigate whether particular ministers or officials also have disproportionate influence or even influence beyond what one would expect based on their formal positions. For example, our own individual archival research brought to our attention the disproportionate influence of Chancellor of the Exchequer Neville Chamberlain—who was even more influential in matters of foreign affairs than Foreign Secretary Sir John Simon or even Prime Minister Stanley Baldwin—in the Baldwin government in the mid-1930s. Likewise, Minister of Agriculture Ariel Sharon was more influential than Foreign Minister Yitzhak Shamir in Menachem Begin's second government. Therefore, it is incumbent upon the researcher to utilize primary and secondary sources to determine which actors are more influential within the FPE.[73]

Hitler (Bloomington: Indiana University Press, 1989); and V. M. Zubok and Konstantin Pleshakov, Inside the Kremlin's Cold War: From Stalin to Khrushchev (Cambridge, MA: Harvard University Press, 1996).

71. In the decision to bomb Iraq's nuclear reactor in June 1981, for example, Begin required that the entire cabinet vote. However, the decision was essentially made in the Ministerial Committee and not in the larger Cabinet, given that many in the latter group turned to members of the Ministerial Committee, which had been deliberating on the matter for a long time, to guide their decision. Yehuda Ben Meir, National Security Decisionmaking: The Israeli Case (Boulder, CO: Westview, 1986); and Jonathan Renshon, Why Leaders Choose War: The Psychology of Prevention (Westport, CT: Praeger, 2006), pp. 41–58.

72. Shlomo Nakdimon, First Strike: The Exclusive Story of How Israel Foiled Iraq's Attempt to Get the Bomb (New York: Summit, 1987), pp. 158–168.

73. Norrin M. Ripsman and Jack S. Levy, "Wishful Thinking or Buying Time? The Logic of British Appeasement in the 1930s," International Security, vol. 33, no. 2 (2008), pp. 148–181; Steven E. Lobell, "Bringing Balancing Back In: Britain's Targeted Balancing, 1936-1939," Journal of Strategic Studies, vol. 35, no. 6 (2012), pp. 747–773; and idem., "Balance of Power, Components of Power, and International Relations," unpublished manuscript, University of Utah, n.d.

To determine the boundaries of the FPE, the researcher must consult secondary sources on foreign policy making in the state in question during the period under investigation to assess, a priori and deductively, the positions and actors who one would expect to be part of a central foreign policy decision-making inner circle. These individuals might include the positions that Graham Allison identifies as chiefs.[74] In democratic states, these individuals are easier to identify, by asking the following questions. Do these individuals participate in the deliberations in which major diplomatic, military, or economic options are evaluated? In situations where there are formal or informal votes on policy, do these individuals have a vote? Do these individuals have privileged access to secret information and the advice of foreign policy experts? Are these individuals at the senior level in their department? Can these individuals challenge the position of a sitting president or prime minister? Do these individuals provide more than professional expertise, information, and data?

In non-democratic states, it is more difficult to ascertain where decisions are made, as members of the legislature and cabinet ministers are often figureheads or have limited influence. In this instance, the researcher should examine decision makers who are close to the dictator or crown, which might include loyal family or tribal members. There is likely to be variation across different types of authoritarian regimes. For example, the membership and the boundaries of the FPE in a highly bureaucratized one-party regime, such as China after Mao Zedong's death or the Soviet Union after Josef Stalin's death, comprised at a half-dozen officials.[75] It is not unreasonable to assume the members of a military junta, such as the ones that ruled Argentina from 1976 to 1983 or the "regime of the colonels" in Greece from 1967 to 1974, are members of the FPE. In so-called personalist or strongman dictatorships, however, the membership of the FPE is highly idiosyncratic.[76] Dictators like Stalin, Mao, Hitler, and Saddam Hussein often made major strategic decisions secretly and outside of formal policymaking bodies, without necessarily consulting a broader group

74. Graham T. Allison, *Essence of Decision: Explaining the Cuban Missile Crisis* (Boston: Little Brown, 1971), pp. 294–313.

75. In the cases of post-Mao China, the FPE would generally comprise the Standing Committee of the Politburo and the Central Military Commission of the Chinese Communist Party (CCP). See Jean-Pierre Cabestan, "China's Foreign-and Security-Policy Decision-Making Processes under Hu Jintao," *Journal of Current Chinese Affairs*, vol. 38, no. 3 (2009), pp. 63–97. In the post-Stalin USSR, the FPE was largely synonymous with the CPSU Politburo.

76. On the characteristics of "personalist" (or strongman) regimes versus the characteristics of juntas and "non-personalist machine regimes," see Jessica L. P. Weeks, *Dictators at War and Peace* (Ithaca, NY: Cornell University Press, 2014), pp. 6–7.

of ministers or military leaders.[77] In such cases, the researcher would need to focus exclusively on the leader, if adequate sources are available.

Of course, when the researcher begins his/her detailed case analysis of the particular issue area, he/she might need to revise the initial estimate of who matters. There are two possible findings that should inspire revisions. The first is the dog that does not bark. In other words, while the researcher might have expected an individual to matter based on his/her position in the government or cabinet, the archival research and interviews demonstrate that the individual in fact had little or no voice in the decision-making process. In this instance, even though a priori one would have expected the individual to matter, their policy positions and stances have little influence. Books and archives are full of accounts of such actors. For instance, the literature on appeasement often highlights the role of Nevile Henderson, Britain's ambassador to Germany from 1937 to 1940. However, Henderson's positions, papers, and stances had little influence on the decision-making process.[78]

The second finding that should inspire revisions is the mouse that roared, or individuals one would not expect a priori to influence policy, based on their position in the government or administration, actually having meaningful influence over policy. This might include a member of an opposition party, an individual who occupied a minor Cabinet position, an influential friend of the leader, or an individual who has remained private or secret about his/her role after leaving the government. In this instance, such individuals are difficult to find before investigating the case and reading the archival documents. For example, President Franklin D. Roosevelt's friend Harry Hopkins was his chief emissary to the British and the Soviet governments during World War II. Moreover, as he lived in the White House for three-and-a-half years during the war, he arguably had greater influence over Roosevelt's foreign policy than many within government, including Secretary of State Cordell Hull.[79] Yet, as he held no official position in the Roosevelt administration after his resignation

---

77. See, for example, Ian Kershaw, *Hitler*, 1st American ed., 2 vols. (New York: W. W. Norton, 1999); Walter Warlimont, *Inside Hitler's Headquarters, 1939–45*, (New York: Praeger, 1964); and Simon Sebag Montefiore, *Stalin: The Court of the Red Tsar*, 1st American ed. (New York: Knopf, 2004); Jerrold M. Post, Amatzia Baram, and USAF Counterproliferation Center, *Saddam Is Iraq: Iraq Is Saddam* (Maxwell Air Force Base, AL: USAF Counterproliferation Center, Air War College, Air University, 2002).

78. See, for example, Peter Neville, *Appeasing Hitler: The Diplomacy of Sir Nevile Henderson, 1937–39* (London: MacMillan, 2000); and Ripsman and Levy, "Wishful Thinking or Buying Time?," p. 163.

79. See Cordell Hull and Andrew Henry Thomas Berding, *The Memoirs of Cordell Hull* (New York: Macmillan, 1948); Christopher D. O'Sullivan, *Harry Hopkins: FDR's Envoy to Churchill and Stalin* (Lanham, MD: Rowman and Littlefield, 2014).

as secretary of commerce in September 1940, it would be easy to omit Hopkins from an a priori list of FPE members. Similarly, National Security Advisor Henry Kissinger had more influence over the Nixon administration's foreign policy decisions than Secretary of Defense Melvin Laird and Secretary of State William Rogers.[80]

It is of great importance to determine who the important actors are, as the integrity of the study's conclusions depends on it. For example, it would be remiss to quote a statement of a backbencher in the British Parliament as an authoritative statement of the FPE's intentions to explain the government's rationale for a major foreign policy decision, choice, or action, as that backbencher might be oblivious to the FPE's true rationale. It would be similarly inappropriate to ignore an influential FPE member whose policy preferences may have determined the direction of policy. Of course, scholars may disagree over the exact composition of the FPE, though there should be wide consensus on most of the members.

Given the sensitive nature of security topics, there might be limited access to cabinet, presidential, or prime ministerial papers. One consequence is that the researcher must examine the writings, memoirs, and interviews of foreign policy experts to assess the decision making of the inner cabinet. Of course, there are risks associated with this strategy since the experts do not attend all of the sessions of the inner cabinet, may not understand the dynamics of the small group (some of whom have relationships dating back decades), and may only hear about but not witness the deliberations. Nevertheless, it is useful to have the testimony of the experts about the FPE, since they had greater access to the FPE than most other individuals.

SELECTING ALTERNATIVE EXPLANATIONS

To determine whether a hypothesis or theoretical model advances our understanding of the phenomenon under investigation, it is useful to test it against appropriate alternative explanations. But how should the researcher select an appropriate set of alternative explanations? This is an important issue, as the selection of weak alternatives—i.e., straw

---

80. See, for example, Asaf Siniver, *Nixon, Kissinger, and U.S. Foreign Policy Making: The Machinery of Crisis* (Cambridge: Cambridge University Press, 2008), pp. 40–70; William Burr and Henry Kissinger, eds., *The Kissinger Transcripts: The Top Secret Talks with Beijing and Moscow* (New York: New Press, 2000); William P. Bundy, *A Tangled Web: The Making of Foreign Policy in the Nixon Presidency*, 1st ed. (New York: Hill and Wang, 1998).

men—which a priori do not seem likely to provide much explanatory leverage on the question would undermine the credibility of the test and confidence in the conclusions. This choice should depend on the nature of the research question or empirical puzzle.

If the research question or empirical puzzle is not new and the researcher has developed his/her theoretical framework as an improvement on existing approaches to that question, the choice is easy. The model should be tested against those existing approaches to see if there is indeed any value-added to the theoretical innovation. For example, balance-of-power theory serves as both the structural realist baseline and the most likely source of alternative hypotheses for Dueck's neoclassical realist theory of US grand strategic adjustment.[81]

In the case of a novel research question, which has not heretofore been investigated directly, there will be no conventional answers to that specific question to use as foils. Nonetheless, if similar questions in different issue areas have been investigated, the researcher can test his/her model against relevant theories that have been used in that context. Narang's study of the nuclear postures of regional powers is illustrative. The research questions he poses about states' nuclear posture choices and their likely effects on nuclear deterrence are arguably novel: to date there had been no studies explicitly addressing those questions. Nonetheless, Narang utilizes theories developed to explain related aspects of nuclear proliferation, deterrence, and coercive diplomacy—chiefly offense-defense theory, offensive realism, and deterrence theory—which suggest plausible alternative hypotheses to the ones Narang derives from his posture optimization theory.[82]

Where there is no body of research on similar questions in cognate issue areas, the researcher will have to be more creative in an attempt to identify credible alternative explanations. In particular, he/she will need to draw out the logical implications of theories devised for other contexts and suggest hypotheses regarding the issue in question for empirical testing. This was Ripsman's strategy for testing his two-staged model of regional peacemaking. While neither realist nor liberal, nor constructivist theories made explicit predictions about the conditions under which regions could transform from regions of conflict to regions of war, Ripsman drew out the implications of relevant theories, such as democratic peace theory, balance-of-power theory, and institutionalism, to construct hypotheses that he tested against the experiences of Western European and Middle

---

81. Dueck, *Reluctant Crusaders.*
82. Narang, *Nuclear Strategy in the Modern Era.*

East peacemaking.[83] In some cases, however, where the issue area is novel and no existing theories speak to it, it would be appropriate to test only the researcher's theory, without comparing its performance against alternative explanations.

HISTORIOGRAPHY, PROCESS TRACING, AND STANDARDS OF EVIDENCE

Since neoclassical realism requires researchers to investigate, among other factors, the role of idiosyncratic state institutions and processes on policy choices, it lends itself to careful, qualitative case studies, rather than large-N quantitative analysis. Quantitative methods are useful for discerning general patterns of correlation, and they can be useful as a reality check to confirm the generalizability of findings based on small-N case studies, but while they may be able to shed light on the sequencing of processes, they cannot determine whether hypothesized independent variables actually had any causal impact on the policy choices of any individual state in a large-N study. To discern a causal impact on foreign policy choices, however, one would need to examine the decision-making processes of particular states to determine why they did what they did and whether the researcher's variables of interest were at all relevant to their decisions.[84] For example, using a dataset evaluating domestic institutions, such as POLITY IV, to provide information on one of the intervening variables we discuss in Chapter 3, a researcher could determine the degree to which states with more constrained executives engage in alliances rather than internal balancing to pursue security.[85] Nonetheless, to determine whether executive constraints or institutional checks and balances actually explain alignment decisions or bargaining strategies with existing allies at any particular period in time, it would be necessary to do case research to assess whether domestic constraints on the executives of specific states were in any way responsible for alliance policies.[86]

83. Norrin M. Ripsman, *Peacemaking from Above, Peace from Below: Ending Conflict between Regional Rivals* (Ithaca, NY: Cornell University Press, 2016).

84. See, for example, Russett, "International Behavior Research."

85. "POLITY IV: Political Regime Characteristics and Transitions, 1800–2013," http://www.systemicpeace.org/polity/polity4.htm (accessed December 7, 2015).

86. See, for example, Galen Jackson, "The Showdown that Wasn't: U.S.-Israeli Relations and American Domestic Politics, 1973–75," *International Security*, vol. 39, no. 4 (2015), pp. 130–169.

The most appropriate strategy for investigating causal chains in specific cases is the process-tracing method described by Alexander George and Andrew Bennett.[87] As George and Bennett write, "The general method of process tracing is to generate and analyze data on the causal mechanisms, or processes, events, actions, expectations, and other intervening variables, that link putative causes to observed effects."[88] In essence, it involves the detailed study of a case to determine: whether or not the hypothesized causal variables were present and/or reached the thresholds specified by the theory being tested; whether they were temporally linked (and appropriately sequenced) with any hypothesized intervening variables and the changes in the dependent variable that one is trying to explain; and whether there is evidence that the purported causal mechanism, and not other factors, actually brought about those changes. For this task, since it is not sufficient merely to look for the correlation of hypothesized variables or even multiple correlations over time, it is necessary to specify the causal mechanisms identified and then carefully discern whether the independent and intervening variables brought about the observed changes in the dependent variable.[89]

Because neoclassical realism requires researchers to answer questions about the reasons why particular policies were selected, it requires them to get inside the black box of the state to be able to answer these questions with reasonable certainty. For this reason, it is incumbent upon researchers, where possible, to go beyond secondary historical sources to do so. There are four key limitations to relying exclusively on secondary sources from historians and political scientists. First, historians often ask different questions from the ones that political scientists ask. Therefore, their accounts might omit or brush over the most useful information for reaching judgments about the key questions neoclassical realists must answer. Second, relying primarily on the research of other political scientists, who

87. George and Bennett, *Case Studies and Theory Development in the Social Sciences*, pp. 205–232; Stephen Van Evera, *Guide to Methods for Students of Political Science*, (Ithaca, NY: Cornell University Press, 1997), pp. 64–67; and James Mahoney, "Process Tracing and Historical Explanation," *Security Studies*, vol. 24, no. 2 (2015), pp. 200–218.

88. Andrew Bennett and Alexander L. George, "Process Tracing in Case Study Research," a paper presented at the MacArthur Foundation Workshop on Case Study Methods, Belfer Center for Science and International Affairs (BCSIA), Harvard University, October 17–19, 1997, Columbia International Affairs Online, http://www.ciaonet.org/wps/bea03/index. html (accessed January 12, 2014). While process tracing can be useful to improve upon simple correlations by searching for multiple congruence over time—or evidence of correlation between the hypothesized IV and the DV at different temporal points of the case study—in effect to cumulate observations of correlation within the same case, its real value added is to uncover evidence of causation, as we discuss below. See Van Evera, *Guide to Methods for Students of Political Science*, pp. 58–67.

89. See Mahoney, "Process Tracing and Historical Explanation," pp. 207–210.

have their own theoretical positions at stake in their analyses, might inadvertently bias the conclusions. Third, while historians may consult tens of thousands of pages of documents in course of their research, they still have to condense their findings into articles and books, which means that readers are encountering only a small fraction of the evidence that pertains to the case, depending on the historian's personal judgment. Fourth, historical accounts often disagree, and present competing accounts citing plausible evidence. If the researcher were merely to read these secondary accounts, he/she would have no way to choose between them, except on the basis of his/her own theoretical predispositions. Consequently, that would lead to a biased and unscientific basis for choosing empirical accounts. Only by engaging the primary source evidence can one truly evaluate the conclusions reached by historians and others on an evidentiary basis and make credible judgments about their plausibility.

The best way for a neoclassical realist researcher to be certain that he/she understands the reasons why state decision makers took the policies that they did, therefore, would be to consult primary sources—such as government documents, memoirs, speeches, decision-maker interviews, and oral histories—in addition to secondary sources. This is far easier in the digital age than it used to be.[90] Whereas in earlier eras primary source research required extensive and expensive visits to multiple government archives, today many primary sources are available easily online and in published volumes in local university libraries. Here we largely focus on government document collections and archival resources in the United States and the United Kingdom, in part because we have individually worked extensively with them and in part because those resources are readily accessible to scholars.[91]

A researcher conducting research on US foreign policy could access the edited document collection *Foreign Relations of the United States* (*FRUS*) either in book form or online.[92] The *FRUS* series is the official

90. See Hal Brands, "Archives and the Study of Nuclear Politics," *H-Diplo/ISSF Forum*, no. 2 (2014), http://issforum.org/ISSF/PDF/ISSF-Forum-2.pdf, pp. 66–76 (accessed May 13, 2015).

91. For an extensive guide to various primary sources in several countries see Marc Trachtenberg, *The Craft of International History: A Guide to Method* (Princeton, NJ: Princeton University Press, 2006), pp. 216–255.

92. Office of the Historian, Bureau of Public Affairs, United States Department of State http://history.state.gov/historicaldocuments, last accessed March 16, 2015. The full *FRUS* volumes for the Truman, Eisenhower, Kennedy, Johnson, Nixon, Ford, and Carter administrations are currently available online in PDF form, along with *1914, Supplement: The World War* and *1917–1972: Public Diplomacy*. Most US federal depository libraries subscribe to bound copies of *FRUS*, dating back to 1861. Digitized versions of earlier *FRUS* volumes are available online and searchable at the University of Wisconsin's Digital Collection http://digital.library.wisc.edu/1711.dl/FRUS, last accessed January 5, 2016.

compilation of government documents pertaining to major US foreign policy decisions and significant diplomatic activities from 1861 to the present. The researcher should also consult the National Security Archive online.[93] Two other online repositories of declassified US documents are the Cold War International History Project (CWIHP) and the Nuclear Proliferation International History Project (NPIHP).[94]

The websites of thirteen US presidential libraries (Herbert Hoover to George W. Bush) have finding aids to their archival holdings and oral history collections, as does the main website for the US National Archives and Record Administration (NARA) in Washington, DC, and College Park, Maryland.[95] NARA and some of the presidential libraries have online document collections. Additionally, the Library of Congress (LOC) in Washington, DC, and certain university libraries and archives across the United States hold the papers of various cabinet and subcabinet officials. These institutions also have finding aids to their archival holdings available online.[96] Finally, researchers can request the declassification of specific classified documents under the 1966 Freedom of Information Act (FOIA), the 1974 Privacy Act, and Mandatory Declassification Review (MDR) per Executive Order 12958.[97]

Those studying British foreign policy could access different published document collections, depending on the era, as well as the UK National Archives website, which includes many key document groups, such as Cabinet meeting minutes.[98] The official and private papers of some British politicians are held in private collections or archives at

93. The National Security Archive www.nsarchive.gwu.edu, headquartered in the Gelman Library at the George Washington University, is one of the leading nonprofit users of the Freedom of Information Act.

94. CWIHP and NPIHP are under the auspices of the Woodrow Wilson International Center for Scholars at the Smithsonian Institution. CWIHP http://www.wilsoncenter.org/program/cold-war-international-history-project and NPIHP http://www.wilsoncenter.org/program/nuclear-proliferation-international-history-project, accessed 9 April 9, 2015.

95. Presidential Libraries Online Finding Aids, US National Archives and Records Administration (NARA), http://www.archives.gov/presidential-libraries/research/finding-aids.html, accessed January 20, 2015. NARA oversees all thirteen presidential libraries and museums.

96. For example, the papers of Henry A. Kissinger and Alexander M. Haig are held at the Library of Congress. The Seeley G. Mudd Manuscript Library at Princeton University holds the papers of John Foster Dulles and James V. Forrestal.

97. See National Archives and Records Administration Freedom of Information Act (FOIA) Reference Guide, http://www.archives.gov/foia/foia-guide.html, accessed March 16, 2015. The websites of most executive branch departments and agencies, as well as those of the presidential libraries, have online guides to submitting FOIA, Privacy Act, and MDR requests.

98. British cabinet papers, including minutes and memoranda from 1915 to 1986, have been digitized and can be located at the National Archives, http://nationalarchives.gov.uk/cabinetpapers, accessed May 11, 2015.

university libraries. These readily available sources can often provide sufficient insight into governmental decisions. Where possible, these could be supplemented by additional research in governmental archives or by interviewing decision-makers and bureaucrats involved in governmental policy during the time under investigation.[99]

Of course, those studying closed societies, which do not publish or even allow reliable access to government documents, will have to lower their standards of evidence, while still striving for a means of opening up the black box of the state in question to understand the causal logic motivating their decisions. Thus, for example, those studying contemporary China or Iran will have to rely on methods deemed appropriate by the leading scholars who study those states, including interviews with government officials, critical reading of government media and press statements, and the use of secondary sources.[100] Those studying historical cases involving closed societies could compensate for a lack of access to government archives by consulting documentary materials made available by outside sources and by gaining third-party insight into the decisions of these states by consulting the archives of governments that interacted with these states. Thus, for example, scholars studying the security policies of Imperial or Nazi Germany could consult the documents translated and edited by Karl Kautsky after World War I, or the documents captured by the Allies after World War II and published by Raymond Sontag and James Beddie.[101] Those studying the Cold War policies of the Soviet Union and China and their respective allies and satellite states could utilize the documents translated and posted on the internet by the CWIHP, the NPIHP, and the National Security Archives and then follow up with US government sources, such as CIA assessments, internal memoranda and reports, diplomatic cables, and correspondence published in *FRUS* or available at the US presidential libraries, NARA, and private paper collections at various other libraries. A valuable resource for scholars studying Iraq's foreign policy during the period of Saddam Hussein's dictatorship (1979–2003) was the collections of captured documents maintained by the Conflict Records

---

99. See various chapters in Layna Mosley, ed., *Interview Research in Political Science* (Ithaca, NY: Cornell University Press, 2013).

100. See, for example, Narang, *Nuclear Strategy in the Modern Era*, pp. 121–153; and Juneau, *Squandered Opportunity*, pp. 92–103.

101. Max Montgelas and Walther Schucking, eds., *Outbreak of the World War: German Documents Collected by Karl Kautsky* (New York: Oxford University Press, 1924); and Raymond James Sontag and James Stuart Beddie, eds., *Nazi-Soviet Relations, 1939–1941: Documents from the Archives of the German Foreign Office* (Washington, DC: United States Department of State, 1948).

Research Center (CRRC) of the National Defense University (NDU). The CRRC, however, closed its door to researchers on June 19, 2015, due to the termination of funding from the Department of Defense.[102] While sample records (often with full English translations of the original Arabic) from the Saddam Hussein Regime Collection and the al Qaeda and Associated Movements Collection remain accessible on the CRRC's website on the NDU server as of this writing (July 2015), the future of the CRRC and its archival collection remain to be determined.[103]

A scholar studying the decision-making process of a country in whose language he/she has little or no facility should follow a similar strategy. While it would be preferable to examine the decision-making documents in their original language to ascertain that one understands their meaning correctly, scholars who cannot do so should make every effort to assess the decision-making rationale, including some of the following: (1) consulting published translations available as appendices in secondary sources or on the web through a center such as the CWIHP; (2) hiring a research assistant fluent in the language in question to conduct research and translate documents or conduct interviews; (3) engaging a co-author who can conduct that component of the research; and/or (4) assessing the information that can be gleaned from the archives and sources of another country with insight into the country of focus's decisions. The goal, in other words, is not to take shortcuts, but to make an earnest effort to uncover the true motivations of the state and the relative causal impact of the systemic independent and domestic-level intervening variables identified by neoclassical realism and the specific neoclassical realist theory being tested versus that of other variables highlighted by contending approaches to foreign policy and international politics.

At the same time, while comprehensive analysis of all available primary source materials would be ideal, we are not advocating that neoclassical researchers must all become historians or spend years of exhaustive research on each of their case studies to make certain that they have consulted every last document available on each case. Nor is it necessary for every researcher to engage in expensive archival research in multiple locations and, potentially, countries. That would be too onerous a standard and would actually impede scholarship. Instead, we recommend the

102. Michael R. Gordon, "Archive of Captured Enemy Documents Closes," *New York Times*, June 21, 2015, http://www.nytimes.com/2015/06/22/world/middleeast/archive-of-captured-terrorist-qaeda-hussein-documents-shuts-down.html?_r=0.

103. Conflict Records Research Center (CRRC), Institute for National Strategic Studies, National Defense University, http://crrc.dodlive.mil/2014/11/13/crrc-status-update-november-2014/, accessed July 2, 2015.

following steps. First, conduct an extensive search of the secondary literature on the case to determine areas of consensus, axes of debate, and key questions that remain unaddressed or unresolved. Second, consult available published document collections, online archives, and memoirs to see what they indicate about the scholarly debates and the researcher's essential research questions that might remain unaddressed or inadequately addressed by the secondary literature—and, of course, whether documentary materials challenge or undermine the conventional wisdom— as well as whether there remain key questions about which they fail to provide adequate information. Third, determine whether additional archival research would be feasible, desirable, and worth the additional time and expense. Finally, after conducting any additional research (if any was deemed necessary), report findings with an acknowledgement that access to additional sources might conceivably have altered the case findings. It would then be for subsequent researchers—both historians and political scientists—to verify the conclusions based on the material consulted, as well as additional relevant materials that might not have been consulted. That would be the qualitative research equivalent of replication.[104]

All of this means, of course, that researchers cannot hope to achieve certainty in their research. As mentioned earlier, soft positivism implies that researchers cannot conclusively "prove" or "disprove" the broader theoretical claims they investigate; the best they can do is offer strong confirming or disconfirming evidence. But even their understandings of the cases they study must necessarily be subject to a discount rate, since they cannot be certain that accessing additional information would not alter their conclusion. Therefore, the research should not speak in terms of certainty, but instead attempt to reach plausible conclusions and make plausible arguments consistent with the evidence.

Finally, the researcher must be scientific and open-minded about the research. While he/she might have forged the theory based on deductive expectations, if the case studies indicate that the hypothesized causal mechanism did not bring about the case outcome and that other mechanisms did, the only legitimate courses of action open are to discard or modify the theory to explain the case results. In this regard, the detailed case studies may provide an opportunity to revisit the theoretical assumptions through an additional process of induction based on careful research.

104. See Andrew Bennett and Colin Elman, "Case Study Methods and the International Relations Subfield," *Comparative Political Studies*, vol. 40, no. 2 (2007), pp. 170–195, at pp. 188–189.

CONCLUSION

This chapter has provided a discussion of the process of neoclassical realist research. It details every major step of the research process from selecting a research question and theory construction to case studies and empirical analysis. The next chapter will consider the value-added of neoclassical realism by concentrating on four key debates in the international relations literature and analyzing how a neoclassical realist approach could resolve these debates. In the process, we will utilize and illustrate the methodological advice that we developed in this chapter.

CHAPTER 6

Resolving Key Theoretical Debates Using Neoclassical Realism

In this chapter, we demonstrate the utility of neoclassical realist theory by considering how it could be used to elucidate and even resolve several persistent debates in international relations. To this end, we consider what our approach would add to the debates between realists over the survival strategies of threatened states, between balance-of-power realists and power preponderance theorists over whether hegemony leads to cooperation or balancing, between liberals and economic nationalists over whether states prefer free trade or protectionism, and between ideational theorists and materialists over whether ideas or material interests determine states' policy choices.

We choose these debates because they have the potential to demonstrate the uniqueness and value added of neoclassical realist theory vis-à-vis a broad spectrum of other approaches to international relations. Specifically, we show that attention to the unique domestic circumstances of states can add greater nuance to realist theories of state behavior and systemic outcomes, while a focus on whether states face permissive or restrictive international environments can elucidate when ideational and economic interests are able to determine policy choices and outcomes. Along the way, we build upon our discussion of methodology in Chapter 5, including the formulation of research questions, the selection of appropriate structural realist baselines for the phenomena to be explained, and the identification of the relevant intervening variables for neoclassical realist theory. Our purpose here is not to conduct detailed case studies, which would detract from the theory-building focus of the book, but rather to provide illustrative examples of how neoclassical realism might be used to clarify or resolve these central debates.

We selected these debates for several reasons. First, they reflect some of the core and unresolved theoretical debates in the field of international relations, both within and across approaches. Second, these debates vary along a number of continuums including so-called high politics and low politics, state security strategies and trade policy, permissive and restrictive international environments, and materialist and ideational models of international politics. Third, the diversity of these issue areas allows us to demonstrate that neoclassical realism has a distinct explanation and consistency across these debates, including the primacy of systemic-structure over domestic-unit level pressures, the significance of the variation in strategic environments, and the conditions under which domestic politics and ideas can matter.

SURVIVAL STRATEGIES FOR THREATENED STATES: THE IMPORTANCE OF THE THREATENED STATE'S POLICY ENVIRONMENT

Neoclassical and structural realists agree that states are responsive to shifts in the relative distribution of material capabilities. The core hypothesis of Kenneth Waltz's balance-of-power theory is that threatened states tend to balance against dangerous accumulations of power by forging alliances with weaker states (external balancing), by increasing their own military capabilities (internal balancing), or in some cases, through a combination of the two. Stephen Walt's refinement, balance-of-threat theory, posits that states do not merely respond to shifts in the distribution of material capabilities, but instead respond to shifts in the level of external threat, which is a composite of other states' aggregate power, offensive military capabilities, proximity, and perceived intent. In general, states tend to balance against threatening states or coalitions.[1] Thus two major structural realist theories see balancing behavior and the reoccurrence of systemic balances of power as general tendencies in international politics. Moreover, they also see balancing behavior as a normative ideal for the foreign and security policies of threatened states.[2]

---

1. Kenneth N. Waltz, *Theory of International Politics* (Reading, MA: Addison-Wesley, 1979), pp. 124–128; and Stephen M. Walt, *The Origins of Alliances* (Ithaca, NY: Cornell University Press, 1987), pp. 28–33.

2. See Jack S. Levy, "Balances and Balancing: Concepts, Propositions, Concepts, and Research Design," in *Realism and the Balancing of Power: A New Debate*, ed. John Vasquez and Colin Elman (Upper Saddle River, NJ: Pearson, 2002); and Daniel Nexon, "The Balance of Power in Balance," *World Politics*, vol. 62, no. 1 (2009), pp. 330–359.

Several key questions remain unresolved. When do states respond to external threats by balancing and when do they employ other strategies, such as bandwagoning? When states do balance, under what conditions are they more likely to do so internally and when will they rely on others? In other words, how do vulnerable states make trade-offs between arms build-ups, which offer the advantage of increasing that state's own military power without a loss of autonomy, but which are also costly and take time to bring to fruition, and alliance formation, which offers the advantage of an affordable short-term capability aggregation against a common adversary, but also entails a loss of autonomy vis-à-vis allies?[3] When do states choose balancing over bandwagoning? To this point, the debate between structural realism and *Innenpolitik* theories divides solely on external/internal lines. Structural realists argue that the choice is highly constrained and depends on the state's position in the international system. Thus, while Waltz argues that states should always prefer to balance against more powerful states or coalitions rather than bandwagon with them, Walt argues that the choice between balancing and bandwagoning depends solely on the nature of the external environment states face.[4] States generally balance against threats, unless faced with constraints related to the international system or their position in it. In particular, they will select a strategy of bandwagoning with the threatening state only if they are too small to add enough material power to tip the balance against the challenger, if there are no available alliance partners, or if it is too late to avoid war.[5]

In contrast, *Innenpolitik* approaches argue that states respond to similar external threats in different ways, depending on the nature of their dominant governing coalition and its parochial interests.[6] For example, Benjamin Fordham contends the United States' decision to balance against the Soviet Union with a militarized version of containment between 1949 and 1951 resulted from bargaining among different economic sectors (e.g., manufacturing exporters, banks with large international loans, and investment firms), the Truman administration, and the Congress over the distribution of benefits, rather than simply a "strategic"

---

3. On the trade-offs between arms (internal balancing) and alliance formation (external balancing), see James D. Morrow, "Arms Versus Allies: Trade-Offs in the Search for Security," *International Organization*, vol. 47, no. 2 (1993), pp. 207–233.

4. Waltz, *Theory of International Politics*, pp. 125–128.

5. Walt, *Origins of Alliances*, pp. 28–33.

6. The term *Innenpolitik* subsumes several different research programs (e.g., democratic peace, diversionary theories, bargaining theories, etc.). Here our focus is largely on political economy theories or models of grand strategic adjustment and foreign policy behavior.

response to the military capabilities of the Soviet Union and its allies.[7] Kevin Narizny argues that the leaders of rising and declining great powers are not neutral arbiters of the "national interests," but instead act as agents of domestic coalitional interests. In his view, the economic interests that back governing parties largely determined whether the United States and Great Britain pursued expansionist or status quo policies, such as balancing, in their respective cores and peripheries from the 1860s until the outbreak of World War II.[8] Similarly, Peter Trubowitz contends that the subjective costs and benefits of investing in defense over social welfare policies that benefit economic sectors generally override international systemic pressures (the degree of "geopolitical slack") in the formulation of the United States' grand strategy. Balancing strategies, whether in the form of rearmament or defensive war, are likely only when the United States has scarce geopolitical slack and when the party in power in Washington favors "guns" over "butter." Conversely, when the United States has scarce geopolitical slack, but the governing party favors welfare policies that benefit specific economic sectors, the United States pursues satisficing strategies such as appeasement, external balancing (alliance formation), or buck passing.[9]

Neoclassical realism suggests that timely and efficient balancing strategies are more difficult for states to undertake and are probably a less common phenomenon in international politics than either balance-of-power theory or balance-of-threat theory would predict.[10] Instead of being the "default" strategic response to aggregate shifts in relative power or the level of external threat, the ability and the willingness of threatened states to balance is contingent upon both systemic and unit-level factors.[11]

7. Benjamin O. Fordham, *Building the Cold War Consensus: The Political Economy of U.S. National Security Policy, 1949–51* (Ann Arbor: University of Michigan Press, 1998).

8. Kevin Narizny, *The Political Economy of Grand Strategy* (Ithaca, NY: Cornell University Press, 2007).

9. Peter Trubowitz, *Politics and Strategy: Partisan Ambition and American Statecraft* (Princeton, NJ: Princeton University Press, 2011), pp. 16–37.

10. A variety of historians and international relations theorists—both realists and critics of realism—question the prevalence of balancing behavior and the recurrence of power equilibrium in modern Europe, as well as in various (historical) non-European international systems. See Paul W. Schroeder, *The Transformation of European Politics, 1763–1848* (Oxford and New York: Oxford University Press, 1994); Stuart J. Kaufman, Richard Little, and William Curti Wohlforth, eds., *The Balance of Power in World History* (New York: Palgrave Macmillan, 2007); and David C. Kang, *East Asia Before the West: Five Centuries of Trade and Tribute* (New York: Columbia University Press, 2010).

11. One neoclassical realist does see systemic balances of power as a natural equilibrium and contends that major powers will eventually balance against the United States (the current unipole). See Christopher Layne, *The Peace of Illusions: American Grand Strategy from 1940 to the Present* (Ithaca, NY: Cornell University Press, 2006).

Moreover, neoclassical realism can mediate between structural realism and *Innenpolitik* theories by building upon the insights of both in a systematic manner, privileging international structure.

Neoclassical realist theory specifies the strategic circumstances under which vulnerable states, or more properly the foreign policy executives (FPEs) that act on their behalf, might consider balancing or bandwagoning strategies in the first place. Unlike Waltz's balance-of-power theory and Walt's balance-of-threat theory, which portray the choice between balancing and bandwagoning as solely a function of position in the international system, neoclassical realism posits that in the first instance, states make alignment choices with reference to their external environment, namely anticipated shifts in the relative distribution of power or levels of external threat. However, rather than simply explaining deviations from the predictions of balance-of-power and balance-of-threat theories, neoclassical realism accounts for variation in the timing, the intensity, and the specific components of the balancing strategies pursued.

As noted in Chapter 2, permissive strategic environments entail relatively minor external impediments on a state's ability to use material power to achieve its interests in the international arena, no imminent or high-level threats, a broad range of strategies that might be appropriate, and longer time horizons for states to respond to potential threats and opportunities. Restrictive strategic environments entail greater systemic impediments on a state's use of material power, serious and imminent threats, shorter time horizons for responding to threats and seizing opportunities, and therefore a more restricted set of viable strategic responses. All else being equal, neoclassical realism suggests that a state's FPE may choose to balance or select another strategy in a permissive strategic environment but is more likely to balance or to bandwagon as their strategic environments become more restrictive. This should especially be true in a restrictive environment under conditions of high clarity, when the system provides clear information about the nature of the threat, its time frame, and the optimal policy response.

Yet, in any strategic environment, the domestic intervening variables we identified in Chapter 3 can shape and constrain the nature of the state's responses to external pressures. Aaron Friedberg, William Wohlforth, and Thomas Christensen, for example, conclude that elite calculations and perceptions of power play a key intervening role between systemic imperatives and the formulation of foreign and defense policies.[12] More

---

12. See Gideon Rose, "Neoclassical Realism and Theories of Foreign Policy," *World Politics*, vol. 51, no. 1 (1998), pp. 144–172; Aaron L. Friedberg, *The Weary Titan: Britain and the Experience of Relative Decline, 1895–1905* (Princeton, NJ: Princeton University Press,

recent neoclassical realist works take these insights further by explicat-
ing how the degree of elite consensus (or lack thereof) about perceptions
of external threat, the components of other states' capabilities seen as
most dangerous, and the time frame for anticipated power shifts influence
states' willingness to pursue either balancing or various non-balancing
strategies.

Schweller's underbalancing theory posits elite consensus about the
nature and the magnitude of external threats as a proximate cause of the
states' response or non-response to changes in a state's strategic environment. Schweller argues, "Balancing behavior requires the existence of a
strong consensus among elites that an external threat exists and must be
checked by either arms or allies or both."[13] He does not expect states to
balance against threats when there is: "(1) significant elite disagreement
in terms of threat perception; (2) elite consensus that a threat exists, but
disagreement over the appropriate remedy . . . or (3) elite consensus to
adopt other policy options such as appeasement, bandwagoning, buck-
passing, or bilateral or multilateral binding strategies."[14]

Elite perception and consensus about the nature and magnitude of
external threat are merely preconditions for states to undertake timely
balancing strategies. Neoclassical realism's second contribution to the
balancing versus bandwagoning debate pertains to the politics of resource
extraction and domestic mobilization. Balance-of-power and balance-
of-threat theories assume that states can simply mobilize their material
and human resources in response to international threats and opportunities. This is especially the case for the great powers. Waltz argues that
"the economic, military, and other capabilities of nations cannot be sec-
tored and separately weighted."[15] Whether or not a state ranks among
the great powers depends on how it scores on all of the following: "size of
population and territory, resource endowment, economic capability, military strength, political stability and competence."[16] However, he never
addresses the question of why some great powers are better able to translate their resource endowments and economic capabilities into actualized

1988); William Curti Wohlforth, *The Elusive Balance: Power and Perceptions During the
Cold War* (Ithaca, NY: Cornell University Press, 1993); and Thomas J. Christensen, *Useful
Adversaries: Grand Strategy, Domestic Mobilization, and Sino-American Conflict, 1947–1958*
(Princeton, NJ: Princeton University Press, 1996).

13. Randall L. Schweller, "Unanswered Threats: A Neoclassical Realist Theory of
Underbalancing," *International Security*, vol. 29, no. 2 (2004), pp. 159–202, at 170–171;
and idem., *Unanswered Threats: Political Constraints on the Balance of Power* (Princeton,
NJ: Princeton University Press, 2006), pp. 47–48.

14. Schweller, *Unanswered Threats*, p. 49.

15. Waltz, *Theory of International Politics*, p. 131.

16. Ibid.

military capabilities than are others. Nor does he elaborate on what constitutes political stability and competence. While Walt argues that states tend to balance against threats rather than simply power, his theory does not explain how vulnerable states mobilize their own resources to undertake balancing strategies. Meanwhile, he views bandwagoning as a strategy of last resort for militarily weak states and/or states that lack potential allies.[17]

Neoclassical realists directly address the importance of resource mobilization. Zakaria and Christensen draw a distinction between national power—which encompasses the economic, technological, and human resources within society—and state power (or national political power)—which is a function of national power and state strength and reflects the state's ability to mobilize those resources in support of policy.[18] Subsequent neoclassical realists further develop the concept of state power. Friedberg, for example, examines how the US federal government extracted (or failed to extract) money and manpower and then mobilized arms manufacturing, industry, and technological development in order to confront the Soviet threat during the early Cold War. The strategies pursued resulted from elite threat perception as well as a series of political bargains reached among the Truman, Eisenhower, and Kennedy administrations, the Congress, and various economic sectors and interest groups, all of whom subscribed to what Friedberg terms an anti-statist ideological tradition.[19] Taliaferro suggests that the willingness and the ability of states to emulate the successful military technologies and practices of the great powers (a form of internal balancing) are functions of levels of external vulnerability as mediated through the extractive and mobilization capacity of existing state institutions.[20] In addition to a lack of elite consensus and cohesion, Schweller argues that vulnerable states' tendency to underbalance external threats is also a function of the degree of social fragmentation and regime vulnerability. Extremely incoherent states, defined by Schweller as "oversized, ethnically stratified states, which typically reside in the Third World," are likely to underbalance in response to external threats due to their incapacity to leverage resources,

17. Walt, *Origins of Alliances*, pp. 263–266.

18. Fareed Zakaria, *From Wealth to Power: The Unusual Origins of America's World Role* (Princeton, NJ: Princeton University Press, 1998), pp. 37–39; and Christensen, *Useful Adversaries*, pp. 14–22.

19. Aaron L. Friedberg, *In the Shadow of the Garrison State: America's Anti-Statism and Its Cold War Grand Strategy* (Princeton, NJ: Princeton University Press, 2000), pp. 40–75.

20. Jeffrey W. Taliaferro, "Neoclassical Realism and Resource Extraction: State Building for Future War," in *Neoclassical Realism, the State, and Foreign Policy*, ed. Steven E. Lobell, Norrin M. Ripsman, and Jeffrey W. Taliaferro (Cambridge: Cambridge University Press, 2009), pp. 194–226.

with a "high probability of further state disintegration (e.g., civil war or revolution)."[21]

Thus, for neoclassical realists, a state's response to external threats is determined by an interaction between the external environment and unit level constraints. Like structural realists, we assume that, all things being equal, states (i.e., their FPEs) would prefer to balance rather than under-balance or bandwagon, and prefer internal balancing to external balancing.[22] Nonetheless, they cannot always do so, because of a failure to agree on the nature of the external environment. Furthermore, depending on state-society relations, domestic institutions, and strategic culture, they cannot always mobilize the necessary resources to pursue the balancing strategy they prefer. Consequently, structural realists are incorrect because states cannot balance as fluidly and automatically as they expect. Yet, *Innenpolitik* approaches incorrectly assume that the external environment does not impose preferred strategies on states. Instead, the emergence of an external threat does condition state behavior, but the policy effects of that threat will be moderated by the unit-level intervening variables we identify in Chapter 3.

THE CONSEQUENCES OF HEGEMONY: THE IMPORTANCE OF THE HEGEMON'S POLICY ENVIRONMENT

A related debate between realist scholars concerns the consequences of unipolarity for other states and for the international system as a whole.[23]

---

21. Schweller, *Unanswered Threats*, p. 63.

22. Not all neoclassical realists would subscribe to balancing theories as a baseline behavior, as we indicate in Chapter 5. For example, Brooks and Wohlforth contend that unipolarity is durable and that extreme concentration of power in the hands of the United States is unlikely to provoke balancing responses. Stephen G. Brooks and William C. Wohlforth, "Assessing the Balance," *Cambridge Review of International Affairs*, vol. 24, no. 2 (2011), pp. 201–219; and idem., *World out of Balance: International Relations and the Challenge of American Primacy* (Princeton, NJ: Princeton University Press, 2008), pp. 23–50, 60–97. Elsewhere, Wohlforth and his collaborators (who include both self-described realists and critics of realism) conduct eight case studies of balancing and balancing failure in international systems that comprise 2,000 years of international politics in the Middle East, the Mediterranean basin, Central and South America, East and South Asia. They find that, contrary to balance-of-power theory, hegemonies form regularly and that second tier states rarely pursue sustained balancing strategies. William C. Wohlforth et al., "Testing Balance-of-Power Theory in World History," *European Journal of International Relations*, vol. 13, no. 2 (2007), pp. 155–188; and Kaufman, Little, and Wohlforth, *Balance of Power in World History*.

23. This debate is related to the previous discussion because the response to hegemony represents a special case of responding to external threats either through balancing

Power preponderance theorists, such as Robert Gilpin and William Wohlforth, argue that unipolarity offers the greatest prospects for both durability and peace in an anarchic international system.[24] When one state possesses a preponderance of political, economic, and military resources, it can use its power to provide order and predictability to the world. In particular, it provides public goods and can establish global rules and norms, and enforce these by providing selective political and economic incentives to those who follow them and coercing those who do not. Since they are considerably weaker than the hegemon, other states have little choice but to cooperate with the unipole's rules, or at least refrain from direct challenges. Needless to say, the hegemon is not altruistic. It provides stability because it benefits most from order, which perpetuates its power, especially as it sets rules that benefit itself disproportionately.[25] Only when a rising challenger threatens the hegemon's dominance do instability and the risk of war rise, either because the challenger tries to topple the leader or because the hegemon initiates a preventive war against the challenger to preserve its dominance.[26] According to this view, therefore, unipolarity is constructive and desirable.[27]

Conversely, Waltz and other balance-of-power theorists assume that unipolarity is fleeting, dangerous, and rare. Under unipolarity, the dominant state has no check on its power. Consequently, it can act in a

(competition), bandwagoning (cooperation), or some other strategy. Nonetheless, our discussion differs in three important ways. First, the debate here is not about the threatened state's strategic response, but about the systemic outcome of hegemony in terms of its durability and peacefulness. Consequently, it represents a shift in emphasis to the longer-term range of our dependent variable. Second, our explanation here will hinge upon the threatening state's (i.e., the hegemon's) domestic constraints, rather than those of the threatened state, as our discussion in the previous section did. Finally, because of the longer time-frame associated with systemic outcomes rather than national policy responses, the intervening variables that we draw upon in our discussion are somewhat different, with more of an emphasis on strategic culture, institutions, and state-society relations than perceptual variables, which played an important role in our previous discussion.

24. We follow Nuno Monteiro in eschewing the vague term "stability" in favor of the more precise elements of durability and peace. Nuno P. Monteiro, "Unrest Assured: Why Unipolarity Is Not Peaceful," *International Security*, vol. 36, no. 3 (2011–2012), pp. 9–40.

25. Robert Gilpin, *War and Change in World Politics* (Cambridge: Cambridge University, 1981); William Wohlforth, "The Stability of a Unipolar World," *International Security*, vol. 24, no. 1 (1999), pp. 5–41; and Brooks and Wohlforth, *World out of Balance*.

26. For the variant of power transition theory that blames war on the rising powers, see A. F. K. Organski, *World Politics*, 2nd ed. (New York: Alfred A. Knopf, 1968); and A. F. K. Organski and Jacek Kugler, *The War Ledger* (Chicago: University of Chicago Press, 1980). Gilpin argues that the declining hegemon is more likely to wage a preventive war. Gilpin, *War and Change in World Politics*.

27. Stephen G. Brooks, G. John Ikenberry, and William C. Wohlforth, "Don't Come Home, America: The Case against Retrenchment," *International Security*, vol. 37, no. 3 (2012), pp. 5–51.

predatory manner toward all other states with impunity, as no other state or combination of states has the capacity to resist its power. "The powerful state may, and the United States does, think of itself as acting for the sake of peace, justice, and the well-being of the world," Waltz observes, "These terms, however, are defined to the liking of the powerful, which may conflict with the preferences and interests of others."[28] For example, in March 2003, the United States invaded Iraq despite the vocal opposition of some its longstanding NATO allies, principally France and Germany, and without the sanction of the United Nations Security Council, where permanent members Russia and China signaled they would veto any resolution authorizing the use of force to remove Saddam Hussein's regime. A hegemon thus represents by far the greatest threat to the survival of other states, particularly those on the cusp of becoming great powers or suspected of acquiring nuclear weapons.[29] For this reason, Waltz expects states eventually to balance against any state that threatens to approach global hegemony and to unite against any state that were to obtain system dominance, in order to restore an international balance as soon as possible. Instead, he argues that an international balance of power, preferably a bipolar one, is far more stable than unipolarity.[30]

Is it possible to square these two positions? Are they completely irreconcilable or can we discern conditions under which each argument is valid? We contend that neoclassical realist theory can provide guidance on when hegemony is likely to lead to war and turmoil, and when it is likely to enhance peace and durability. In essence, the problem is that the impact of unipolarity on other states and the behavior of the system as a whole are indeterminate unless one considers the domestic political context of the dominant state.[31]

Unlike structuralists, such as Waltz and Gilpin, neoclassical realists maintain that the international distribution of power rarely dictates a single behavioral response or grand strategic approach for states to

28. Kenneth N. Waltz, "Structural Realism after the Cold War," in *America Unrivaled: The Future of the Balance of Power*, ed. G. John Ikenberry (Ithaca, NY: Cornell University Press, 2002), p. 52.

29. Nuno P. Monteiro, *Theory of Unipolar Politics* (New York: Cambridge University Press, 2014), pp. 179–204.

30. Kenneth N. Waltz, "The Emerging Structure of International Politics," *International Security*, vol. 18, no. 2 (1993), pp. 44–79; and John J. Mearsheimer, *The Tragedy of Great Power Politics* (New York: W. W. Norton, 2001), pp. 415–416. For similar arguments, see Duncan Snidal, "The Limits of Hegemonic Stability Theory," *International Organizations*, vol. 39, no. 4 (1985), pp. 579–614.

31. See, for example, Norrin M. Ripsman, "Domestic Practices and Balancing: Integrating Practice into Neoclassical Realism," in *International Practices*, ed. Vincent Pouliot and Emanuel Adler (Cambridge: Cambridge University Press, 2011), pp. 200–228, at pp. 206–207.

pursue. While unipolarity presents unparalleled opportunities for the hegemon to expand and pursue its interests in a maximalist and predatory manner, Waltz makes unwarranted assumptions about the ability of any potential hegemon to extract and utilize its resources for unlimited expansion.[32]

As we have argued in Chapter 3, however, different domestic political structures and circumstances, reflected in our four clusters of intervening variables, affect states' capacities to enact policy and mobilize national resources to implement policy. If the hegemon's strategic culture would enable aggressive expansion and its FPE would be unencumbered by restrictive domestic institutions or state-society networks, the hegemon would indeed be able to act as Waltz expects, with the attendant consequences for stability within the international system, if it wished to do so. If the Soviet Union had emerged as the winner of the Cold War, for example, its less-constrained security executive, which for decades was able to take and implement decisions with few domestic constraints and which had pursued an aggressive policy within its sphere of influence, should have alarmed other states and provoked balancing and resistance. Similarly, if we were to imagine a thought experiment in which contemporary China were the global hegemon and not the United States, we would expect the dynamics of international politics to be qualitatively different.

Nonetheless, if the dominant state's strategic culture would act as a brake on unlimited expansion and/or if state-society relations and domestic political institutions would restrict the FPE's ability to embark upon and mobilize resources for a policy of predation, the degree of threat that the hegemon would pose to the system and to other states would be muted. Under these circumstances, over time other states would recognize the hegemon's domestic constraints and fear it less. The risks associated with continued unipolarity would thus diminish for other states, which could then seek the gains that hegemonic stability theorists identify by cooperating with the unipole.

The American experience in the post–Cold War world is instructive in this regard. In the 1990s, despite overwhelming preponderance and the absence of a great power competitor on the horizon, the George H. W. Bush and Clinton administrations faced considerable domestic constraints. In the absence of any serious international threats, facing a very permissive environment, the US national security state had been

---

32. As Waltz observes, "A dominant power acts internationally truly when the spirit moves it." Waltz, "Structural Realism after the Cold War," p. 63.

scaled back, with a domestic preference for reduced defense spending and a focus on the domestic economy.[33] Consequently, Congress and even the media and US interest groups—long considered largely irrelevant to the conduct of foreign policy during the Cold War—began to play a greater role in the construction of policy.[34] The checks and balances on US foreign policy, which had been incrementally restored after the excesses of the Vietnam War, could now operate with confidence given the low threat, permissive environment.[35] The result was a more constrained, consultative hegemon, which eschewed unilateralism for greater multilateralism. The administration of George H. W. Bush did wage war against Iraq in 1991, but it did so within a broad coalition endorsed by the UN Security Council. The Clinton administration made multilateral consultation a hallmark of its foreign policy.[36] As a result, other states— particularly Western liberal states, which perceived little threat from such a constrained hegemon—were relatively comfortable with American leadership and cooperated with it.

In this regard, John Owen explains the absence of a balancing coalition against the United States in the 1990s not in terms of hegemony itself, but of the liberal and restrained character of American hegemony and the extent to which it consulted and cooperated with its allies, rather than taking advantage of them.[37] In his view, due to restrained American hegemony, "Liberal elites the world over tend to perceive a relatively broad coincidence of interest between their country and other liberal countries. They tend to interpret the United States as benign and devote few resources to counterbalancing it."[38] John Ikenberry echoes Owen's

33. Laurence J. Korb, "U.S. Defense Spending After the Cold War: Fact and Fiction," in *Holding the Line: U.S. Defense Alternatives for the Early 21st Century*, ed. Cindy Williams (Cambridge, MA: MIT Press, 2001), pp. 35–54, at p. 47.

34. See James McCormack, "Interest Groups and the Media in Post-Cold War US Foreign Policy," in *After the End: Making US Foreign Policy in the Post-Cold War World*, ed. James M. Scott (Durham, NC: Duke University Press, 1998), pp. 170–198.

35. On the post-Vietnam, post-Watergate constraints on US foreign policy, see Andrew Rudalevige, *The New Imperial Presidency: Renewing Presidential Power after Watergate* (Ann Arbor: University of Michigan Press, 2006), pp. 101–138; and David P. Auerswald and Peter F. Cowhey, "Ballotbox Diplomacy: The War Powers Resolution and the Use of Force," *International Studies Quarterly*, vol. 41, no. 3 (1997), pp. 505–528.

36. Secretary of State Madeleine Albright described Clinton's foreign policy as "assertive multilateralism." Madeleine K. Albright, "Myths of Peacekeeping, Statement before the Subcommittee on International Security, International Organizations, and Human Rights of the House Committee on Foreign Affairs, 24 June 1993," *State Department Dispatch*, vol. 4, no. 26 (1993), p. 464.

37. John M. Owen IV, "Transnational Liberalism and US Primacy," *International Security*, vol. 26, no. 3 (2001–2002), pp. 117–152; and idem., *Liberal Peace, Liberal War: American Politics and International Security* (Ithaca, NY: Cornell University Press, 1997).

38. Ibid., p. 121.

argument to some extent, arguing that the liberal character of the United States—which makes American decision making more transparent—coupled with the liberal international institutions that bind the United States from without, restrain the United States as a hegemon.[39]

Our neoclassical realist argument is different, however, from Owen's and Ikenberry's liberal argument that the United States poses little threat to others because of its liberal democratic nature. Instead, we argue that any hegemon—democratic or other—would pose less of a threat to the other states of the system to the extent that it faces domestic political constraints on its use of power. We are thus closer to T. V. Paul, who couches his argument in terms of domestic constraints, rather than liberal democracy. He contends that other leading states in the early post–Cold War world engaged in soft balancing against the United States, rather than traditional military-oriented hard balancing, in part because of domestic political constraints on the US national security state which prevent overly aggressive, predatory behavior that threatens the sovereignty of other states. He writes, "U.S. power seems to be limited by a multitude of internal and external factors, thus making the United States a 'constrained hegemon.'"[40] While liberal democratic states may, on average, face greater constraints than others, this is not always the case.[41] Thus, contra Owen and Ikenberry, liberalism should not always be a guarantee of restraint.

In this regard, in the wake of the September 11 terrorist attacks the United States, although still a liberal democracy, has begun to escape its domestic constraints.[42] Consequently, US hegemony has grown more threatening to other states. As a consequence of these attacks, the institutional restraints on American national security policy diminished, to be replaced by the Patriot Act, the Bush Doctrine emphasizing "pre-emption" and the use of force, and norms that discouraged domestic interference with executive efforts to secure the United States from al-Qaeda

39. G. John Ikenberry, *After Victory: Institutions, Strategic Restraint, and the Rebuilding of Order after Major Wars* (Princeton, NJ: Princeton University Press, 2001), pp. 61–79.

40. T. V. Paul, "Soft Balancing in the Age of U.S. Primacy," *International Security*, vol. 30, no. 1 (2005), pp. 46–71, quote at p. 53.

41. Norrin M. Ripsman, *Peacemaking by Democracies: The Effect of State Autonomy on the Post-World-War Settlements* (University Park: Penn State University Press, 2002).

42. Some, like Eric Hamilton, argue that domestic institutions are shaped by the external environments that states face. Therefore, states in dangerous international environments are likely to develop institutions that provide maximal autonomy over foreign affairs. In contrast, those that face permissive environments are likely to develop more constraining domestic institutions. See, for example, Eric J. Hamilton, "International Politics and Domestic Institutional Change: The Rise of Executive War-Making Autonomy in the United States," PhD diss., School of International Relations, University of Southern California, 2015. For the purposes of this book, we are not engaging this debate and are simply treating existing domestic arrangements as exogenous.

and global terrorism. The George W. Bush administration was subsequently able to flex its military might at will, replacing multilateralism with unilateralism and displaying a willingness to use force in the face of opposition from not only the UN, but also American allies within NATO. A consequence has been decreased cooperation from Washington's allies in the Western world—witness French, German, and Belgian efforts to stymie American efforts to build a coalition against Iraq—and increasing challenges from China and Russia. And relations between the United States and non-liberal great powers China and Russia have deteriorated considerably.[43]

In recent years, the domestic constraints on US power have started to increase again. In particular, the Bush administration faced record federal budget deficits, heightened partisanship in Congress—which has persisted and grown in the Obama administration—greater congressional scrutiny of the executive branch, and the 2008 financial crisis. This reassertion of US domestic constraints, ironically, could portend a less threatening hegemony in the future.

A neoclassical realist approach, which considers not only systemic pressures, but also the intervening domestic-level variables that act as a transmission belt for systemic stimuli, thus provides a clearer picture of the implications of unipolarity than purely systemic theories.

FREE TRADE VERSUS PROTECTIONISM: THE INTERACTION BETWEEN THE SECURITY ENVIRONMENT AND DOMESTIC COALITIONS

When do states pursue free trade as opposed to protectionist trade policies? Liberal approaches maintain that trade policy depends on the domestic coalition of interests that capture the state.[44] An internationalist

---

43. See, for example, Robert Anthony Pape, "Soft Balancing Against the United States," *International Security*, vol. 30, no. 1 (2005), pp. 7–45; Paul, "Soft Balancing in the Age of U.S. Primacy"; Judith Kelley, "Strategic Non-Cooperation as Soft Balancing: Why Iraq Was Not Just About Iraq," *International Politics*, vol. 42, no. 2 (2005), pp. 153–173; and Weiqing Song, "Feeling Safe, Being Strong: China's Strategy of Soft Balancing through the Shanghai Cooperation Organization," *International Politics*, vol. 50, no. 5 (2013), pp. 664–685.

44. Peter Gourevitch, *Politics in Hard Times: Comparative Responses to International Economic Crises* (Ithaca, NY: Cornell University Press, 1986); Jeffrey A. Frieden, *Debt, Development, and Democracy: Modern Political Economy and Latin America, 1865–1985* (Princeton, NJ: Princeton University Press, 1991); Fordham, *Building the Cold War Consensus*; Etel Solingen, *Regional Orders at Century's Dawn: Global and Domestic Influences on Grand Strategy* (Princeton, NJ: Princeton University Press, 1998); Peter Trubowitz, *Defining the National Interest: Conflict and Change in American Foreign*

coalition will favor freer trade, as it will profit from greater international engagement; a nationalist coalition will favor protectionism, isolationism, and even disengagement from the international trading order. In contrast, realists argue that states will be wary of the risks of dependence and the relative gains inherent in freer trade.[45] Consequently, states will always prefer protectionism, unless they expect to gain disproportionately from freer trade.

Neoclassical realism provides a more nuanced understanding of the choice between freer trade and protection. The foreign economic policies of great powers will depend on the geostrategic environment they inhabit. In a restrictive international environment, all great powers are more concerned about the security externalities associated with free trade and, therefore, should be more reluctant to embrace freer trade, regardless of their domestic make-up.[46] In a highly restrictive environment or when security is extremely scarce, states will pursue autarchic practices, withdraw from the international trading order, and favor beggar-thy-neighbor trade policies and currency devaluation.[47] Moreover, in this environment, neoclassical realists anticipate that all major powers will pursue policies to maximize security, favor relative power gains, and emphasize independence and protectionism.

In a more permissive strategic environment, however, where security is abundant and the security externalities of economic exchange are less important, whether states opt for freer trade or protectionism should depend on their domestic political and economic environments. In states dominated by a nationalist coalition of economic and other interests that benefit from protectionism, and especially where inward-oriented factors, sectors, and firms dominate the state, neoclassical realists would expect the FPE to eschew free trade. After all, nationalists support tariffs, duties,

---

Policy (Chicago: University of Chicago Press, 1998); Steven E. Lobell, *The Challenge of Hegemony: Grand Strategy, Trade, and Domestic Politics* (Ann Arbor: University of Michigan Press, 2003); and Narizny, *Political Economy of Grand Strategy.*

45. Waltz, *Theory of International Politics,* pp. 129–160; and Joseph M. Grieco, *Cooperation among Nations: Europe, America, and Non-Tariff Barriers to Trade* (Ithaca, NY: Cornell University Press, 1990).

46. Joanne Gowa and Edward D. Mansfield, "Power Politics and International Trade," *American Political Science Review,* vol. 87, no. 2 (1993), pp. 408–420; and Joanne Gowa, *Allies, Adversaries, and International Trade* (Princeton, NJ: Princeton University Press, 1995).

47. Of course, as Gowa points out, this dynamic should be most acute in a multipolar system. In a bipolar system and, presumably, in a unipolar one, states will refrain from inter-alliance trade. Nonetheless, given the lack of a credible exit option—which makes it unlikely for allies to take the gains of trade to another alliance—they will continue to engage in intra-alliance trade. Joanne Gowa, "Bipolarity, Multipolarity, and Free Trade," *American Political Science Review,* vol. 83, no. 4 (1989), pp. 1245–1256.

and subsidies to exclude foreign competition from the home market. High tariffs mean that they will enjoy sectoral monopolies and a settled share of the domestic market. Import competing nationalists favor capital controls and oppose foreign lending because it would strengthen their competition and encourage growth abroad. Nationalists also tend to stress the need for domestic production of goods for strategic reasons and favor state intervention in the domestic economy. Consequently, where nationalists exert a disproportionate influence over the state, states should prefer protectionism to freer trade.

In contrast, in states where internationalists and exporters dominate the domestic political environment, and especially where outward-oriented factors, sectors, and firms predominate, the FPE is likely to pursue foreign economic policies of freer trade and laissez-faire domestic policies. Furthermore, internationalists will also encourage coordination and collaboration with foreign governments and business cohorts on matters of international trade, monetary, and security policy to achieve mutual economic gains.[48] This means participating in multilateral international organizations, conventions, treaties, and collective security arrangements.

In this regard, as we indicate in Table 6.1, we argue that in the 1930s, when multiple European states faced restrictive international environments and perceived security to be scarce, these states all opted for protectionism. Let us consider the case of Britain in particular, though, because it is the hard case for our argument of a historically liberal hegemon that provided the public goods necessary for a liberal international trading order. As the international environment shifted from permissive to highly restrictive, London too abandoned free trade. Specifically, London retreated from its traditional laissez-faire economic policies and abandoned the gold standard (1931), placed informal embargos upon capital issues for non-Empire borrowers, and adopted imperial preferences (1932). The British government embraced greater protectionism even in the face of opposition from powerful commercial centers in the City of London, including the internationally oriented banking, financial services, shipping, and insurance sectors, as well as overseas merchants and those who earned income from capital invested overseas.[49]

By 1937, in a highly restrictive environment, London abandoned its previous opposition to a Defense Loan of £400 million (the maximum to be borrowed over the next five years), which was amended in 1939 to

---

48. Solingen, *Regional Orders at Century's Dawn*, pp. 26–29; and Fordham, *Building the Cold War Consensus*, p. 3.
49. See Lobell, *Challenge of Hegemony*, pp. 105–111.

Table 6.1. FREE TRADE VERSUS PROTECTIONISM: THE INTERACTION BETWEEN
THE SECURITY ENVIRONMENT AND DOMESTIC COALITIONS

	Abundant Security	Scarce Security
Inward Coalition	Protection, Japan 1990s	Protection, Europe 1930s (Germany)
Outward Coalition	Free trade, US 1990s	Protection, Europe 1930s (Great Britain)

£800 million. Official opinion also crystallized against the policy of business as usual and non-intervention in the economy. Indeed, at the behest of the Air Staff, which was the first of the Services to call for the deliberate interference with normal business methods, in 1937 the government abandoned the practices of Treasury Control over finance and non-intervention in the economy, in order to direct labor and capital toward aircraft production. After Germany occupied Austria in March 1938, the Treasury backed away from the rationing of finance and the Cabinet cancelled the rule that rearmament should not interfere with normal civil industry and the course of normal trade.[50] Clearly, a high-threat environment led even the great power with the most liberal history of economic policies to close itself off from the world economy and pursue a protectionist trade policy.

In contrast, when security is abundant, trade preferences depend on the domestic coalitions that capture the state, a key component of our state-society relations cluster of intervening variables, which we identified in Chapter 3. In the aftermath of the Cold War, both Japan and the United States faced permissive strategic environments, yet Japan pursued protectionism while the United States favored a freer trade policy. In the 1980s and 1990s, Japanese agricultural policy was highly protectionist and agricultural interests, cooperatives, and farm organizations demanded continued protection. Agricultural interests, which are disproportionately represented in the Japanese political system, lobbied Japanese decision makers and the Diet for tariffs, quotas, and non-tariff barriers, and domestic subsidies to protect the commodity sector. Agricultural interests also resisted the Uruguay Round of multilateral trade negotiations (1986–1994), which called for a reduction in tariff rates and agricultural

50. J. P. D. Dunbabin, "British Rearmament in the 1930s: A Chronology and Review," *Historical Journal*, vol. 18, no. 3 (1975), p. 601; Steven E. Lobell, "Bringing Balancing Back In: Britain's Targeted Balancing, 1936–1939," *Journal of Strategic Studies*, vol. 35, no. 6 (2012), pp. 747–773; and Norrin M. Ripsman and Jack S. Levy, "Wishful Thinking or Buying Time? The Logic of British Appeasement in the 1930s," *International Security*, vol. 33, no. 2 (2008), pp. 148–181, at p. 179.

liberalization, and Japan's loss of a GATT case concerning import restrictions on agricultural goods. In the case of rice, by 1994, Japan abandoned its policy of prohibiting the import of rice and allowed "minimum access," but countered soon after by erecting a high tariff.[51]

In the 1990s, US trade policy was dominated by a broad and logrolled coalition of outward-oriented internationalists who favored freer trade including bilateral and multilateral trade agreements. Internationalists included large agribusiness, multinational companies, the US Chamber of Commerce, the service sector, and export-oriented industry. A much weaker inward-oriented nationalist bloc called for greater trade protection and included labor, farm groups, unions, and heavy manufacturing. The internationalist and nationalist blocs clashed over the North American Free Trade Agreement (NAFTA), which called for eliminating trade and investment barriers between the United States, Canada, and Mexico. Pro-NAFTA internationalists campaigned to ratify the treaty and argued that it would create new jobs, expand exports, and increase American international competitiveness. Anti-NAFTA nationalists opposed the treaty on the grounds that it would harm labor and undermine environmental standards. In ratifying the treaty, the internationalist bloc captured the distributional gains from NAFTA and further hastened the structural shift in the US economy toward capital intensive and global oriented sectors, and away from labor intensive and inward-oriented sectors.[52]

A neoclassical realist explanation for a state's trade orientation improves on realist and liberal accounts about when states will pursue protectionist and free trade policies. We maintain that when a state confronts a restrictive environment, it will pursue protection, even if the outward-oriented internationalist bloc dominates over the nationalist bloc. When a state confronts a permissive environment, domestic trade coalitions are freer to compete and the more powerful bloc will dictate the state's trade orientation.

MATERIALISM VERSUS IDEALISM: IDEAS AND IDEOLOGY MATTER IN PERMISSIVE SECURITY ENVIRONMENTS

The final debate we address is between materialism and idealism. In some respects, this debate between theories that privilege material variables

51. Yoshihisa Godo, "Reforming Japan's Agricultural Policies," WTO Millennium Round Issues, October 5, 2000, http://fordschool.umich.edu/rsie/Conferences/CGP/Oct2000Papers/Godo.pdf, accessed May 13, 2015.

52. Frederick W. Mayer, *Interpreting NAFTA: The Science and Art of Political Analysis* (New York: Columbia University Press, 1998); Maxwell A. Cameron and Brian W. Tomlin,

(at the systemic or unit-level) in explaining foreign policy and international outcomes, on the one hand, and theories that privilege ideational variables (again at the systemic or unit-level), on the other hand, has always been present in one form or another since the emergence of international relations as a discipline after World War I. The current iteration began with the end of the Cold War and the dissolution of the Soviet Union, which many scholars judged to be a major empirical anomaly for neorealism, especially Waltz's balance-of-power theory.[53] During this period, constructivism emerged as a major ontological and epistemological approach to the study of international relations. For the past twenty years, proponents of constructivism and related ideational or cultural theories have claimed that those theories offer superior explanations for observable political behavior than do materialist alternatives, such as structural realism and neoliberalism.[54]

Leaving aside questions of ontology and epistemology, much of the current debate revolves around two issues: (1) the relative importance of ideational variables and material structures in determining the foreign policy behavior of states and the patterns of international bargaining

The Making of NAFTA: How the Deal Was Done (Ithaca, NY: Cornell University Press, 2000); and Kerry A. Chase, *Trading Blocs: States, Firms, and Regions in the World Economy* (Ann Arbor: University of Michigan Press, 2005).

53. See, for example, Richard Ned Lebow and Janice Gross Stein, *We All Lost the Cold War* (Princeton, NJ: Princeton University Press, 1994); Richard K. Herrmann and Richard Ned Lebow, *Ending the Cold War: Interpretations, Causation, and the Study of International Relations*, 1st ed. (New York: Palgrave Macmillan, 2004); Janice Gross Stein, "Political Learning by Doing: Gorbachev as Uncommitted Thinker and Motivated Learner," *International Organization*, vol. 48, no. 2 (1994), pp. 155–183; Rey Koslowski and Friedrich V. Kratochwil, "Understanding Change in International Politics: The Soviet Empire's Demise and the International System," *International Organization*, vol. 48, no. 2 (1994), pp. 215–247; Stephen G. Brooks and William C. Wohlforth, "Economic Constraints and the End of the Cold War," in *Cold War Endgame*, ed. William C. Wohlforth (University Park: Pennsylvania State University Press, 2002); idem., "From Old Thinking to New Thinking to Qualitative Research," *International Security*, vol. 26, no. 4 (2002), pp. 93–111; idem., "Power, Globalization, and the End of the Cold War: Reevaluating a Landmark Case for Ideas," *International Security*, vol. 25, no. 3 (2000), pp. 5–53; and Randall L. Schweller and William C. Wohlforth, "Power Test: Evaluating Realism in Response to the End of the Cold War," *Security Studies*, vol. 9, no. 3 (2000), pp. 60–107.

54. Seminal constructivist works in IR include Alexander Wendt, *Social Theory of International Politics* (Cambridge: Cambridge University Press, 1999); Nicholas G. Onuf, *World of Our Making: Rules and Rule in Social Theory and International Relations* (Columbia: University of South Carolina Press, 1989); Emanuel Adler, "Seizing the Middle Ground: Constructivism in World Politics," *European Journal of International Relations*, vol. 3, no. 3 (1997), pp. 319–363. We recognize that constructivism refers to an ontology, rather than to a school of IR theory, per se. Since we also recognize that some proponents of theories positing ideational, cultural, or psychological variables eschew the constructivist label, we try to avoid that term in this section. Instead, we use "materialism" and "idealism," despite their imprecision.

outcomes; and (2) whether or not self-described realist theories (including neoclassical realism) can assign any causal role to ideational variables without violating the hard core assumptions of structural realism.[55] Since we address the latter issue at length in Chapters 2, 3, and 7, here we concentrate on the former.

For neoclassical realism, the operative questions are not whether or not collectively held ideas "matter" in foreign policy or whether material structure always trumps ideology, or vice versa, in determining international outcomes. Instead, the central question becomes: Given the causal primacy of systemic (material) variables, under what conditions are collective ideational variables at the unit level more likely to play an intervening role between systemic pressures, on the one hand, and the specific foreign and security strategies states pursue at a given time?

Neoclassical realism suggests the following. When states confront restrictive strategic environments, systemic (material) variables largely override ideational variables in determining states' foreign and security policies. Moreover, where such restrictive environments persist for long periods, we would expect to see broad continuities in the types of external strategies that states pursue, regardless of ideological differences within and between states.

Consider, for example, some underlying continuities in the foreign policies of pre- and post-revolutionary Iran. Although the fall of Shah Mohammad Reza Pahlavi in late 1978 and the 1979 revolution brought to power Shiite clerics who perceived the United States and Israel as their main adversaries, the new Islamic Republic of Iran nonetheless cooperated with Israel and the United States on a number of issues of mutual interest. Revolutionary Iran found itself in a restrictive strategic environment in the early 1980s due to a combination of the Soviet Union's occupation of neighboring Afghanistan, the strain of fighting a full-scale war against Saddam Hussein's Iraq (which in turn received substantial military and/or economic assistance from the United States, France, Jordan, Morocco, and the Arab states of the Persian Gulf), and its growing isolation from most of the other states in the greater Middle East.[56] The vast ideological distance separating Tehran from Washington and Jerusalem did not prevent Iran from negotiating secret arms deals with the United

---

55. Kitchen observes, "Much of IR theory is overly concerned with epistemology and ontology, to the extent that arguments over the status of subjects come to subsume the subjects, and the analysis, themselves." See Nicholas Kitchen, "Ideas of Power and Power of Ideas," in *Neoclassical Realism and European Politics: Bringing Power Back in*, ed. Asle Toje and Barbara Kunz (Manchester: Manchester University Press, 2012), p. 85. We tend to agree.

56. Stephen M. Walt, *Revolution and War* (Ithaca, NY: Cornell University Press, 1996), pp. 222–224 and 237–250.

States and Israel, which only became public with the Iran-Contra scandal in 1986.[57]

When states confront more permissive strategic environments, our theory expects ideas and ideology to exert a greater influence on states' foreign policies. Consider the case of the Soviet Union during the inter-war period. Like the leaders of revolutionary Iran in 1979–1980, the Bolsheviks who seized power in November 1917 had a radically different ideology and worldview than the Russian provisional government and the tsarist regime they replaced. Bolshevik Russia (formally the Soviet Union from 1922) confronted a relatively permissive strategic environment following the end of the Russian Civil War in 1924, especially since the disarmament and reparations clauses of the Versailles Treaty reduced the near-term military threat posed by Germany. In this environment, Moscow had the luxury of allowing purely ideological concerns to shape its foreign policy; the Comintern was given free rein in its efforts to subvert capitalist states in Europe.

However, as the USSR's strategic environment became more restrictive in the mid to late 1930s, with the rising military threats from Germany in the west and from Japan in the east, considerations of relative power and anticipated power shifts largely drove Soviet foreign and security policies. The Kremlin began to pursue strategies quite consistent with *Realpolitik* calculations, including signing a five-year nonaggression pact with Nazi Germany in August 1939 (as a means to buy time for Soviet rearmament) and a neutrality treaty with Japan in March 1941.[58] When faced with the "ultimate" restrictive strategic environment following Germany's invasion of June 22, 1941 (Operation Barbarossa), the Soviet Union not only forged a wartime alliance with Britain and the United States (the two main capitalist powers) but also supported Chiang Kai-shek's Kuomintang government in China, which had fought an intermittent civil war with the Chinese Communist Party of Mao Zedong for almost two decades at that point.[59]

Despite the devastation the USSR suffered at the hands of Germany in the "Great Patriotic War" and the United States' (short-lived) monopoly

---

57. Gawdat Bahgat, "The Islamic Republic and the Jewish State," *Israel Affairs*, vol. 11, no. 3 (2005), pp. 517–534.

58. Timothy W. Crawford, "Powers of Division: From the Anti-Comintern to the Nazi-Soviet and Japanese Soviet Pacts, 1936–1941," in *The Challenge of Grand Strategy: The Great Powers and the Broken Balance between the World Wars*, ed. Jeffrey W. Taliaferro, Norrin M. Ripsman, and Steven E. Lobell (New York: Cambridge University Press, 2011), pp. 246–278.

59. Geoffrey Roberts, *Stalin's Wars: From World War to Cold War, 1939–1953* (New Haven, CT: Yale University Press, 2006), pp. 284–287.

on atomic weapons and long-range bombers, and tremendous advantages in economic capacity and technology, the Kremlin arguably faced a more permissive strategic environment after 1945. The defeat of Germany and Japan created power vacuums in Eastern and Central Europe and on the East Asian mainland. In this more permissive environment for the USSR, the ideological mission returned to Soviet foreign policy. Notably, the Soviet Union not only imposed its political and economic system on the Eastern European states liberated by the Red Army, but also resumed actively supporting communist insurgencies and communist parties in Western Europe and the Balkans. Thus, in accordance with neoclassical realist expectations, allowing ideology to determine foreign policy and grand strategy was a luxury that could only be allowed when the Soviet Union faced a permissive strategic environment.

Overall, then neoclassical realism can explain the variance in the ideological behavior of states to a greater extent than both materialist theories that treat ideology as largely irrelevant or ideational theories that privilege ideology over material interests.

CONCLUSION

In this chapter, we have examined four diverse and persistent debates or problems in international relations and demonstrated that neoclassical realism can help resolve them. While this is not an exclusive list, the diversity of these debates—drawn from security studies, foreign policy analysis, and international political economy—illustrates the immense promise of neoclassical realism, utilized as a theory of international politics, to provide considerable added value for international relations scholars. In the final chapter of this book, we will consider other potential uses of our approach, after distinguishing it from other approaches that operate across levels of analysis and responding to critics of neoclassical realism.

CHAPTER 7

The Future of the Neoclassical Realist Research Agenda

In the preceding chapters, we argued that neoclassical realist theory is more than simply the logical extension of structural realism. Rejecting the artificial distinction that Kenneth Waltz draws between theories of international politics and theories of foreign policy, we made the case that neoclassical realism can offer explanatory and predictive theories of phenomena ranging from short-term crisis behavior, to foreign policy, to patterns of grand strategic adjustment by individual states, up to broader long-term patterns of international outcomes and structural change. We explicated the independent variable, clarified and organized the unit-level intervening variables, and specified the full range of potential dependent variables for neoclassical realist theories. In addition, we addressed various aspects of neoclassical realist theory construction and methodology and demonstrated how neoclassical realist theory can be used to resolve longstanding puzzles and debates in international relations theory.

In this final chapter, we undertake the following tasks. First, we draw a distinction between neoclassical realism and other schools of international relations theories, including eclecticism, liberalism, constructivism, foreign policy analysis (FPA), and classical realism, which also posit independent and intervening variables at multiple levels of analysis. These areas of overlap require us to clear up potential confusion over the boundaries of neoclassical realism and its distinctness from these approaches.

Second, we respond to various criticisms of neoclassical realism as a research venture. Critics variously fault neoclassical realism for allegedly: (1) incorporating unit-level variables in an ad hoc manner; (2) prioritizing descriptive accuracy over parsimony and explanatory power; (3) repudiating the core assumptions of structural realism and the broader

Realpolitik tradition; (4) being incapable of producing generalizable theories; and (5) demonstrating a bias toward the United States and past great powers in case selection. We contend that each of these criticisms is either mistaken or has been rectified in this book.

Finally, we conclude the chapter with a brief discussion of several future research agendas for neoclassical realism.

DISTINGUISHING NEOCLASSICAL REALISM FROM OTHER THEORETICAL APPROACHES

In recent years, neoclassical realism has grown in popularity among international relations scholars, principally as an approach to the study of foreign policy. Leading journals of international relations and political science and various edited volumes have published articles and chapters that advance different neoclassical realist hypotheses on phenomena such as alliance behavior, defense policy, crisis decision-making, and foreign economic policy.[1] Other articles and book chapters address neoclassical realism's status as an emerging research program and raise questions about its epistemology, methodology, and the relationship between neoclassical realism and other (non-realist) empirical and normative theories.[2] A growing number of single-authored books advance various neoclassical realist theories of foreign policy and grand strategic adjustment.[3]

1. See for example, Anders Wivel, "Explaining Why State X Made a Certain Move Last Tuesday: The Promise and Limitations of Realist Foreign Policy Analysis," *Journal of International Relations and Development*, vol. 8, no. 4 (2005), pp. 355–380; Conor Loughlin, "Irish Foreign Policy During World War II: A Test for Realist Theories of Foreign Policy," *Irish Studies in International Affairs*, vol. 19 (2008), pp. 99–117; Balkan Devlen and Özgür Özdamar, "Neoclassical Realism and Foreign Policy Crises," in *Rethinking Realism in International Relations: Between Tradition and Innovation*, ed. Annette Freyberg-Inan, Ewan Harrison, and Patrick James (Baltimore: Johns Hopkins University Press, 2009), pp. 136–163; Nicholas Kitchen, "Systemic Pressures and Domestic Ideas: A Neoclassical Realist Model of Grand Strategy Formation," *Review of International Studies*, vol. 36, no. 1 (2010), pp. 117–143; Victor D. Cha, "Powerplay: Origins of the U.S. Alliance System in Asia," *International Security*, vol. 34, no. 3 (2009–2010), pp. 158–196; and Evan N. Resnick, "Strange Bedfellows: U.S. Bargaining Behavior with Allies of Convenience," *International Security*, vol. 35, no. 3 (2010), pp. 144–184.

2. Stefano Guzzini, "The Enduring Dilemmas of Realism in International Relations," *European Journal of International Relations*, vol. 10, no. 4 (2004), pp. 533–566; Jonathan D. Caverley, "Power and Democratic Weakness: Neoconservatism and Neoclassical Realism," *Millennium: Journal of International Studies*, vol. 38, no. 3 (2010), pp. 593–614; Eben Coetzee and Heidi Hudson, "Democratic Peace Theory and the Realist-Liberal Dichotomy: The Promise of Neoclassical Realism?," *Politikon*, vol. 39, no. 2 (2012), pp. 257–277; and Adam Quinn, "Kenneth Waltz, Adam Smith, and the Limits of Science: Hard Choices for Neoclassical Realism," *International Politics*, vol. 50, no. 2 (2013), pp. 159–182.

3. See Christopher Layne, *The Peace of Illusions: American Grand Strategy from 1940 to the Present* (Ithaca, NY: Cornell University Press, 2006); Colin Dueck, *Reluctant*

Scholars have been drawn to neoclassical realism for two key reasons. First, it offers a unique solution to the levels-of-analysis problem that has plagued international relations theorists and foreign policy analysts by positing not simply a multilevel approach, but by prioritizing international stimuli in the formulation of national foreign policy objectives, while acknowledging that whether and how states respond to international pressures depends on domestic political institutions, state-society relations and other unit-level variables.[4] Second, Types I and II neoclassical realism's focus on mid-range theorizing to explain tangible foreign policy behavior and patterns of grand strategic adjustment, as opposed to highly abstract and general patterns of international political outcomes, has made it more approachable as a means of shedding light on practical policy problems.

Nonetheless, there is still some confusion about the nature of neoclassical realism and the manner in which it incorporates unit-level variables. In this section, we seek to clear up the confusion by distinguishing neoclassical realism from other theoretical approaches that utilize both state- and individual-level variables.

i. Eclecticism

A recent trend in international relations is the movement toward theoretical eclecticism.[5] Reflecting a concern that rigid adherence to paradigmatic approaches strips much of the nuance and complexity away from international politics and therefore distorts our understanding of the

Crusaders: Power, Culture, and Change in American Grand Strategy (Princeton, NJ: Princeton University Press, 2006); Jeremy Pressman, *Warring Friends: Alliance Restraint in International Politics* (Ithaca, NY: Cornell University Press, 2008); Amelia Hadfield, *British Foreign Policy, National Identity, and Neoclassical Realism* (Lanham, MD: Rowman and Littlefield, 2010); and Stéfanie von Hlatky, *American Allies in Times of War* (Oxford: Oxford University Press, 2013).

4. On the levels-of-analysis problem and the agent-structure debate, see Kenneth N. Waltz, *Man, the State, and War: A Theoretical Analysis* (New York: Columbia University Press, 1959); J. David Singer, "The Level-of-Analysis Problem in International Relations," *World Politics*, vol. 14, no. 1 (1961), pp. 77–92; Alexander E. Wendt, "The Agent-Structure Problem in International Relations Theory," *International Organization*, vol. 41, no. 3 (1987), pp. 335–370; idem., "Levels of Analysis vs. Agents and Structures: Part III," *Review of International Studies*, vol. 18, no. 2 (1992), pp. 181–185; and David Dessler, "What's at Stake in the Agent-Structure Debate?," *International Organization*, vol. 43, no. 3 (1989), pp. 441–473.

5. On eclectic theories, see John A. Hall and T. V. Paul, "Preconditions for Prudence: A Sociological Synthesis of Realism and Liberalism," in *International Order and the Future of World Politics*, ed., T. V. Paul and John A. Hall (Cambridge: Cambridge University Press, 1999), pp. 67–77; and Rudra Sil and Peter J. Katzenstein, *Beyond Paradigms: Analytic Eclecticism in the Study of World Politics* (London: Palgrave Macmillan, 2010).

subject, some theorists have begun to build theories of international politics that reach beyond paradigmatic boundaries.[6] Particularly in the area of regional security complexes, scholars have therefore begun to borrow concepts and variables from realism, liberalism, and constructivism to add explanatory power.[7]

Neoclassical realism, with its attention to variables at multiple levels of analysis and its emphasis on explanatory power over parsimony belongs to this theoretical movement. Nonetheless, it differs from eclectic theory in important ways. Most importantly, it stresses the primacy of the international system. States construct foreign policy with an eye to the external environment above all other considerations, as realists maintain. Whether and how they respond to international challenges may be affected by other variables, be they domestic political variables of the type emphasized by liberals or ideational or cultural variables advanced by constructivists. Nonetheless, neoclassical realists are still realists and privilege realist variables, incorporating variables from other paradigms in a rather regular, pre-specified, and systematic manner. In this regard, neoclassical realism is a realist subset of eclectic or multiparadigmatic theories. All neoclassical realist theories are multiparadigmatic, but not all multiparadigmatic or eclectic theories are neoclassical realist. Thus, for example, Benjamin Miller's innovative theory of regional war and regional peace, which gives primary explanatory power to the degree of underlying state-to-nation congruence in a particular region, is not a neoclassical realist theory, even though he incorporates realist balance-of-power variables to explain the intensity of war or peace outcomes. Indeed, Miller actually reverses the causal logic of neoclassical realism. By arguing that the war proneness of regions depends primarily on domestic and regional factors, such as the state-to-nation balance, and is only modified by the global balance of power and great power behavior, Miller actually posits only an intervening role for systemic variables, while affording causal primacy to unit and region-level variables. His theory therefore, while intriguing, is not neoclassical realist.[8]

6. David A. Lake, "Why 'Isms' Are Evil: Theory, Epistemology, and Academic Sects as Impediments to Understanding and Progress," *International Studies Quarterly*, vol. 55, no. 2 (2011), pp. 465–480.

7. See, for example, Peter J. Katzenstein, *A World of Regions: Asia and Europe in the American Imperium* (Ithaca, NY: Cornell University Press, 2005); Norrin M. Ripsman, "Two Stages of Transition From a Region of War to a Region of Peace: Realist Transition and Liberal Endurance," *International Studies Quarterly*, vol. 49, no. 4 (2005), pp. 669–693; Benjamin Miller, *States, Nations, and the Great Powers* (Cambridge: Cambridge University Press, 2007); and Jonathan Rynhold, "The German Question in Central and Eastern Europe and the Long Peace in Europe after 1945: An Integrated Theoretical Explanation," *Review of International Studies*, vol. 37, no. 1 (2011), pp. 249–275.

8. Miller, *States, Nations, and the Great Powers.*

ii. Liberalism

While its emphasis on unit and subunit variables pertaining to domestic political institutions, decision-making characteristics, and perception have been informed by what Rose labels *Innenpolitik* approaches, neoclassical realism is clearly distinct from the *Innenpolitik* logic, and it cannot be dismissed as reductionist.[9] *Innenpolitik* theories are unit-level approaches, which explain foreign policy primarily in terms of the internal characteristics of states, their domestic political processes, and the preferences of individuals, parties, and coalitions that lead them. Liberal theories, in particular, assume that domestic coalitions, political institutions, and the public at large determine the content of foreign policy and constrain liberal states from selecting policies outside the domestic consensus. While domestic causes do interact with external forces in liberal theory, these domestic variables trump international pressures, such as the distribution of power. Thus, for example, democratic peace theory assumes that public opinion and the public's representatives in the legislature restrain leaders from using force against other democratic states, regardless of the underlying balance of power and the nature of conflictive issues between them.[10] Similarly, societal strands of commercial liberalism posit that states will avoid the use of force against trading partners because business sectors that stand to lose as a result of war will compel the government to avoid disrupting the normal economic relationship, regardless of strategic considerations.[11] In each case, the liberal state is a pluralist entity that responds to the balance of domestic interests and aggregate societal preferences when conducting foreign policy, selecting the policy option that reflects aggregate societal preferences.[12]

9. Gideon Rose, "Neoclassical Realism and Theories of Foreign Policy," *World Politics*, vol. 51, no. 1 (1998), pp. 144–172.

10. See Bruce M. Russett, *Grasping the Democratic Peace* (Princeton, NJ: Princeton University Press, 1993).

11. See, for example, Paul A. Papayoanou, "Interdependence, Institutions, and the Balance of Power: Britain, Germany, and World War I," *International Security*, vol. 20, no. 4 (1996), pp. 42–76; and Galia Press-Barnathan, *The Political Economy of Transitions to Peace* (Pittsburgh, PA: University of Pittsburgh Press, 2009). For the logic of commercial liberalism, see Robert O. Keohane, "International Liberalism Revisited," in *The Economic Limits to Modern Politics*, ed. John Dunn (Cambridge: Cambridge University Press, 1990), pp. 186–187; Michael W. Doyle, *Ways of War and Peace: Realism, Liberalism, and Socialism* (New York: W. W. Norton, 1997), pp. 230–250; and Edward D. Mansfield and Brian M. Pollins, "Interdependence and Conflict: An Introduction," in *Economic Interdependence and International Conflict*, ed. Edward D. Mansfield and Brian Pollins (Ann Arbor: University of Michigan Press, 2003), pp. 1–28, at pp. 2–3.

12. Andrew Moravcsik, "Taking Preferences Seriously: Liberalism and International Relations Theory," *International Organization*, vol. 51, no. 4 (1997), pp. 512–553.

In contrast, neoclassical realists have a markedly different conception of the state.[13] The essence of the state consists of the foreign policy executive (FPE), comprising the head of state or government and the key ministers and officials charged with the conduct of foreign and defense policy.[14] The FPE has access to privileged information about foreign affairs from the diplomatic corps and intelligence services that makes it more aware of the interests of state than other domestic or societal actors. For this reason, the state is distinct from society. Moreover, since the executive is uniquely responsible for state performance and, especially, the security of the state, it will be especially attuned to national interests rather than to sectoral or coalitional interests. Consequently, although state leaders are drawn from society, their attitudes and preferences change when they experience "the view from the top," as the privileged information they receive and the *raison d'état* culture they become imbued in make state actors more than simply representatives of their societal coalition. Thus, it is not uncommon for a candidate for political office to espouse a policy position critical of the incumbent, only to abandon it after assuming power and being briefed by government officials. High-profile examples include President Barack Obama backpedaling on his promise to remove US forces from Iraq in short order and President Bill Clinton doing the same on his commitment to link the extension of Most Favored Nation status to China to Beijing's human rights record.[15]

For neoclassical realism, therefore, the state occupies a critical position at the intersection between the domestic and international arenas. It is uniquely situated to respond to the challenges and opportunities of the international system because of its privileged information. Yet, it may

13. Jeffrey W. Taliaferro, Steven E. Lobell, and Norrin M. Ripsman, "Introduction: Neoclassical Realism, the State, and Foreign Policy," in *Neoclassical Realism, the State, and Foreign Policy*, ed. Steven E. Lobell, Norrin M. Ripsman, and Jeffrey W. Taliaferro (Cambridge: Cambridge University Press, 2009), pp. 1–41, at pp. 23–28.

14. For similar concepts, see Margaret G. Hermann, Charles F. Hermann, and Joe D. Hagan, "How Decision Units Shape Foreign Policy Behavior," in *New Directions in the Study of Foreign Policy*, ed. Charles F. Hermann, Charles W. Kegley, and James N. Rosenau (Boston: Allen and Unwin, 1987), pp. 309–336; David A. Lake, *Power, Protection, and Free Trade: International Sources of US Commercial Strategy, 1887–1939* (Ithaca, NY: Cornell University Press, 1988); Norrin M. Ripsman, *Peacemaking by Democracies: The Effect of State Autonomy on the Post-World War Settlements* (University Park: Pennsylvania State University Press, 2002), pp. 43–44.

15. Nicholas Kitchen, "The Obama Doctrine—Détente or Decline?" *European Political Science*, vol. 10, no. 1 (2011), pp. 27–35; Colin Dueck, *The Obama Doctrine: American Grand Strategy Today* (New York: Oxford University Press, 2015); and Lowell Dittmer, "Chinese Human Rights and American Foreign Policy: A Realist Approach," *Review of Politics*, vol. 63, no. 3 (2001), pp. 421–459.

still misperceive systemic stimuli, such as relative capabilities, whether an adversary's force posture is offensive or defensive, or the time frame of threats they may face. Moreover, while the state is potentially autonomous of societal forces, it is not necessarily so. Depending on domestic political arrangements, states vary in their ability both to enact policy responses to international challenges and to raise revenue and resources to implement policy choices.[16] Less autonomous states must frequently bargain with societal groups and key veto players in the legislature over foreign security policy. Thus, for example, the administrations of George H. W. Bush and George W. Bush spent months garnering domestic support for their respective strikes against Iraq before they felt capable of waging war.[17] Furthermore, while neoclassical realists maintain that the state conducts foreign policy primarily with regard to the international arena, a matter which puts them squarely within the realist camp, they recognize that leaders also must be attuned to threats to their power position from within the state; therefore, in rare times of extreme domestic instability, national leaders might actually conduct foreign policy with greater attention to the domestic audience than to international exigencies.[18] This can explain why leaders whose power positions at home are threatened may launch diversionary wars that might not be in the national interest.[19] Thus, neoclassical realists have a considerably different view of the state than *Innenpolitik* approaches.

16. See Ripsman, *Peacemaking by Democracies*; Jeffrey W. Taliaferro, "State Building for Future Wars: Neoclassical Realism and the Resource-Extractive State," *Security Studies*, vol. 15, no. 3 (2006), pp. 464–495; and Jean-Marc F. Blanchard and Norrin M. Ripsman, "A Political Theory of Economic Statecraft," *Foreign Policy Analysis*, vol. 4, no. 4 (2008), pp. 371–398.

17. For sources on George W. Bush's war mobilization efforts, see Chaim Kaufmann, "Threat Inflation and the Failure of the Marketplace of Ideas: The Selling of the Iraq War," *International Security*, vol. 29, no. 1 (2004), pp. 5–48; Ronald R. Krebs and Chaim Kaufmann, "Correspondence: Selling the Market Short? The Marketplace of Ideas and the Iraq War," *International Security*, vol. 29, no. 4 (2005), pp. 196–207; and Jon Western, "The War over Iraq: Selling War to the American Public," *Security Studies*, vol. 14, no. 1 (2005), pp. 106–139.

18. Norrin M. Ripsman, "Neoclassical Realism and Domestic Interest Groups," in *Neoclassical Realism, the State, and Foreign Policy*, ed. Steven E. Lobell, Norrin M. Ripsman, and Jeffrey W. Taliaferro (Cambridge: Cambridge University Press, 2009), pp. 170–193; and Steven R. David, "Explaining Third World Alignment," *World Politics*, vol. 43, no. 2 (1991), pp. 233–256.

19. Jack S. Levy, "The Diversionary Theory of War," in *The Handbook of War Studies*, ed. Manus I. Midlarsky (Boston: Unwin Hyman, 1989), pp. 259–288; Alastair Smith, "Diversionary Foreign Policy in Democratic Systems," *International Studies Quarterly*, vol. 40, no. 1 (March 1996), pp. 133–153; and Sara McLaughlin Mitchell and Brandon C. Prins, "Rivalry and Diversionary Uses of Force," *Journal of Conflict Resolution*, vol. 48, no. 6 (2004), pp. 937–961.

Furthermore, unlike liberal theories, neoclassical realists assume that not only the state, but also societal actors themselves must frame their policy preferences in reference to the international challenges and opportunities they face. Given the importance of security in an anarchic international environment, states should be unwilling to adopt policies advanced by societal forces that could jeopardize national security, despite the domestic political fallout they expect. Therefore, domestic groups that seek to maximize their interests by directing foreign policy in a manner disconnected from the international environment the state faces are likely to be unsuccessful. Thus, for neoclassical realists, the international system focuses and frames the state's foreign policy response, although the domestic arena will tailor the shape it will take. For this reason, the approach remains realist and distinct from liberalism.[20] In this vein, Brawley demonstrates that in the 1920s and early 1930s Great Britain, France, and the Soviet Union all identified impending German recovery as the leading threat to their security, but their unique societal considerations led them to adopt distinctly different strategies to respond to the threat.[21]

iii. Classical Realism

As its name suggests, neoclassical realism revives classical realism's concern for domestic politics, the statesman, and institutions, and its emphasis on the quality of diplomacy as a means of explaining the foreign security policy of states.[22] Neoclassical realism departs from classical realism, however, by providing clearly stated, testable hypotheses, aspiring to the positivistic scientific rigor that structural realism introduced to

---

20. Rose, "Neoclassical Realism and Theories of Foreign Policy."

21. Mark R. Brawley, "Neoclassical Realism and Strategic Calculations: Explaining Divergent British, French, and Soviet Strategies toward Germany between the World Wars (1919–1939)," in *Neoclassical Realism, the State, and Foreign Policy*, ed. Steven E. Lobell, Norrin M. Ripsman, and Jeffrey W. Taliaferro (Cambridge: Cambridge University Press, 2009), pp. 75–98.

22. On the importance of domestic politics and political institutions, see E. H. Carr, *The Twenty Years' Crisis, 1919–1939: An Introduction to the Study of International Relations* (London: Macmillan, 1961), pp. 85–87, 124–129, and 132–138; Reinhold Niebuhr, *The Structure of Nations and Empires* (New York: Charles Scribner's, 1959); Raymond Aron, *Peace and War: A Theory of International Relations*, trans. Richard Howard and Annette Baker Fox (London: Weidenfeld and Nicolson, 1966), pp. 597–600; and Hans J. Morgenthau, *Dilemmas of Politics* (Chicago: University of Chicago Press, 1958), pp. 68–75. On the importance of the quality of diplomacy as a component of material power and a determinant of foreign policy, see Hans J. Morgenthau, *Politics among Nations: The Struggle for Power and Peace*, 5th ed., rev. (New York: McGraw-Hill, 1978), pp. 146–150.

realism, and specifying the causal primacy of the anarchic international system.[23] In our previous work, we briefly discussed how neoclassical realism seeks to build upon classical realism by incorporating some theoretical concepts and insights, such as the complex relationships between states (that is, the administrative apparatus of government) and domestic societies, into causal theories of foreign policy and grand strategic adjustment.[24] Here, we further explicate the areas of convergence and the areas of divergence between classical realism and neoclassical realist theory.

It is important to be clear about what we mean by classical realism. The labels "classical realism" and "neorealism" did not come into widespread use until the journal *International Organization* published Richard Ashley's 1984 review article of Waltz's *Theory of International Politics*. Ashley sought to draw a sharp distinction between Waltz and other leading structural theorists of international politics in the United States during the 1970s and 1980s, on the one hand, and proponents of the older "European" tradition of classical realist thought principally associated in the postwar United States with writings of Hans J. Morgenthau, Reinhold Niebuhr, Henry A. Kissinger, and John Herz, on the other hand.[25]

Classical realism refers to a centuries-old philosophical approach to international politics, rather than a research program. Classical realists were preoccupied with the primacy of power and conceived of politics— both domestic and international—as an endless struggle by self-interested actors coping with scarcity and uncertainty. When proponents of neoclassical realism claim to draw upon or incorporate insights from classical realism, they generally make explicit reference to Morgenthau, Niebuhr, Herz, and Kissinger, as well their contemporaries, such as Raymond Aron, E. H. Carr, Walter Lippmann, George F. Kennan, Nicholas Spykman, A. J. P. Taylor, and Arnold Wolfers.[26]

---

23. See Patrick James, *International Relations and Scientific Progress: Structural Realism Reconsidered* (Columbus: Ohio State University Press, 2002), pp. 14–20.

24. Taliaferro, Lobell, and Ripsman, "Introduction," esp. pp. 13–21.

25. Richard K. Ashley, "The Poverty of Neorealism," *International Organization*, vol. 38, no. 2 (1984), pp. 225–286. Besides Waltz, Ashley's list includes Robert Keohane, Stephen Krasner, Robert Gilpin, Robert Tucker, George Modelski, and Charles Kindleberger, among others, as the leading proponents of "North American structuralism" or "neorealism."

26. Taliaferro, Lobell, and Ripsman, "Introduction," pp. 14–16. This list is not a representative sample of twentieth-century classical realists, but rather a list of those more frequently cited by self-described neoclassical realists. Other prominent classical realists would include Bernard Brodie, Herbert Butterfield, Frederick S. Dunn, E. M. Earle, Edward Vose Gulick, Otto Hintze, William T. R. Fox, Friedrich Meinecke, Leopold von Ranke, Friedrich L. Schuman, William W. Thompson, Martin Wight, and Quincy Wright. See Jonathan Haslam, *No Virtue Like Necessity: Realist Thought in International Relations since Machiavelli* (New Haven, CT: Yale University Press, 2002).

Joseph M. Parent and Joshua M. Baron contend that much of the indictment that Waltz, Mearsheimer, and other structural realists level against classical realism—chiefly that the latter is insufficiently theoretical and structural and that it privileges human nature (the first image) over the anarchic nature of the international system (the third image) as the permissive cause of conflict—is grossly overstated and inaccurate. We agree with some of Parent and Baron's criticisms of the standard narrative about the alleged "sins" of classical realism.[27] Nonetheless, we identify two main areas of divergence between neoclassical realism and classical realism: (1) the causal primacy of systemic variables, and (2) a commitment to social science methodology.

Neoclassical realism privileges systemic variables over unit-level variables in accounting for patterns of international outcomes, grand strategic adjustment, and foreign policy decision-making, whereas classical realism was agnostic on the matter. While Morgenthau, Herz, Spykman, Aron, and other classical realists did write extensively about anarchy and the distribution of power as causes of international political outcomes and the external strategies of individual states, they also wrote extensively about human nature and drew parallels between domestic politics and international politics. Even for Morgenthau, who is often identified as the exemplar of "human nature realism" because of his oft-quoted reference to the *animus dominandi*, human nature is not the central explanation of why states seek power maximization. Nonetheless, he does give primacy to human nature, which compels states to maximize power as an end, rather than simply a means.[28] Neoclassical realist theory's prioritization of the international system similarly distinguishes it from recent European attempts to return to classical realism—or at least an ideational interpretation of it—that some mistakenly conflate with neoclassical realism.[29]

In addition, neoclassical realism, unlike classical realism, adheres to widely accepted notions of social science methodology. Neoclassical realists

27. Joseph M. Parent and Joshua M. Baron, "Elder Abuse: How the Moderns Mistreat Classical Realism," *International Studies Review*, vol. 13, no. 2 (2011), pp. 193–213.

28. Ibid., pp. 197–198; and Ashley J. Tellis, "Reconstructing Political Realism: The Long March to Scientific Theory," *Security Studies*, vol. 5, no. 2 (1996), p. 50.

29. This European turn, which we term "European ideational realism," relies heavily on Michael Williams's study of Morgenthau's ideational underpinnings. In particular, see Michael C. Williams, "Why Ideas Matter in International Relations: Hans Morgenthau, Classical Realism, and the Moral Construction of Power Politics," *International Organization*, vol. 58, no. 4 (2004), pp. 633–665; Dario Battistella, "Raymond Aron: A Neoclassical Realist before the Term Existed?" in *Neoclassical Realism in European Politics: Bringing Politics Back In*, ed. Alse Toje and Barbara Kunz (Manchester: Manchester University Press, 2012), pp. 117–137; and Michael C. Williams, ed., *Realism Reconsidered: The Legacy of Hans Morgenthau in International Relations* (Oxford: Oxford University Press, 2007).

seek to develop empirical theories that explain foreign policy behavior and international outcomes that generate testable hypotheses. Since neoclassical realism's independent, intervening, and dependent variables are located at different levels-of-analysis, neoclassical realists are careful to identify causal mechanisms and to specify the predictions (or observable implications) of their hypotheses. As we stated in Chapter 5, neoclassical realist theory proceeds from a soft-positivist epistemology, which would have been antithetical to the approach adopted by the scholars and practitioners now called classical realists, who were not social scientists and did not adhere to what are now widely accepted standards of social science methodology.[30]

iv. Foreign Policy Analysis (FPA)

Foreign policy analysis (FPA) has been conceptualized both as a distinct subfield of international relations and, more narrowly, as a distinct theoretical perspective or approach within the discipline.[31] Here we focus on the second conception. Valerie Hudson writes that FPA has "an actor-specific focus, based upon the argument that all that occurs between nations and across nations is grounded in human decision makers acting singly or in groups."[32] In addition to this emphasis on agent-oriented theory, according to Hudson, the other defining characteristics of the FPA literature are that it "views the explanation of foreign policy decision making as multifactorial, with the desideratum of examining variables from more than one level-of-analysis (multilevel)" and explicitly incorporates theoretical insights and methodologies from a variety of social science disciplines. FPA thus encompasses studies of foreign policy decision-making grounded in political psychology and organizational behavior, as well as rationalist models of foreign policy decision-making.[33]

FPA theories tend to focus on one or more of the following: (1) the impact of individual and small group psychological dynamics in foreign policy decision-making; (2) variation in organizational decision-making processes in foreign policy; and (3) the relationship between foreign policy elites and the mass public.[34] FPA's relationship with the "mainstream"

30. Haslam, *No Virtue Like Necessity*; and Michael Joseph Smith, *Realist Thought from Weber to Kissinger* (Baton Rouge: Louisiana State University Press, 1986).

31. Juliet Kaarbo, "A Foreign Policy Analysis Perspective on the Domestic Politics Turn in IR Theory," *International Studies Review*, vol. 17, no. 2 (2015), pp. 189–216.

32. Valerie M. Hudson, "Foreign Policy Analysis: Actor-Specific Theory and the Ground of International Relations," *Foreign Policy Analysis*, vol. 1, no. 1 (2005), p. 1.

33. Ibid., p. 2.

34. For other overviews, see Valerie M. Hudson and Christopher S. Vore, "Foreign Policy Analysis Yesterday, Today, and Tomorrow," *International Studies Quarterly*, vol. 39, no. 3

schools of international relations theories is ambiguous, due to the fact that many scholars concurrently work in FPA and across different sub-fields of the international relations discipline (such as security stud-ies, political economy, and international organization) and also, in part, because over the past two decades, even self-described realists, liberals, and constructivists have paid renewed attention to domestic politics and foreign policy decision-making.[35]

We acknowledge areas of overlap and even complementarity between FPA and neoclassical realism. Both schools, for example, pay careful attention to how the preexisting belief systems and cognitive constraints on policymakers influence their perceptions and assessments of inter-national stimuli, as well as to how organizational dynamics within the national security bureaucracy or the degree of institutional autonomy policymakers enjoy might delimit the range of options that they can pur-sue.[36] Indeed, two of us (along with many other neoclassical realists) have explicitly built upon FPA insights, a point that Juliet Kaarbo makes in a recent review article.[37] Nevertheless, there are major areas of disagree-ment between FPA and neoclassical realism.

Neoclassical realism clearly privileges the international system over domestic (or unit-level) variables. The independent variable for any neo-classical realist theory must be located at the international level. FPA the-ories, in contrast, may acknowledge the importance of the international system, but they clearly privilege unit-level variables in foreign policy decision-making. In short, what neoclassical realism treats as the inter-vening variable (specifically what we grouped in the categories of leader

(1995), pp. 209–238; Ryan K. Beasley, Juliet Kaarbo, Charles F. Hermann, and Margaret G. Hermann, "People and Processes in Foreign Policymaking: Insights from Comparative Case Studies," *International Studies Review*, vol. 3, no. 2 (2001), pp. 217–250; Juliet Kaarbo, "Introduction, Foreign Policy Analysis in 20/20: A Symposium," *International Studies Review*, vol. 5, no. 2 (2003), pp. 155–156; and Jean A. Garrison, "Foreign Policymaking and Group Dynamics: Where We've Been and Where We're Going," *International Studies Review*, vol. 5, no. 2 (2003), pp. 156–163.

35. For example, Robert Jervis has made major contributions to foreign policy analysis (especially in political psychology), as well as to the subfields of security studies and intel-ligence studies, and the development of structural realism. For analyses of Jervis's seminal contributions to each of these areas of study, see James W. Davis, ed., *Psychology, Strategy and Conflict: Perceptions of Insecurity in International Relations* (New York: Routledge, 2012).

36. See Kaarbo, "A Foreign Policy Analysis Perspective," p. 204. For an earlier call to incor-porate insights from behavioral decision theory, cognitive, social, and evolutionary psy-chology, and information processing explicitly into realist theories, see James M. Goldgeier and Philip E. Tetlock, "Psychology and International Relations Theory," *Annual Review of Political Science*, vol. 4, no. 1 (2001), pp. 67–92.

37. See Kaarbo, "A Foreign Policy Analysis Perspective," pp. 204–205.

images, strategic culture, domestic institutions, and state-relations in Chapter 3), various FPA theories treat as independent variables.[38]

FPA and neoclassical realism disagree over exactly how, when, and under what circumstances domestic politics might influence a state's external behavior. Kaarbo observes that "FPA presents a more contingent view of the relationship between domestic and international politics. Executives (or leaders') responses to domestic and international pressures are conditioned by a number of factors, including their own beliefs and perceptions."[39] Thus FPA and neoclassical realism represent separate but related research agendas.

v. Constructivism

Before addressing constructivism's relationship to neoclassical realism, we need to make two disclaimers. First, we recognize that constructivism refers to an ontological position, as well as to a broad (and diverse) school of international relations theories. As Jeffrey Checkel observes, constructivism is "not a theory but an approach to social inquiry based upon two assumptions: (1) the environment in which agents/states take action is social as well as material; and (2) this setting can provide agents/states with understandings of their interests (it can 'constitute' them)."[40] In this section, we are mainly interested in constructivism as a distinct theoretical school. Second, although some constructivist theories focus on the social construction of underlying dynamics of international politics and shared norms at the systemic level, we are mainly interested in constructivist theories that purport to explain why the foreign policies of states appear to defy the expectations of liberal and (structural) realist theories.[41]

---

38. Ibid., pp. 203–205.

39. Ibid., p. 204.

40. Jeffrey T. Checkel, "The Constructivist Turn in International Relations Theory," *World Politics*, vol. 50, no. 2 (1998), p. 325; and see also Nicholas G. Onuf, "Constructivism: A User's Manual," in *International Relations in a Constructed World*, ed. Vendulka Kubálková, Nicholas G. Onuf, and Paul Kowert (Armonk, NY: M. E. Sharpe, 1998), pp. 58–78, esp. pp. 58–64.

41. Examples of the former include Nicholas G. Onuf, *World of Our Making: Rules and Rule in Social Theory and International Relations* (Columbia: University of South Carolina Press, 1989); and Alexander Wendt, *Social Theory of International Politics* (Cambridge: Cambridge University Press, 1999). Examples of the latter include Jeffrey Legro, *Cooperation under Fire: Anglo-German Restraint during World War II* (Ithaca, NY: Cornell University Press, 1995); Peter J. Katzenstein, *Cultural Norms and National Security: Police and Military in Postwar Japan* (Ithaca, NY: Cornell University Press, 1996); Jeffrey Legro, *Rethinking the World: Great Power Strategies and International Order* (Ithaca, NY: Cornell University Press,

A frequent criticism of neoclassical realist theory is that most of the causal work is done by leaders' perceptions, ideology, and strategic culture, rather than by the relative distribution of material capabilities. Therefore, some critics claim that neoclassical realism is unnecessary since constructivism incorporates these ideational variables more efficiently.[42] This line of criticism is mistaken on several counts, not the least of which is that constructivism and neoclassical realism proceed from different epistemological positions. While constructivists acknowledge that there is an "objective" reality outside of the actors, they also hold that reality is indeterminate. Instead, it is the intersubjective interpretations of the actors that constitute both reality and the actors themselves. As Steve Smith notes, "social construction starts from the assumption that actors make their worlds, and this assumption lies behind most of the foreign policy analysis literature."[43]

In contrast, neoclassical realism starts from two premises. First, there is an "objective" reality or environment (in this case, the international system) that exists independently of actors (territorial states). Second, that environment's properties—namely the relative distribution of material capabilities among the actors—delimit the range of possible strategies any actor can pursue, as well as the range of possible bargaining outcomes among those actors. As we stated in Chapter 2 of this book, as well as in the Introduction to our 2009 edited volume, neoclassical realism is an environment-based body of theory.[44] States cannot transcend their external environment. While leader images or strategic culture may impede the "optimal" assessment of international systemic pressures and opportunities, it is ultimately systemic level variables, chiefly the relative distribution of power and power trends, that account for most of the variation in states' external behaviors and ultimately patterns of international bargaining outcomes.

If neoclassical realist theory posits an intervening role for collective ideational variables at the unit level, then might some type of synthesis between it and constructivism of the type Samuel Barkin proposes be possible?[45] For Barkin, a realist-constructivist synthesis becomes possible

2005); and Mark L. Haas, *The Ideological Origins of Great Power Politics, 1789–1989* (Ithaca, NY: Cornell University Press, 2005).

42. Jeffrey W. Legro and Andrew Moravcsik, "Is Anybody Still a Realist?" *International Security*, vol. 24, no. 2 (1999), pp. 5–55, at pp. 34–39.

43. Steve Smith, "Foreign Policy Is What States Make of It: Social Constructivism and International Relations Theory," in *Foreign Policy in a Constructed World*, ed. Vendulka Kubálková (Armonk, NY: M. E. Sharpe, 2001), pp. 38–55, at p. 38.

44. Taliaferro, Lobell, and Ripsman, "Introduction," pp. 28–29.

45. J. Samuel Barkin, *Realist Constructivism* (Cambridge: Cambridge University Press, 2010), p. 154.

if one returns to classical realism's emphasis on prescription (normative theory) and abandons structural realism's focus on prediction, because the core constructivist commitment to the active role of agency in the production of social arrangements is incompatible with prediction.[46]

Whatever the merits of Barkin's realist-constructivism, such a synthesis would be antithetical to neoclassical realist theory. Indeed, it is not clear what insights his realist-constructivist synthesis might bring to our understanding of the contemporary "real-world" problems and international history that neoclassical realists address.[47] As we noted in Chapter 5, neoclassical realism proceeds from a soft-positivist epistemology. We seek theories that generate testable hypotheses and which can therefore help us draw contingent causal inferences. The explanation of political phenomena, whether contemporary or historical, is the main purpose of neoclassical realism. Therefore, neoclassical realism is a distinctly different enterprise from constructivism.

RESPONDING TO CRITICS OF NEOCLASSICAL REALISM

Since we published our edited book on neoclassical realism in 2009, we have continued to encounter both the objections to the approach we addressed in that book, as well as new concerns. In this section, we respond to these concerns, particularly the claims that the neoclassical realist research program variously: (1) incorporates unit-level variables in an ad hoc manner; (2) does not yield a coherent theory; (3) prioritizes descriptive accuracy over parsimony and explanatory power; (4) repudiates the core assumptions of structural realism and the broader *Realpolitik* tradition; (5) is incapable of producing generalizable theories; and (6) demonstrates a great power or United States-centric bias and therefore has little utility in explaining the behavior of the vast majority of states. Some of these criticisms overlap. Nonetheless, we address them sequentially for the sake of clarity.

Ad Hoc Inclusion of Unit-Level Variables

Jeffrey Legro and Andrew Moravcsik criticized a broad range of writings—including many we classify as neoclassical realist—claiming

---

46. Ibid., pp. 103–104.
47. Chris Brown, "Realism: Rational or Reasonable?" *International Affairs*, vol. 88, no. 4 (2012), pp. 857–866.

to belong in the realist tradition as involving ad hoc additions of variables such as perception, domestic political arrangements, and international norms to fix what they view as a failing realist core.[48] For similar reasons, John Vasquez charges that this emendation of realist theory to save a flawed core theory is testimony to the degenerative nature of the entire realist research paradigm.[49] Stephen Walt charged that "Neoclassical realism tends to incorporate domestic variables in an ad hoc manner, and its proponents have yet to identify when these variables have greater or lesser influence." Moreover, he continues, it "has yet to offer a distinct set of explanatory hypotheses" and "has given up generality and predictive power in an attempt to gain descriptive accuracy and policy relevance."[50]

While it is possible that some who incorporate domestic variables in the service of a more powerful realism may do so in an ad hoc manner, well-specified neoclassical realist theories are not susceptible to the charge of being ad hoc. Theories such as Randall Schweller's theory of underbalancing, Taliaferro's theory of emulation and mobilization, and Ripsman's theory of structural autonomy, for example, all stem from a deductive theoretical analysis of the circumstances under which state behavior is likely to deviate from structural realist expectations. Consequently, they begin with a priori identifications of the relevant variables on theoretical grounds, rather than ad hoc selections to rationalize anomalous findings.[51] Indeed, one of the distinct missions of the new generation of neoclassical realists is to generate a set of clearly specified propositions regarding exactly when domestic political and leadership variables will have greater causal effect and when policies and outcomes are determined primarily by systemic variables.[52] In addition, since Type II and Type III

---

48. Legro and Moravcsik, "Is Anybody Still a Realist?"

49. John A. Vasquez, "The Realist Paradigm and Degenerative versus Progressive Research Programs: An Appraisal of Neotraditional Research on Waltz's Balancing Proposition," *American Political Science Review*, vol. 91, no. 4 (1997), pp. 899–912.

50. Stephen M. Walt, "The Enduring Relevance of the Realist Tradition," in *Political Science: State of the Discipline*, ed. Ira Katznelson and Helen Milner (New York: W. W. Norton, 2002), pp. 197–230, at p. 211.

51. Randall L. Schweller, *Unanswered Threats: Political Constraints on the Balance of Power* (Princeton, NJ: Princeton University Press, 2006); Jeffrey W. Taliaferro, "Neoclassical Realism and Resource Extraction: State Building for Future War," in *Neoclassical Realism, the State, and Foreign Policy*, ed. Steven E. Lobell, Norrin M. Ripsman, and Jeffrey W. Taliaferro (Cambridge: Cambridge University Press, 2009), pp. 194–226; and Ripsman, *Peacemaking by Democracies*.

52. Daniel L. Byman and Kenneth M. Pollack, "Let Us Now Praise Great Men: Bringing the Statesman Back In," *International Security*, vol. 25, no. 4 (2001), pp. 107–146; and Norrin M. Ripsman, "Neoclassical Realism and Domestic Interest Groups," in *Neoclassical Realism, the State, and Foreign Policy*, ed. Steven E. Lobell, Norrin M. Ripsman, and Jeffrey W. Taliaferro (Cambridge: Cambridge University Press, 2009), pp. 170–193.

neoclassical realist theories seek to do more than simply explain away anomalies and pathologies in structural realism and aspire to construct clearly testable models, they cannot be labeled "degenerative."[53]

Throughout this volume, we have explicitly addressed the charge that neoclassical realist theory incorporates unit-level intervening variables in an ad hoc manner. We devoted a large portion of Chapter 3 to organizing the hitherto disparate list of intervening variables into four broad categories—leader images, strategic culture, state-society relations, and domestic institutional arrangements—which we selected a priori, based on the effects they should have on the critical intervening-level processes of perception, decision making, and policy implementation. In Chapters 4 and 5, we further specified the circumstances under which each of the four categories of intervening variable would likely have a discernable effect on the dependent variables. Finally, in Chapter 5, we suggested two ideal strategies—one deductive and the other inductive—for identifying appropriate intervening variables for neoclassical realist theories. Thus, our use of unit-level intervening variables is hardly ad hoc.

Neoclassical Realism Is Not a Coherent Theory

In many public presentations of our research, some critics have complained that neoclassical realism is not a coherent theory. This charge is not fair. The neoclassical realism described by Gideon Rose, Randall Schweller, and us—even in this book—amounts to a research program, rather than a single theory.[54] Like other approaches—such as structural realism, liberalism, and constructivism—neoclassical realism presents a set of common assumptions that unites a variety of disparate theorists and theories, which may generate competing hypotheses and predictions. It should be evaluated by its logic, the degree to which its assumptions are coherent and reflect the real world, and the performance of well-specified theories that begin with its assumptions.

53. See Randall L. Schweller, "The Progressiveness of Neoclassical Realism," in *Progress in International Relations Theory: Appraising the Field*, ed. Colin Elman and Miriam Fendius Elman (Cambridge, MA: MIT Press, 2003), pp. 311–347.

54. Rose, "Neoclassical Realism and Theories of Foreign Policy"; Schweller, "The Progressiveness of Neoclassical Realism"; Taliaferro, Lobell, and Ripsman, "Introduction"; and Norrin M. Ripsman, Jeffrey W. Taliaferro, and Steven E. Lobell, "The Future of Neoclassical Realism," in *Neoclassical Realism, the State, and Foreign Policy*, ed. Steven E. Lobell, Norrin M. Ripsman, and Jeffrey W. Taliaferro (Cambridge: Cambridge University Press, 2009), pp. 280–299.

The Delicate Balance between Parsimony and Explanatory Power

Another key challenge that neoclassical realism is susceptible to is the charge that it is comparatively inefficient. By including domestic political and perceptual variables within their models of foreign policy and international relations, neoclassical realist theories are less parsimonious than structural realist theories.[55] For Waltz—who prides himself on parsimony—explaining important elements of international politics and state behavior with a single variable (the distribution of capabilities; Waltz's other variable, system structure, does not actually vary, since the system has been anarchic for centuries and is not likely to change, as states are reluctant to surrender their sovereignty), this would be a considerable disadvantage of neoclassical realism.[56]

Neoclassical realists counter, however, that while structural realism is a useful starting point, it sacrifices too much explanatory power at the altar of parsimony. The inclusion of unit-level variables, provided it is done in a careful, scientific manner, can add significantly to our ability to explain past events and predict future state behavior.[57] Since theories of international relations are intended not only for their esoteric value but to serve policymakers as guides for action, the more precision we can generate in a systematic manner in our theories about how a particular state is likely to react in a particular set of international circumstances, the more useful the theory is.

Moreover, we would argue that the reification of parsimony in international relations theory, and even the way realist scholars understand the concept, is problematic. Based on the principle of Occam's razor, if two theories can explain the same phenomenon, we should rely on the simpler one, since there is no added value in adding greater complexity.[58] Simpler is better, though, only if the simpler theory can explain the phenomenon

55. Walt, "The Enduring Relevance of the Realist Tradition," p. 211; and Annette Freyberg-Inan, Ewan Harrison, and Patrick James, "Ways Forward," in *Rethinking Realism in International Relations: Between Tradition and Innovation*, ed. Annette Freyberg-Inan, Ewan Harrison, and Patrick James (Baltimore: Johns Hopkins University Press, 2009), pp. 253–265, at p. 259.

56. Kenneth N. Waltz, *Theory of International Politics* (Reading, MA: Addison-Wesley 1979), chapters 5–6; and idem., "Reflections on *Theory of International Politics*: A Response to My Critics," in *Neorealism and Its Critics*, ed. Robert O. Keohane (New York: Columbia University Press, 1986), pp. 322–346, at p. 330.

57. Taliaferro, Lobell, and Ripsman, "Introduction," p. 23.

58. See, for example, Carl Hempel, "Empiricist Criteria of Cognitive Significance: Problems and Changes," in *The Philosophy of Science, Part I*, ed. Richard Boyd, Philip Gasper, and J. D. Trout (Cambridge, MA: MIT Press, 1991), pp. 71–84, at p. 79.

(or as much of it) as effectively as the more complex theory. Under these circumstances, parsimony is a virtue. If, however, the simpler theory explains less than the more complex one—i.e., it explains less variance— then the principle of Occam's razor no longer applies. It is a more challenging issue to determine which theory is preferable and, indeed, which is more parsimonious. If the more complex theory explains only marginally more than the simpler, more elegant theory explains, and if the simpler theory has far fewer moving parts and variables, one may well still consider the simpler theory more useful and parsimonious. Conversely, if adding slightly more complexity yields considerably more explanatory power, then doing so would be preferable and it would be misleading to view a simpler theory as more parsimonious. When faced with trade-offs of this sort, therefore, the challenge is to achieve a reasonable balance between simplicity and explanatory power.

We contend that neoclassical realism adds considerably more explanatory power than purely structural or *Innenpolitik* theories. This additional explanatory power justifies the greater complexity of the approach.

Is Neoclassical Realism Realist?

Some critics of neoclassical realist theories question whether they are truly consistent with the logic of realism, particularly structural realism. According to Legro and Moravcsik, by shifting the causal logic away from the international system, realist theorists who incorporate domestic-level variables in their analysis are, in effect, abandoning the realist tradition and cannot properly be labeled "realists."[59]

Neoclassical realism falls squarely within the realist camp. Theories properly designated as neoclassical realist in accordance with the principles set out in this book all share common assumptions that attest to their structural realist origins. Specifically, they assume: (1) that the international system is anarchic and, consequently, that states must rely on themselves to ensure their survival; (2) that survival is the most important national interest in an anarchic realm; and (3) that anarchy makes cooperation difficult, as it leads states to prefer relative over absolute gains.[60] Indeed, it is precisely these structural realist assumptions that lead neoclassical realists to take as their starting point the primacy of the international system—i.e., that states conduct foreign security policy first

---

59. Legro and Moravcsik, "Is Anybody Still a Realist?" p. 30.
60. See Benjamin Frankel, "Restating the Realist Case: An Introduction," *Security Studies*, vol. 5, no. 3 (1996), pp. ix–xx.

and foremost with an eye to the anarchic international system because failing to do so could jeopardize national security, the state's overriding priority—utilizing auxiliary domestic-level variables not as independent variables, but as intervening variables between systemic constraints and national policy responses. Hence, neoclassical realism is a direct descendant of structural realism and is consistent with the underlying principles of realism.

As we discuss in Chapter 5, there are several structural realist baselines, derived from different theories, which researchers can begin with when constructing their neoclassical realist theories. This baseline, in effect, amounts to the independent (systemic) variable(s) unmoderated by domestic-level intervening variables. This choice is of great consequence, as the selection of an inappropriate baseline will yield an ineffective theory. Admittedly, our discussions of how neoclassical realism might resolve four longstanding theoretical debates in Chapter 6 all begin with baselines derived from balancing theories. Nonetheless, we reiterate that there is nothing to prevent future researchers from identifying appropriate baselines from the hegemonic (or power preponderance), offense-defense, power transition, or offensive realism. Furthermore, in Chapter 5, we establish various criteria by which a researcher might identify an appropriate structural realist baseline for his or her neoclassical realist theory.

Adam Quinn argues that in seeking to explain law-like patterns of behavior arising from the interaction of systemic and unit-level variables, neoclassical realism breaches the outer limits of what Waltz considers tolerable in a theory of international politics. For Quinn, there is an inherent and unresolved tension between neoclassical realism's claim to build upon Waltz's insights about the constraining effects of international structure, on the one hand, and the methodological approach and theoretical claims of self-styled neoclassical realists, on the other hand. Quinn writes that for "Waltz's theory . . . to hold, states must be systematically punished for failing to respond appropriately to systemic imperatives."[61] Consequently, he claims that neoclassical realism now finds itself at a crossroad: it can either confine itself to explaining anomalous cases of foreign policy behavior within Waltzian structural realism or it can attempt to identify new rules of international politics that ultimately call the primacy of Waltz's systemic imperatives into question.[62]

---

61. Quinn, "Kenneth Waltz, Adam Smith, and the Limits of Science," p. 161.
62. Ibid., p. 178.

By his own admission, Quinn's first theoretical path would relegate neoclassical realism to a subsidiary status within structural realism: a collection of mid-level theories that only purport to explain anomalous foreign policy behavior.[63] This is what we call Type I neoclassical realism. Quinn's second path would boldly cast neoclassical realism as a "behaviourally oriented counter-revolutionary push against Waltz's effort to establish parsimonious system theory at the centre of the realist agenda."[64] In this volume, we embrace the second path. We do not see neoclassical realist theory as being subsidiary to structural realism. Rather, we seek to establish neoclassical realism as a coherent realist research program (or school of theories) alongside structural realism as a part of a broader *Realpolitik* tradition.

Building Generalizable Theories

A temptation that neoclassical realists must avoid succumbing to is to focus excessively on a single case or small set of cases. Since the approach requires painstaking qualitative empirical analysis, usually involving archival and other primary sources, this may lead the researcher to focus excessively on the idiosyncratic trees of his/her cases, rather than the more theoretically interesting forest it is part of. While thick description of an important case is interesting in and of itself, without generalizability those insights will not allow the researcher to make inferences beyond the time, space, and unique context of the case and therefore allow for predictions about the future or for policy relevant advice. Walt therefore criticizes neoclassical realism's emphasis on "descriptive accuracy" rather than generalizability.[65]

We argue that the success of neoclassical realism as an approach to the study of international politics and foreign policy will depend on its ability to generate generalizable theories about phenomena of great policy relevant importance (such as nuclear strategy, fighting terrorism, peacemaking, human security, etc.) that can be tested against leading structural realist contenders, as well as those of other approaches. To this end, we provided the primer on building and testing neoclassical realist theories in Chapter 5. To the extent that these and other neoclassical realist theories can demonstrate the utility of combining systemic independent variables and unit-level intervening variables by outperforming

---

63. Ibid., pp. 171–173, 178.
64. Ibid., p. 177.
65. Walt, "The Enduring Relevance of the Realist Tradition," p. 211.

conventional explanations in systematic tests, our faith in this approach will be vindicated.

Is Neoclassical Realism an Approach for Great Powers or for All?

Since the publication of our 2009 edited volume, we have encountered yet another line of criticism of neoclassical realism at various conference panels and during our respective presentations at invited conferences. Some fellow panelists and audience members have observed that the extant neoclassical realist literature shows a marked bias toward historical cases involving the great powers, especially the United States. Others have questioned whether neoclassical realism is even relevant for explaining the foreign policy behavior of non-great powers or the dynamics of contemporary international politics outside of North America and Western Europe. We offer the following responses to this line of criticism.

The four books that Rose claimed as constituting a new theoretical school—those of Christensen, Schweller, Wohlforth, and Zakaria—examined cases involving the United States, the Soviet Union, and former great powers of Europe and East Asia during the early twentieth century. Many of the other works that we classify herein as exemplifying Type I and Type II neoclassical realism, including our own respective books and our two previous co-edited volumes, explicitly deal with grand strategic adjustment by the great powers. After all, neoclassical realism arose in reaction to Waltz's *Theory of International Politics* in 1979 and the ensuing debate between structural realism and neoliberal institutionalism in the 1980s and early 1990s. It is also not surprising since most, if not all, of the early neoclassical realists earned their PhDs in the leading political science departments in the United States in the 1990s.

The fact that many neoclassical realist scholars have studied cases involving the United States and past great powers is perfectly in keeping with a long tradition in realist thought. Realists of all stripes are united by the assumption that power matters in international politics and that therefore the more powerful states are the more consequential players on the international stage. This does not mean, however, that neoclassical realism is exclusively a theory of great power politics and that it has little relevance in the explaining behavior of the vast majority of the world's states. On the contrary, we would expect the independent variables—the relative distribution of power, the clarity of the international system, the relative permissiveness or restrictiveness of a state's strategic environment—as well as the four groups of unit-level intervening variables—leader images, strategic culture, state-society relations, and domestic institutions—to shape the external behavior of and the patterns of interaction among small and middle powers, as well as the great power(s) in the current international system and in past interstate systems.[66] Throughout this book, we have cited dozens of recent books and articles that present neoclassical realist theories that purport to explain the strategic behavior of middle and small powers.[67]

AN AGENDA FOR FUTURE RESEARCH

Adherents of neoclassical realism contend that the approach represents a significant improvement on existing approaches to international relations and foreign policy. In the preceding chapters, we have made the case that Type III neoclassical realism generates predictive and explanatory theories for a range of phenomena up to and including international systemic outcomes. There remain several potential avenues for future research. To begin with, it would be useful to test the claim that neoclassical realism adds sufficient explanatory power to warrant the inclusion of a raft of unit-level variables. To this end, studies that engage in careful and systematic testing of neoclassical realist models vis-à-vis leading structural realist and systemic liberal alternatives would be extremely helpful. Similarly, it would be useful to test the assumption that states conduct foreign policy primarily with a view to the international arena with careful tests of the comparative utility of neoclassical realist theories vis-à-vis various *Innenpolitik* approaches.

Although some of the recent scholarship mentioned in this book has begun to address Walt's charge that neoclassical realism focuses more on post hoc idiosyncratic explanation of particular historical cases than

---

66. This applies to regional subsystem, as well as great power politics. See Steven E. Lobell, Kristen P. Williams, and Neal G. Jesse, "Why Do Secondary States Choose to Support, Follow, or Challenge?" *International Politics*, vol. 52, no. 2 (2015), pp. 146–162.

67. See for example, Schweller, *Unanswered Threats*, pp. 85–102; Vipin Narang, *Nuclear Strategy in the Modern Era: Regional Powers and International Conflict* (Princeton, NJ: Princeton University Press, 2014); Devlen and Özdamar, "Neoclassial Realism and Foreign Policy Crises"; Tom Dyson, *Neoclassical Realism and Defence Reform in Post-Cold War Europe* (New York: Palgrave Macmillan, 2010); Hans Mouritzen and Anders Wivel, *Explaining Foreign Policy: International Diplomacy and the Russo-Georgian War* (Boulder, CO: Lynne Rienner, 2012); Lorenzo Cladi and Mark Webber, "Italian Foreign Policy in the Post-Cold War Period: A Neoclassical Realist Approach," *European Security*, vol. 20, no. 2 (2011), pp. 205–219; and Hyon Joo Yoo, "Domestic Hurdles for System-Driven Behavior: Neoclassical Realism and Missile Defense Policies in Japan and South Korea," *International Relations of the Asia-Pacific*, vol. 12, no. 2 (2012), pp. 317–348.

on the construction of generalizable theories, for neoclassical realism to develop into a useful approach for explaining categories of events and to serve as a guide for policymakers, it will be necessary to demonstrate that it is not merely a realm of case narratives, but can also operate as a basis for contextually informed theory. In this regard, Nicholas Kitchen's efforts to construct a neoclassical realist theory of grand strategic formation and change, utilizing domestic culture and ideas as intervening variables, is encouraging, as it is purely a deductive theoretical enterprise, rather than case driven.[68]

Another area where neoclassical realism can potentially distinguish itself from other branches of realism is in its treatment of international organizations (IOs). Structural realists typically assume that IOs do not have independent effects on international politics, but are epiphenomenal of great power politics.[69] Neoclassical realists would largely agree, except that they would allow that IOs might be able to produce independent results when they interact with our intervening variables. In other words, if the statements or decisions taken by an IO were to co-opt domestic opinion in a less-autonomous state, that would constrain the state's policy options and, consequently affect its policy choice. If that state's choice has a consequential effect on an international outcome, then the IO could be of more consequence than realists typically acknowledge.[70] Thus, for example, since the French, German, Belgian, and Canadian publics were persuaded that the United Nations (UN) weapons inspectors should be given more time to verify whether Saddam Hussein was illegally pursuing unconventional weapons before resolving to use force against Iraq in 2003, they limited their government's ability to support the American initiative, and effectively precluded a UN- or NATO-sanctioned strike against Iraq. The scope of IO influence within neoclassical realism thus deserves some study.

Similarly, neoclassical realism should also be able to clarify the impact of international nongovernmental organizations (INGOs) on the international stage. Unlike other realists, who view INGOs as largely inconsequential, neoclassical realists recognize that, to the extent that these organizations can generate domestic political pressure in a particular state and to the extent that the state lacks governmental autonomy,

---

68. Kitchen, "Systemic Pressures and Domestic Ideas."

69. John J. Mearsheimer, "The False Promise of International Institutions," *International Security*, vol. 19, no. 3 (1994), pp. 5–49; Kenneth N. Waltz, "Globalization and Governance," *PS: Political Science and Politics*, vol. 32, no. 4 (1999), pp. 693–700; and idem., "Structural Realism after the Cold War," *International Security*, vol. 25, no. 1 (2000), pp. 5–41.

70. See Norrin M. Ripsman, "Neoclassical Realism and International Organizations," unpublished manuscript, Concordia University, n.d.

INGOs may occasionally be able to affect the strategic behavior of states. Consequently, in rare circumstances, they might have a meaningful impact on international politics. This remains an undertheorized area, however, which would be a fruitful avenue of research.

In addition to IOs and INGOs, the relationships between states and other categories of non-state actors suggest possible research avenues for neoclassical realism. Consider, for example, the emergence of private security and military companies (PSMCs).[71] One recent study advances a neoclassical realist theory to explain how high domestic mobilization hurdles for the George W. Bush administration and British Prime Minister Tony Blair's government constrained their response to the need for "more boots on the ground" in Iraq and Afghanistan. For the US and British militaries, PSMCs served as "operational force multipliers."[72] Future research might better specify the conditions under which FPEs use private military contractors as a means to overcome high domestic mobilization hurdles and the circumstances under which PSMCs actually serve as "operational force multipliers" in fighting external and internal adversaries.

Another topic for neoclassical realism is the emerging powers of Brazil, Russia, India, China, and South Africa (BRICS) and the implications of their rise for system-wide and regional conflict. Some of the pressing questions include whether the BRICS's rise will be peaceful, whether they will challenge the status quo, how the extant great powers will respond, whether historic rivalries will re-emerge, and how secondary and tertiary states in the locales will react. Theorizing about regional and small power dynamics has added complexity, due to the possible involvement of extra-regional actors. The levels of engagement by extra-regional powers, the number of regional powers in the locale, and which states are waning and waxing, all impose constraints and create opportunities for secondary and tertiary states. Their responses are filtered through unit- or subunit-level intervening variables.[73] A related matter is whether the "Thucydides

71. Deborah D. Avant, *The Market for Force: The Consequences of Privatizing Security* (Cambridge: Cambridge University Press, 2005); P. W. Singer, *Corporate Warriors: The Rise of the Privatized Military Industry*, updated ed. (Ithaca, NY: Cornell University Press, 2008); Andrew Alexandra, Deane-Peter Baker, and Marina Caparini, eds., *Private Military and Security Companies: Ethics, Policies and Civil-Military Relations* (London and New York: Routledge, 2008); and Thomas C. Bruneau, *Patriots for Profit: Contractors and the Military in U.S. National Security* (Stanford, CA: Stanford University Press, 2011).

72. Eugenio Cusumano, "Bridging the Gap: Mobilisation Constraints and Contractor Support to US and UK Military Operations," *Journal of Strategic Studies*, vol. 38, no. 5 (2015), pp. 1–29.

73. Kristen P. Williams, Steven E. Lobell, and Neal G. Jesse, eds. *Beyond Great Powers and Hegemons: Why Secondary States Support, Follow, or Challenge* (Stanford, CA: Stanford University Press, 2012); and T. V. Paul, ed., *Accommodating Rising Powers: Past, Present, Future* (Cambridge: Cambridge University Press, 2016).

Trap," or a major war between a rising China and a hegemonic United States, is inevitable. President Xi Jinping and even some American officials maintain that China's emergence need not cause conflict with the United States.[74] Researchers might investigate the role of domestic unit-level intervening variables (in China and the United States) in escaping the Thucydides Trap.

Finally, neoclassical realists would do well to heed Shiping Tang's call for more research on the domestic politics of international cooperation in order to shed what he refers to as the "competition bias" of neoclassical realism.[75] While Tang's criticism is overstated, as studies do utilize neoclassical realist approaches to explain cooperative issue areas—such as Ripsman's study of interstate peacemaking or Taylor Fravel's study of the willingness of China to compromise on territorial disputes—Tang is correct that much of the neoclassical realist literature focuses on interstate competition rather than cooperation.[76] Since realism does not preclude cooperation, there is no reason to believe that neoclassical realism would be better suited as a tool to explain conflict than cooperation.[77] A more balanced set of empirical foci is therefore warranted.

On a broader theoretical level, neoclassical realism may help researchers understand and incorporate time as a variable in international relations. Currently, time and time horizons feature prominently in power transition theory, which posits that differential growth rates across states over time drives changes in relative power and provides declining states with incentives to wage preventive war.[78] Institutional theories of cooperation point to the utility of iteration as a means of extending the shadow

74. Steven E. Lobell, "Can the United States and China Escape the Thucydides Trap?" *China International Strategy Review* (Beijing: Center for International and Strategic Studies, Peking University, 2015).

75. Shiping Tang, "Taking Stock of Neoclassical Realism," *International Studies Review*, vol. 11, no. 4 (2009), pp. 799–803, at pp. 799–800.

76. Ripsman, *Peacemaking by Democracies*; and M. Taylor Fravel, *Strong Borders, Secure Nation: Cooperation and Conflict in China's Territorial Disputes* (Princeton, NJ: Princeton University Press, 2008).

77. On realism and cooperation, see Kenneth A. Oye, "Explaining Cooperation under Anarchy: Hypotheses and Strategies," in *Cooperation under Anarchy*, ed. Kenneth A. Oye (Princeton, NJ: Princeton University Press, 1986), pp. 1–24; and Peter D. Feaver et al., "Brother, Can You Spare a Paradigm? (Or Was Anybody Ever a Realist?)," *International Security*, vol. 25, no. 1 (2000), pp. 165–193, at p. 174.

78. See, for example, Robert Gilpin, *War and Change in World Politics* (Cambridge: Cambridge University Press, 1981); Jack S. Levy, "Declining Power and the Preventive Motivation for War," *World Politics*, vol. 40, no. 1 (1987), pp. 82–107; Stephen Van Evera, *Causes of War: Power and the Roots of Conflict* (Ithaca, NY: Cornell University Press, 1999); and Dale C. Copeland, *The Origins of Major War* (Ithaca, NY: Cornell University Press, 2000).

of the future.[79] Theories of electoral cycles and foreign policy expect that a leader's time horizon will typically extend only to the next election, whereas retiring or term-limited leaders will be freer to focus on the state's longer-term interests rather than their parochial interests of power preservation.[80] In recent years, scholars have begun to question the simplified assumptions of time and intertemporal tradeoffs that underlie conventional theories of international politics of foreign policy.[81] Type III neoclassical realists suggest additional dimensions of time as a variable to gain leverage on state behavior and international politics. In particular, it considers time not only as an element of the independent and intervening variables that condition state behavior, but also as an element of the dependent variable, since the impact of international pressures and domestic constraints grows over time—as, consequently, does the scope of what neoclassical realism can explain. Thus this research program suggests that a reconsideration of time and its impact on international politics would be in order.

Following the release of our 2009 edited volume, *Neoclassical Realism, the State, and Foreign Policy,* neoclassical realism has emerged as a major theoretical approach to the study of foreign policy. In the concluding chapter of that volume, we wrote, "neoclassical realism will continue to flourish as a research program precisely because its proponents have not lost sight of the 'political' in the study of international politics, foreign policy, and grand strategy."[82]

In this volume, we advanced the neoclassical realist research program. We moved beyond Type I neoclassical realism, which merely purports to explain pathological foreign policy behavior by individual states. We also moved beyond Type II neoclassical realism, which purports to generate general theories of foreign policy. By incorporating systemic-level independent variables and intervening unit-level variables in a deductively

---

79. Robert Axelrod, *The Evolution of Cooperation* (New York: Basic Books, 1984); and Oye, "Explaining Cooperation under Anarchy."

80. See, for example, Bruce Russett, *Controlling the Sword: The Democratic Governance of National Security* (Cambridge, MA: Harvard University Press, 1990).

81. David M. Edelstein, "Managing Uncertainty: Beliefs about Intentions and the Rise of Great Powers," *Security Studies,* vol. 12, no. 1 (2002), pp. 1–40; Monica D. Toft "Issue Indivisibility and Time Horizons as Rationalist Explanations for War," *Security Studies,* vol. 15, no. 1 (2006), pp. 34–69; Philip Streich and Jack S. Levy, "Time Horizons, Discounting, and Intertemporal Choice," *Journal of Conflict Resolution,* vol. 51, no. 2 (2007), pp. 199–226; and Ronald R. Krebs and Aaron Rapport, "International Relations and the Psychology of Time Horizons," *International Studies Quarterly,* vol. 56, no. 3 (2012), pp. 530–543.

82. Norrin M. Ripsman, Jeffrey W. Taliaferro, and Steven E. Lobell, "Conclusion: The State of Neoclassical Realism," in *Neoclassical Realism, the State, and Foreign Policy,* ed. Steven E. Lobell, Norrin M. Ripsman, and Jeffrey W. Taliaferro (Cambridge: Cambridge University Press, 2009), pp. 280–299, at p. 299.

consistent manner, Type III neoclassical realism can explain phenomena ranging from the short-term crisis behavior of states, to foreign and defense policies, to near-to-medium-term patterns of grand strategic adjustment, up to and including longer-term patterns of international (systemic) outcomes. It arguably meets the criteria for progressive research programs in international politics set forth by scholars who have been critical of previous neoclassical realist theorizing.[83] In short, Type III neoclassical realism allows international relations scholars to answer "big and important" questions, on which existing theoretical approaches—including structural realism, liberalism, and constructivism—cannot shed sufficient light. We believe, therefore, that neoclassical realist theory of international politics unleashes the full explanatory power of realism.

---

83. Vasquez, "The Realist Paradigm and Degenerative versus Progressive Research Programs."

INDEX